# About Pfeiffer

Pfeiffer serves the professional development and hands-on resource needs of training and human resource practitioners and gives them products to do their jobs better. We deliver proven ideas and solutions from experts in HR development and HR management, and we offer effective and customizable tools to improve workplace performance. From novice to seasoned professional, Pfeiffer is the source you can trust to make yourself and your organization more successful.

**Essential Knowledge**   Pfeiffer produces insightful, practical, and comprehensive materials on topics that matter the most to training and HR professionals. Our Essential Knowledge resources translate the expertise of seasoned professionals into practical, how-to guidance on critical workplace issues and problems. These resources are supported by case studies, worksheets, and job aids and are frequently supplemented with CD-ROMs, websites, and other means of making the content easier to read, understand, and use.

**Essential Tools**   Pfeiffer's Essential Tools resources save time and expense by offering proven, ready-to-use materials—including exercises, activities, games, instruments, and assessments—for use during a training or-team-learning event. These resources are frequently offered in looseleaf or CD-ROM format to facilitate copying and customization of the material.

Pfeiffer also recognizes the remarkable power of new technologies in expanding the reach and effectiveness of training. While e-hype has often created whizbang solutions in search of a problem, we are dedicated to bringing convenience and enhancements to proven training solutions. All our e-tools comply with rigorous functionality standards. The most appropriate technology wrapped around essential content yields the perfect solution for today's on-the-go trainers and human resource professionals.

*Essential resources for training and HR professionals*

Instructors are invited to download a FREE Instructor's Manual with tools and information for using *Learning in 3D* in a college course. The instructor's manual includes sample course outlines and syllabi, study and discussion questions, student assignments, classroom activities, PowerPoint slides, and other helpful resources. Please visit www.wiley.com/college/kapp to download your copy.

# LEARNING IN 3D

## Adding a New Dimension to Enterprise Learning and Collaboration

Karl M. Kapp
Tony O'Driscoll

**Pfeiffer**

**A Wiley Imprint**
www.pfeiffer.com

Published by Pfeiffer
An Imprint of Wiley
989 Market Street, San Francisco, CA 94103-1741   www.pfeiffer.com

For additional copies/bulk purchases of this book in the U.S. please contact 800-274-4434.

Pfeiffer books and products are available through most bookstores. To contact Pfeiffer directly call our
Customer Care Department within the U.S. at 800-274-4434, outside the U.S. at 317-572-3985, fax
317-572-4002, or visit www.pfeiffer.com.

Pfeiffer also publishes its books in a variety of electronic formats. Some content that appears in print
may not be available in electronic books.

**Library of Congress Cataloging-in-Publication Data**

Kapp, Karl M.
   Learning in 3D: adding a new dimension to enterprise learning and collaboration / Karl M. Kapp,
Tony O'Driscoll.
      p.   cm.
   Includes bibliographical references and index.
   ISBN 978-0-470-50473-4 (cloth)
      1. Organizational learning.   2. Computer networks.   3. Organizational change.
   I. O'Driscoll, Tony II. Title.
   HD58.82.K37 2010
   658.3'12404—dc22

                                                                    2009043622

Acquiring Editor: Matthew Davis                    Editor: Rebecca Taff
Director of Development: Kathleen Dolan Davies      Editorial Assistant: Lindsay Morton
Production Editor: Dawn Kilgore                     Manufacturing Supervisor: Becky Morgan


Printed in the United States of America

*Printing* 10   9   8   7   6   5   4   3   2   1

# Contents

# Foreword

CONTENT HAS ALWAYS BEEN the center of the human-computer interface. We have lived now for decades with the "desktop" and the "filing cabinet" being the primary metaphor for the human–computer interaction. In learning, we spent years implementing learning management systems that are essentially prisons for learning content. We had to be sure the data about our students was properly tracked and scored—we missed the point about learning. We had a focus on content that reflected the hierarchy of our organizations and of our learning models that were available at that time. Now with the emergence of live avatar-based virtual environments, we have the opportunity to move beyond content, beyond rigid hierarchies, beyond the desktop, to a learning environment focused on the context of learning. Now learning in context will become the most empowering component for learning and collaboration for humans and the human–computer interface will be more naturalistic.

Why do business and learning professionals need to consider virtual immersive environments seriously for learning and collaboration? Why is a new computer–human interface important? Consider the following:

- Recently, scientists, using the most advanced instrumentation, have informed us that the universe is 13.73 billion years old, give or take 120 million years.

- The generally accepted age for the Earth, and the rest of the solar system, is about 4.55 billion years.

- Biological life has been flourishing on our pale blue planet for a significant portion of that 4.55 billion years, with relatively intelligent mammalian bipeds showing up only a few hundred thousand years ago.

- I've only been able to buy cool used guitars online for the past ten years or so.

It's time to move forward in the learning and development field. To this point, the book you are about to read paints a straight arrow of truth toward that future. You will read a grand sweeping vision of how social production and distributed learning will change culture and business as we know it. You will also see iteration points along this early timeline in the form of specific examples and case studies. Throughout, you will witness the convergence of collaboration and learning to create the new immersive Internet. I believe this new Internet will have an important impact on the enterprise as we know it. Modern work life, as we experience it today, is like drinking from a giant fire hose of data. An avalanche of content rains down on our inbox, mobile device, and browser, but data does not give us meaning.

Human interaction is what gives us meaning. And as the consumer social networking and gaming worlds have shown us, our children have already evolved their fathers' Internet from a digital billboard to a PLACE where people go to end their personal isolation. A place they go to find meaning. This powerful new context will be a foundation upon which we will build a new economy, one in which rapidly iterated context shapes the information and data flows of our lives into contextual meaning.

This will not be a nice-to-have option in the "post-depression" economy. The only competitive advantage any organization can hope to leverage in this brave new world is the efficiency (speed) and efficacy (retention/focus) of knowledge transfer, and the 3D Internet aids both." Knowledge transfer is the ultimate currency of the future. It will flow most effectively when collaboration and learning move beyond time-bound "events" where data is downloaded. To a new contextual "always on" sphere of connectivity, where content and context flow like the signals between neurons in a massive and highly adaptive communal brain.

Learning has been and always will be the mechanism of adaptation for us. It is the means by which knowledge is transferred. But now in these most difficult times, organizations must do it very quickly, or be obliterated by Darwinistic market forces. We must now learn top down, bottom up, and side to side, breaking down traditional hierarchies and organizational boundaries. Collaboration and learning will merge to create a powerful "knowledge network" effect, obsolescing traditional organizational hierarchies and functional silos. Learning professionals have an opportunity to leverage this shift to gain a more strategic seat at the executive table.

The two men who have collaborated to write this book, Dr. Tony O'Driscoll, Professor of the Practice at Duke's Fuqua School of Business, and Dr. Karl M. Kapp, Professor of Instructional Technology at Bloomsburg University, are two of the most dynamic minds I have ever met. If you ever earn the honor of a meal with the two of them together, you will instantly feel as if some invisible force has increased your IQ. They have put together a text here that I think will increase the collective IQ for this entire emerging space. As such, I invite you to stay connected with Tony and Karl and this evolving work by joining and contributing to their wiki book and collaborative space at www.learningin3d.info.

The ancient mystics have long taught us that the key to enlightenment is to put some "space" between our thoughts—to be present in the moment to the flow of our ideas, so that we might understand them before we react to them. Had the fallen titans of Wall Street had a similar mechanism for their large and deeply dysfunctional organizations, perhaps the economic crisis we have experienced in recent times may not have happened. Let us use this opportunity in time to create more self-aware organizations, in which we never let blind content rule entire social and financial organizations.

The emerging Immersive Internet holds the promise of a more human net, a more effective way of communicating—one where we can learn to live and work together in new and more sustainable ways.

*Ron Burns*
*CEO*
*ProtonMedia*

# Preface

ANYONE WHO HAS EXPERIENCED the process of building a house has learned first-hand that there is a core set of steps that are absolutely essential for ensuring that the finished product does not disappoint. We believe steps for building an immersive three-dimensional (3D) learning experience are not much different.

The first step in building a house involves active exploration of the possibility space to iteratively determine what is "in" and what is "out" based on criteria such as preferred style, the shape of the land, and the available budget. This step usually culminates with a rough idea of the desirable design elements to be included in the house.

The next step involves working with an architect to craft an integrated blueprint that outlines in great detail how all of the design elements identified in step one converge into a cohesive whole. This step also cycles through a number of iterations based on tradeoffs between preferred layout and architectural constraints.

Once the architectural blueprint is finalized, the final step begins with breaking ground and culminates with a move-in. Whether the experience between these two events is positive or negative is largely a function of how well the plan to move from "blueprint to building" is managed and executed. In any building project, there are always unanticipated circumstances and obstacles that require changes. Without a solid planning process that can accommodate these unanticipated changes, the likelihood of a negative outcome dramatically increases.

This purpose of this book is to describe how to avoid a negative outcome as you work to build engaging 3D learning experiences. As such, the primary steps associated with building a house outlined above provide a good framework to structure the first three parts of this book.

This book contains a great deal of information, tools, models, and advice from the authors and others within this nascent field. The goal of the book is to provide you with a breadth of knowledge so that you begin the process of creating a virtual immersive environment by applying the models and tools provided.

# Getting Started

If you are familiar with virtual worlds and avatars, you can jump right in at Chapter 1. If you are a little less familiar, you might want to review the Appendix and get acquainted with the convergence of e-learning technologies and virtual world technologies into the three-dimensional learning worlds available today. This preface lays the groundwork for understanding terminology and the context in which virtual worlds have begun to be used for learning purposes.

## Part I: Exploring the Possibilities

The first part of this book revolves around three words: Progress, Problems, and Possibilities.

Chapter 1, Here Comes the Immersive Internet, answers the following questions: *What is the Immersive Internet, and how is it impacting the businesses that the learning function serves?* It describes how Immersive Internet technology has **progressed** to a point at which it is beginning to redefine both society and industry. This chapter also examines how business-as-usual is becoming "business unusual" as a result of the convergence of four technology vectors that are driving the business environment toward the creation of new economic platforms based on social production.

Chapter 2, Learning to Change, answers the following questions: *What is wrong with the learning function's current approach to addressing business unusual, and why must it change?* It describes the **problems** that a modern-day organization faces due to its inability to adapt and change as rapidly as the environment within which it operates. This chapter also highlights the growing disconnect between the learning needs of the modern-day enterprise and the ability of the traditional learning function to address them.

Chapter 3, Escaping Flatland, answers the following questions: *What is 3D learning, and why is it better suited to meet the needs of business unusual?* It explores the **possibilities** of a new learning paradigm that is enabled by the same Immersive Internet technologies that are revolutionizing business. This chapter also introduces two vignettes that compare a "Flatland" 2D learning experience to an immersive and engaging 3D learning experience.

As was the case in building a house, once the possibility space has been explored, the next step focuses on architecture.

## Part II: Building a Blueprint

The second part of this book revolves around three words: Principles, Archetypes, and Examples.

Chapter 4, Architecting Learning Experiences, answers the following questions: *What are the 3D learning design principles, and how are they applied to create a 3D learning experience blueprint?* It describes the key design **principles** required to build engaging 3D learning experiences. This chapter also presents a comprehensive 3D learning architecture that can be applied to create a blueprint that ensures alignment and balance in the design of compelling 3D learning experiences.

Chapter 5, Designing by Archetype, answers the following question: *How can learning archetypes be applied as building blocks in the design of engaging 3D learning experiences?* It describes eleven learning **archetypes** that form the basic building blocks for creating 3D learning experiences. This chapter also presents comprehensive definitions of each archetype and provides examples of how the building blocks can be applied to create compelling 3D learning experiences.

Chapter 6, Learning from Experience, answers the following questions: *Who has successfully designed 3D learning experiences, and what can be learned from their experience?* It describes nine case studies of successful 3D learning **experience** designs and maps these designs back to the archetypes that were used to create them.

As was the case in building a house, once the blueprint has been created, the next step focuses on execution.

## Part III: Breaking New Ground

The third part of this book revolves around three words: Process, Adoption, and Rules.

Chapter 7, Overcoming Being Addled by ADDIE, answers the following question: *How does the traditional ADDIE process change when it is applied to create 3D learning experiences?* It describes how the existing ADDIE **process** must be augmented to address the nuances associated with analyzing, designing, developing, implementing and evaluating 3D learning experiences.

Chapter 8, Steps to Successful Enterprise Adoption, answers the following question: *What key steps are required to drive adoption of 3D learning experiences within the enterprise?* It describes the steps required to drive **adoption** of 3D learning experiences by mapping them to the diffusion of innovation attractiveness criteria: Relative Advantage, Compatibility, Complexity, Trialability, and Observability.

Chapter 9, Rules from Revolutionaries, answers the following questions: *Who else has successfully driven 3D learning adoption, and what can be learned from their experience?* It presents four essays from front-line revolutionaries who share their insights on how they changed the **rules** and convinced their organizations to adopt 3D learning.

The final part of this book explores what lies ahead for 3D learning.

## Part IV: Just Beyond the Horizon

The final part of this book revolves around one word: Future.

Chapter 10, Back to the Future, answers the following questions: *What's next for 3D learning, and what will things look like in 2020?* It describes a maturity model that argues that immersive technologies will evolve from learning to eventually encompassing all work activity and how you can move your organization toward that eventuality. It also presents two essays that envision the **future** of 3D learning from two of the industry's leading visionaries.

In short, the ten chapters in this book can be summarized in ten simple words: Progress, Problems, Possibilities, Principles, Archetypes, Examples, Processes, Adoption, Rules, and Future.

## The Best Way to Read This Book

In the spirit of learning from experience, this book is designed to strike a balance between description and prescription. It can be used as a primer or introductory text to introduce the topic of 3D learning, but it is also designed as a practical field-book to help teams that are actually in the midst of designing 3D learning experiences within their workplaces.

If you are reading this book as a primer, it makes the most sense to read the chapters in chronological order. Pause after each part to ensure you understand the key arguments and positions in each chapter and then move on to the next part.

Another approach to consider might be to cover the contents of the book as a team or group. Divide your team, department, or faculty into reading clubs and read a chapter each week. Then, once a week, the group could get together and discuss the salient and thought-provoking points. How can you help the organization design meaningful learning in 3D worlds? What guidelines should we establish for someone teaching in a 3D virtual world? Can we sell 3D virtual worlds to our leadership? How do we implement these ideas?

This group approach will spark discussion, provide insightful solutions, and guide you to develop your own methods of applying the ideas and concepts in this book to your own organization or classroom. It will also begin discussions about the future of learning within your organization that may not have occurred otherwise. These conversations, even when slightly off-topic, will be valuable in strengthening your organization in terms of maximizing the use of virtual immersive environments.

If you are in the midst of designing a 3DLE, we encourage you to become intimately familiar with Part II of the book. Work with your peers on the design team to ensure that you all understand each level of the architecture and test each other to ensure that you have applied the architecture in a way that ensures alignment and balance in the design of instruction.

Graduate and undergraduate students in particular will find this book of interest, as the need to create, interact, and learn within these 3D environments will continue to grow as the generations that have grown up with video games demand interfaces that are just as rich and vibrant in corporate and academic settings. The first part of the book will be of particular interest, as it describes why the change to 3D learning is not cosmetic, but deep and fundamental.

We wish you all the best in your quest to bring a new dimension to learning within your workplace or academic environment!

# Continuing the Discussion

A topic like this does not remain static; it is constantly moving as technology and our understandings of the power of these environments to foster learning and collaboration continue to grow. In an effort to continue the dialogue in real time and to make real progress in helping others understand virtual worlds, we are creating a website (www.learningin3d.info), which contains a space for you to respond to blogs on the subject, a wiki for you to update terms and definitions, and video and podcasts on the topic. You will also find lists of resources and white papers to help you implement and manage 3D learning events. Additionally, you will find the ability to enter into a virtual immersive environment (VIE) and check it out for yourself. You will meet virtual renderings of the authors and interact with others within the space as we have in-world book launches and educational sessions. Most importantly, with these web tools, you will find room to contribute your knowledge, thoughts, and wisdom on the subject. Please visit and share your knowledge and experience of how 3D virtual worlds are impacting you and your organization.

This book provides a list of recommendations and techniques for conducting learning in a 3D virtual learning world. These new and sometimes radical ideas push the knowledge and innovation envelope and sometimes even personal comfort levels. Academic, corporate, and non-profit organizations that adopt 3D virtual worlds for learning will partake in a new and exciting venture that will move online learning far ahead of where it is today.

# Acknowledgments

WE OFTEN TEND TO think of the creative endeavor as a solitary one. The next Einstein, we posit, is holed up in a dark office somewhere just on the cusp of a Eureka moment that will change the world.

My own experience suggests something different. The creative endeavor you hold in your hands is the work of many people. Their respective contributions came together in record time and almost magically found their way into a constantly evolving outline that ebbed and flowed the more we learned in talking to each other and with others. In fact, this book is probably more aptly described as a collective experience, as opposed to a creative endeavor.

However we ultimately describe it, one thing is sure, this book would never have come into existence without:

- My parents, who decided to have a child. Thank you Mum and Dad!

- The countless educators who patiently guided me along the long and winding path to completing my doctoral work. Thanks to all of you.

- My incredibly patient wife and family. Thank you Theresa, Aidan, and Liam.

- A world-class university and a stellar group of administrators at the Fuqua School of Business who supported me in this effort. Thanks Blair, Bill, Jennifer, and Wendy.

- A co-author patient enough to put up with me. Thank you Karl.

- An editor who was willing to allow us the space and time to write the book we wanted to. Thank you Matt.

- A group of selfless Immersive Internet pioneers who willingly shared their insights and wisdom to make this book the best it can be. Thanks to you all.

*Tony O'Driscoll*

*Raleigh, North Carolina*

*September 1, 2009*

Writing is such a rollercoaster experience, the lows of deadlines, writer's block and searching for that darn missing reference and the highs of new knowledge acquired through the collaborative writing process, understandings gained from questioning my assumptions, and new insights developed through shared vision. Writing this book with all the great contributors and my great co-author has been fun. This book is truly a "mash up" of wonderful minds all contributing to the final product.

So I'd like to acknowledge:

- The eLearning Guild for bringing Tony and me together for the essay that started this whole thing.

- My mother for her continued and unfailing belief in me over the years.

- My late father for his sense of patience, thoughtfulness, and dry humor.

- My awesome family. Nancy, Nate, and Nick are simply the best! Special thanks to Nancy.

- All the wonderful students, who question, prod, and push my thinking in continually new directions. You give me such energy.

- Teachers, faculty members, and other educators who have continued to inspire me.

- Bloomsburg University's Department of Instructional Technology. I couldn't ask to work with better faculty and staff at any university. A special thanks to Alexandra Varias, who helped with a variety of last-minute organizational tasks, and to Karen Swartz, who is always helpful.

- Kaplan-EduNeering and Performance Development Group—two clients who continue to provide me with opportunities to apply theory, design, and concepts to solve organizational learning problems.

- Tony, writing this book has been a lot of fun. Really enjoyed sharing ideas, late nights, and impromptu Skype calls. Thanks Tony!

- Thanks to Matthew Davis for our little extension. Always appreciated. And thanks for his vision and forward thinking to bring this book to life.

- And to echo Tony's sentiment: Thanks to a group of selfless Immersive Internet pioneers who willingly shared their insights and wisdom to make this book the best it can be.

*Karl M. Kapp*

*Bloomsburg, PA*

*September 1, 2009.*

# Part One

# Exploring the Possibilities

# Here Comes the Immersive Internet!

"OMG, I AM SO BUSTED! . . . *Mom found the bottle of vodka Tyler got us in the trunk of the car. . . . She is going to tell dad when he gets home. . . . NEED HELP! . . . 17 and my life is already over . . . All hands on deck. . . . Get everyone on FB right NOW. . . . Dad home in 45 minutes. . . . I CAN'T get grounded next weekend. . . . . I am so PSYCHED about going to the dance with Mark."*

Instantly, Jessica's network comes to life. Those not on Facebook are notified via text message. Just to be sure no one is missed, Jessica sends out a tweet: *"Need help right now . . . . mom found vodka . . . .dad home in 45 mins . . . . meet on FB right NOW!"*

Within a minute Jessica's friends are convened. *"When I got busted I worked on my mom to make sure dad didn't ground me for too long,"* says Ashley. *"Yeah but Jessica's mom is not as much of a pushover as your mom,"* says Matt. *"When I got busted I owned up to making a mistake with my dad and that worked better." "But wait, can't we work Tyler into the picture here?"* says Samantha. *"After all, he is Jessica's older brother." "I know,"* says Brittany, *"let's get Tyler to say he got the Vodka for someone else and left it in the car by mistake. . . . Is he online? . . . Let's get him in here now."*

And so it goes on: Each of Jessica's friends bringing his or her respective experience and insights to solve her pressing issue. In twenty short minutes they converge on a story and a set of arguments to maximize the potential that Jessica gets to go on that all-important date with Mark!

Meanwhile, dad pulls into the driveway. Tired from a long day's work and frustrated from the traffic jam on the way home, he asks himself, *"I wonder if there is any way I could slip out to the patio and read the paper in peace for a half-hour before dinner?"*

Little does he know what is waiting for him inside!

## The Invisibly Pervasive Web

On April 22, 1993, the Mosaic web browser was introduced to the world. And, for the past sixteen years, we have collectively surfed the digital domain of the web to a point where it has become so ubiquitous we take it for granted.[1] Just like the air we breathe to stay alive, we only notice the real impact the web has on our lives in its absence.

Skeptical? Pause to consider how many times you access the web each day. Or think about how many e-Vites, LinkedIn, or Facebook invitations you receive weekly. Add to that the number of text messages or tweets you write or receive on a monthly basis and the pervasiveness of how much the web is permeating your life becomes more clear.

The next time the web is "down" at your place of work, closely examine the behavior of your co-workers. Most likely, you will observe groups of people aimlessly wandering the halls behaving as if they have suffered some strange form of collective amnesia as to their roles in the organization and how they add value. Observe today's college students working to complete a research project. If the web went down, these digital natives would have no clue how to navigate the real stacks in an actual library. To them, research means searching on EBSCO[2] and downloading the PDF of the paper to their laptop in a wireless café.

Today, the web has permeated what we do socially, professionally, and educationally to such an extent that we have become oblivious to the profound changes it has brought to how we connect, communicate, coordinate, collaborate, and take collective action. Recognizing that browser software is younger than Jessica in the vignette above, it is daunting to consider just how rapidly the World Wide Web has transformed how we interact socially and collaborate professionally.

As the Internet continues to pervade society, the scarcity paradigm that undergirds most modern economic theory is being challenged. Unlike currency, information is non-appropriable, which essentially means that it can be shared without being given away. Today, information no longer moves in one direction, from the top of the enterprise to the bottom or from teacher to student. Instead, it has a social life all its own.[3] Information travels from place to place based on individuals' desire to interact with it, because they want to make more effective decisions or develop keener insights about a particular situation, or because someone is motivated to learn about a certain topic or how to complete a given task.

We are witnessing the acceleration of the co-evolution of society and technology. In a socio-technical system like the one we are in, information is the currency, individuals are the transport mechanism, interaction is the transfer mechanism, and insight is the value-added outcome. Given this context, we can begin to conceive of the web's own evolution as a pervasive and expanding ecosystem whose central purpose is to facilitate collective action, learning, and growth. In this evolutionary process, it is natural that the three-dimensional web will be a large part of society's increasingly digital future. The societal, professional, and educational consequences of this emerging learning ecosystem are beginning to take shape on a large scale.

Mark Zukerberg, CEO of Facebook, suggests that communication should not be viewed as a way for people to get information. Instead, he proposes that information is a mechanism to foster better communication between people.[4] While the mission of Google is to organize the world's information, it appears that Zukerberg is more focused on leveraging information to organize better interactions between people. It is this subtle yet significant reframing of the relationship between information, communication, and people that allowed Jessica to leverage the Facebook platform to connect with her friends, communicate her pressing issue, collaborate with others at a distance to develop a solution, and take action to ensure that she still got to go on that date with Mark. Poor old dad never had a chance!

To understand the convergence of communication, collaboration, and the inevitable trajectory of the web toward a 3D interface, it is important to understand the transformation of the web and track its maturation as a communication, learning, and collaboration medium. In less than two decades, the commercial web had experienced two full evolutionary waves and is now at the beginning of a powerful third wave that will bring the web into the third dimension.

# Welcome to the Webvolution

*"This could not be more perfect."* Jessica thought to herself as she slow danced to her favorite song with Mark. She looked toward Ashley and Brittany, and they both smiled and gave her a thumbs-up. *"I wish this song would never end."* Jessica thought to herself.

When it did, Mark asked if she wanted to go out to the patio for a chat. As they walked under the stars, she could see Matt, Ashley, and Brittany pointing, giggling, and high-fiving each other out of the corner of her eye. It was clear that they had pulled this off and she was so thankful. She was not sure that their grand plan would work, but she was so desperate to see Mark again that she had been willing to try anything. Now she was very glad she did.

Unfortunately, two nights before the dance, Tyler, Jessica's older brother, blew her cover after they got into a fight. So she and her friends were grounded by their parents and could not attend the dance. As luck would have it, Mark couldn't go to the dance either, as his family had to unexpectedly visit their grandmother, who had broken her hip.

During another Facebook jam session to deal with this turn of events, Matt suggested they set up a virtual dance in the 3D virtual space of Second Life so all the kids who were grounded could attend the event virtually. The friends worked together for a whole day getting the invite list out to all the grounded kids (and Mark), building the virtual dance hall, and figuring out how to pipe the DJ's audio from the actual dance into their online 3D dance hall.

While all the folks were hanging out in "meatspace" at the school gymnasium, Mark and Jessica, while distant from each other physically, could not have felt more together as they chatted on the virtual patio via VoIP. *"I'd really like to see you again when I get home, Jessica. Would you like to go see a movie with me next weekend?"* Jessica smiled, and without trying to sound too eager, replied with a cool, *"Yeah, that might be fun."* She then muted her audio and let out a huge yell *"Yahoooooooo!"* while simultaneously jumping up and down on her bed and Twittering that she got a movie date with Mark!

Dad, still on a mission to read his newspaper in peace, came scurrying up the stairs and pounded on her door *"What are you doing in there? Don't you know you are grounded? Keep it down will you. If you keep this up you will never get to go to a dance again."*

Mark, Jessica and their friends are participating in the third wave of the World Wide Web. They are interacting, communicating, and collaborating within the web. This ability to interact within the web is a hallmark of the third wave of the webvolution. To date, the web has experienced three evolutionary waves:

- Web 1.0 was focused on connecting "TO" the web;
- Web 2.0 is focused on connecting "THROUGH" the web; and
- Web 3.0, which is happening now, is focused on connecting "WITHIN" the web.

The next sections of this chapter explore each wave of the webvolution (see Figure 1.1) and illustrate how we have arrived at this evolutionary convergence of technology, communication, and collaboration.

## Web 1.0: Access and Find

With the arrival of the browser in 1993, Web 1.0 provided society with the opportunity to access more information than ever before. The early "read only" web provided basic text, graphics, and information to anyone who could access it via a browser. As couch potatoes turned into mouse potatoes,

**Figure 1.1.** The Three Webvolution Waves

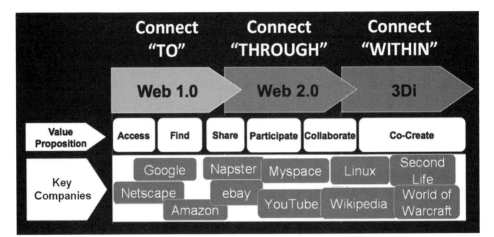

firms in the financial services, banking, and travel industries seized the opportunity to provide their customers with web-based access to information that drove more transactions and generated additional revenues. Information technology (IT) infrastructure and telecommunications companies rode the Web 1.0 wave by building the technical platform that provided web-access to more and more customers. New Internet service provider (ISP) companies such as AOL and Prodigy emerged to provide support and service as an on-ramp to this new medium for a rapidly growing customer base.

As the amount of available content grew exponentially, the need to effectively and efficiently find information on the web became paramount. Initially, search engines with names like Lycos and WebCrawler became popular. Eventually, Yahoo garnered significant traction in meeting the need to quickly find information in the vast repositories of the web. It accomplished its goal by cataloging and organizing web content. By the end of 1994, Yahoo had received over one-million hits.[5]

In the fast-changing world of the web, Yahoo was eventually overthrown by Google. In a few short years, Google became the dominant player in addressing the "Find" value proposition based on Sergey Brin and Larry Page's patented PageRank search algorithm.[6] Thus began Google's ascendancy to the Internet powerhouse it is today. By identifying and addressing an unmet need that emerged from the first wave of the webvolution—the need to "find" information on the web—Google secured its place in business history.

Amazon's Jeff Bezos saw another way to leverage Web 1.0 for economic gain. In so doing, he successfully took on the largest brick-and-mortar bookstores in the world. His idea was that, while most large retail bookstores could offer as many as 200,000 titles, an online bookstore could ultimately offer many more.[7] The lower cost structure of not having to maintain brick-and-mortar retail outlets could be applied toward optimizing the supply chain. In many ways the now familiar concept of long-tail economics, popularized by Chris Anderson at Wired, was at the core of Bezos' vision.[8] More importantly, since the virtual storefront aggregated access for consumers, Amazon's popular book rating and referral system—often cited as a differentiator for Amazon over traditional retail outlets—allowed the company to offer targeted book referrals, driving additional revenues.

If we examine closely the underpinnings of what made both Google and Amazon's value propositions compelling to nascent web users, or "netizens" as they came to be called, it becomes evident that they both leveraged the aggregated behavior of many users to differentiate their respective offerings. Google's page rank system assigns a weight to a web page based on the number of pages that link to it. The more a page is linked to, the higher its relative importance. By aggregating this data as a mechanism for prioritizing search returns, Google provides customers with more effective search results. Similarly, by aggregating the buying patterns of customers, Amazon can make referrals to customers with similar buying patterns that are likely to result in more book purchases.

In both cases, it appears that Bezos, Brin, and Page had, knowingly or not, presaged the next webvolution wave: Web 2.0—The participatory "read-write" web.

## Web 2.0: Share, Participate, Collaborate

During the Web 2.0 wave, the focus shifted from connecting people "to" the web to enabling people to connect "through" the web to share, participate, and collaborate. As outlined in Figure 1.1, file sharing software like Napster serves as a bridge between Web 1.0 and Web 2.0.

In 1999, Shawn Fanning launched Napster, an online music file sharing service.[9] In so doing, he disrupted the existing value chain of the music industry at its core. Suddenly, instead of traveling to a record store to buy a physical piece of media (a CD or cassette), people instantly downloaded an MP3 music file from the web. The key point here is not that people could access music files on the web, but how those music files were made available in the first place. In essence, people took advantage of the all-but-unenforceable illegality of Fanning's peer-to-peer file-sharing technology to share music collections for free. Much has been written on how Napster created a technological discontinuity that fundamentally disrupted the music industry. The Web 2.0 "share" value proposition that was leveraged by people using the Napster platform is what ultimately created this disruption.

Moving from sharing music to sharing video is a logical next step. The music and movie industries have very similar business models and value chain dynamics. One obvious difference is that movies and video programming have a larger digital payload than music files. In the early days of the web there were many skeptics in the movie and broadcast media industry. One of the most notable among them was Stephen Weiswasser, then senior vice president of ABC, who confidently proclaimed, "You are not going to turn passive consumers into trollers on the Internet."[10]

Those of you who have teenagers know all too well that Weiswasser's proclamation was errant. Today's net generation is anything but passive. They want to interact and collaborate on an ongoing basis with their peer networks. They want to be engaged in the creative process rather than just be a consumer of it. They refuse to sit passively digesting broadcast media. Instead, like Jessica and her friends in the earlier vignette, they literally live on social networking sites such as Facebook and MySpace, where they share, create, participate, and collaborate on an ongoing basis.

In September of 2008, Nielsen reported that MySpace had fifty-nine million users and Facebook had thirty-nine million.[11] Less than one year later MySpace has ballooned to 300 million users and Facebook is not far behind with 276 million.[12] To put this in context, if MySpace and Facebook were viewed as virtual countries where netizens reside, MySpace would be the fifth largest country in the world and Facebook would be the sixth.[13]

One of the things that these netizens do in their virtual social habitat is share media. Pictures and videos are instantly uploaded from the cell-phone to the online photo site of Flickr and into the video site, YouTube. These media then begin a social life all their own as they are tagged and commented on by others as they traverse the Web 2.0 landscape at the speed of light.

YouTube, founded in 2005, is a video sharing website that allows users to upload, view, and share video clips.[14] Each day about nine thousand hours of video content is uploaded to YouTube. To put this in context, aggregating all the programming from the three primary networks (ABC, NBC, CBS) for the past sixty years would result in a total of 1.5 million hours of video programming. Those 1.5 million hours are equivalent to less than six months worth of video content submitted to YouTube.[15]

YouTube is a platform that has provided a user-generated alternative to the enterprise studio and broadcast approaches for media access and distribution. In short, with the arrival of Web 2.0 technologies that enable netizens to share, participate, and collaborate, we are witnessing a redefinition of how the media and entertainment industry develops and distributes content. This shift brings with it the need for a redefinition in the industry's enterprise structure and business model to address the threat of the user-generated content.

For those of you who may have an old collection of physical media (vinyl albums, eight-track tapes, or Betamax movies) that are taking up space in your basement or attic, there is still hope! In 1995, eBay founder, Pierre Omidyar's vision was to provide a web-based platform that allowed people to buy and sell goods via an online auction site. Ten short years later, eBay was conducting approximately ten billion web services transactions a year,[16] and more than 700,000 Americans reported that eBay was their primary or secondary source of income.[17] Through eBay, netizens now have the ability to participate in a digital world-wide yard sale, turning their trash into someone else's treasure. Instead of working for eBay, eBay works for them.

As we move into the next wave of the webvolution, we observe a continuing trend in the creation of economic platforms that cultivate new forms of innovative co-creation leading to different forms of wealth creation for those netizens who choose to participate.

If Napster was the bridge from Web 1.0 to Web 2.0, Wikipedia is the bridge from Web 2.0 to the Immersive Internet. In founding Wikipedia in 2002, Jimmy Wales' vision was that every single person on the planet should be given free access to the sum of all human knowledge.[18] Leveraging the ability that Web 2.0 tools brought to allow people to connect "through" the web, Wikipedia derives its value from enabling collaborative action through "crowdsourcing."[19] Crowdsourcing is defined as "the act of taking a task traditionally performed by an employee or contractor and outsourcing it to an undefined, generally large group of people, in the form of an open call."[20]

In the case of Wikipedia, the task that was outsourced to netizens at large was the creation of the world's largest encyclopedia. In the past seven years Wikipedia has grown to twelve million articles written collaboratively by volunteers around the world.[21] This same crowdsourcing phenomenon has been successfully leveraged in the development of open source software such as the Linux operating system. Both Wikipedia and Linux activate the "collaboration" and "co-creation" value propositions of the web—in one case for the development of the world's largest digital encyclopedia and in the other for the creation of an operating system that is gaining significant traction against offerings from traditional IT enterprises such as Microsoft. Thus the application of virtual co-creation is firmly established as a pattern at the edge of Web 2.0 as the third wave approaches.

## The Immersive Internet: Collaborate and Co-Create

Today, the web is in the midst of a migration from the traditional two-dimensional web browser interface to a three-dimensional one. Just as the introduction of the Mosaic browser changed society and business, the impending transformation of the Internet from a static, one-way conduit of information into a three-dimensional virtual environment in which people—as avatars— live, work, and play will have an equally significant transformational impact.

The 3D Internet that was once the dominion of hard-core gamers is rapidly becoming mainstream. To explore how the Immersive Internet is beginning to pervade society and impact the economy, we begin by exploring *World of Warcraft*, one of the world's most popular massively multiplayer online role playing games (MMORPG).

First released in 1994 by Blizzard Entertainment, *World of Warcraft* (WoW) has grown steadily to more than 11.5 million subscribers.[22] As with most MMORPGs, players form teams known as guilds that work together to move through a series of challenges that have increasing levels of difficulty. As game players work together to move through the levels in the game, they gain skills and acquire currency that is tied to their digital personas, or avatars. Players who choose to quit the game have the ability to cash out their currency and even sell their avatars online. This cashing out process is not insignificant. The highest *World of Warcraft* avatar account trade to date was valued at $9,000.[23]

*World of Warcraft* is essentially a game-based economic platform where avatars work through gameplay activities within a virtual economy to develop reputational capital that can then be exchanged for real currency. MMORPG platforms like *World of Warcraft* and *EverQuest* have spawned a new "gold farming" industry in China. In 2007, gold farmers employed more than 100,000 workers. These workers play games in twelve-hour shifts. For each hundred coins gathered, the worker earns approximately $1.25. Their boss sells this virtual loot to an online broker for approximately $3. The online broker ultimately sells the virtual currency coins to an American or European customer for as much as $20 in real currency.[24]

In similar fashion, Second Life (SL), a virtual world developed by Linden Lab, allows its residents to interact with each other through avatars. Second Life residents can socialize, explore, participate in group activities, create items, and trade virtual property and services with one another. Second Life has its own currency, the Linden Dollar, that can be used to buy and sell virtual items within the virtual world. Linden Dollars can be exchanged for real dollars at currency exchanges such as IGE.[25] Anshe Chung is probably the most famous Second Life entrepreneur. She was featured on the cover of *BusinessWeek* in May of 2006, and she is widely reported to be the first real-life Second Life millionaire.[26]

It turns out Anshe is not alone in the business of selling virtual assets. In 2007, people spent over $1.5 billion on virtual items.[27] Many people find it difficult to believe people would spend real money to buy an avatar or a virtual piece of real estate that is essentially nothing more than a digital bucket of bits and bytes. However, if you conceive of the trade, not as a transaction for an object, but as a payment for a service, it may be less difficult to comprehend. In essence, people buying *World of Warcraft* avatars or a fully decked-out Second Life island complete with waterfalls and dolphins are not paying for the digital product but for the services rendered to create it.

The Immersive Internet opens up a world of opportunity for innovative collaboration and co-creation where avatars inhabiting 3D versions of Facebook and MySpace can participate in a marketplace for virtual goods and services on an ongoing basis or even attend a dance together.

Wharton professor Dan Hunter, an expert on law and virtual worlds, suggests that this generalized access to a range of virtual services could have significant impact on future employment patterns, "I confidently predict that my kids (currently six and four years old) will end up working within one or more of these worlds."[28] He is not alone in this predication. Edward Castronova, author of the seminal work *Synthetic Worlds,* writes about the emergence of economic marketplaces that exist only in virtual worlds and the day when virtual gold pieces are traded for real goods like diamonds.[29]

As the webvolution migrates from Web 1.0 through Web 2.0 to the Immersive Internet, each wave builds on the previous one, leading us to a point at which virtual economies have essentially become real. The arrival of the Immersive Internet as a pervasive and persistent environment within which avatars interact will no doubt usher in new forms of innovative co-creation, business and learning opportunities that create new vehicles of wealth generation and development that cannot even be imagined today.

# Social Production Comes of Age

The second and third webvolution waves have ushered in a number of new value exchange platforms that will be critical to the future of organizations, work, and learning. Platforms like Wikipedia enable the coordination and orchestration of capabilities around specific endeavors, as opposed to the command and control of resources by a central authority. In contrast to most real-world enterprises, whose revenue is often correlated with the size of their employee base, companies like Amazon, Google, eBay, MySpace, and Linden Lab hire a relatively small number of employees to manage their value exchange platforms and attract a large number of members or citizens who leverage the platform in unique ways to create and capture market value.

As communication costs have decreased and the quality of web-based interactivity has increased, communities of co-creators no longer need to rely on a formal organization to become organized. Rather than employing an enterprise infrastructure to plan ahead of time, they leverage the pervasive and immersive affordances of the web to coordinate their activities in real time. In so doing, these savvy netizens are creating a new economic transactional framework that Yochai Benkler calls "social production" (see Figure 1.2).[30]

Social production is the means by which a software operating system or a digital encyclopedia can be created without the need for a large centralized hierarchy. In essence, the web platform itself allows members to participate in a given endeavor as much or as little as they choose. In the past such forms of social production were limited and bounded in nature. Computer

**Figure 1.2.** The Webvolution Encourages Social Production

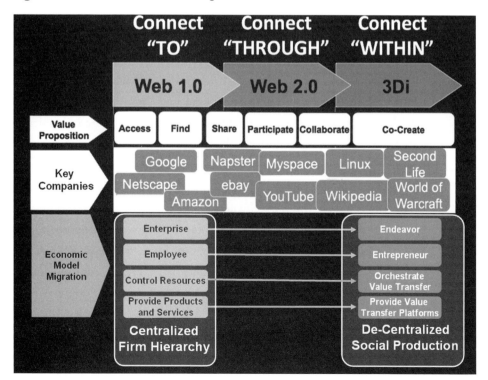

hobbyists in a given city might have gathered monthly to discuss the potential of a new operating system. They might even work together to develop some code. However, now that this kind of work activity can be aggregated and coordinated via the World Wide Web, it is starting to produce significant economic impact. Today, these platforms allow for the orchestration of capable and independent entrepreneurs around a given endeavor, where they can create and capture value from others who participate on that platform.

Virtual worlds like Second Life tap into the talent and creativity of their residents in a unique way. Joe Miller from Linden Lab provides a useful illustration of how much value his company derives from the social production of its residents. Since Second Life provides these residents with the tools to create their own virtual assets, Linden Lab is essentially incenting members to participate in the ongoing development of the Second Life environment. In 2007, Second Life logged about 350,000 hours of use per day. Approximately 25 percent of this time is spent by residents creating new content within the platform. That amounts to 87,500 hour per day of development time spent. Put differently, Second Life residents donate about $1.6 billion worth of free work per year building out the Second Life grid. This equates to a 16,000-person content development team that is not employed by Linden Lab.[31] That is social production in action.

Today, social production is being leveraged much less by the traditional enterprise than it is by the entrepreneurial start-up. These pioneering entrepreneurs are creating and leveraging social production-based platforms for their own benefit as well as for those who participate in their use. These platforms are built on economic models that incent participation without requiring employment. eBay works for eBayers, not the other way around. The deeper we go into the webvolution, the more we will witness the development of economic platforms that allow individuals to operate independently of enterprises to generate value propositions that result in income.

# The Immersive Internet Singularity

In an increasingly digitally interconnected world, technology and enterprise structure are co-evolving at an accelerated rate. If you track the architecture of organizations over the past five decades, moving from centralized bureaucratic hierarchies with rigid boundaries to flatter topological structures with more permeable boundaries, it becomes increasingly evident that there is a syncopation with the IT architectures that underpin these enterprises: From the monolithic centralized mainframes, to the client-server model, to the peer-to-peer decentralized web that constitute today's enterprise IT infrastructures.

Furthermore, technology works through indirection and iteration. This essentially means that it builds on its past success and failures and learns from them to get faster at what it does over and over and over again. This iterative and accelerative cycle is what enables technology to expand and diffuse through society and industry at exponential rates. Moore's law, often articulated as the observation that computers double in speed every eighteen months, is but one example of technology's exponential growth through indirection. In fact, the phenomenon of computer speed doubling has been maintained from the time of vacuum tubes and will no doubt continue once we move from silicon-based transistors to molecular computing.

At present, four discrete software arenas are converging toward a point of technological singularity that will enable the next-generation Immersive Internet infrastructure (see Figure 1.3) or create an "immernet"—the delivery of the immersive characteristics of 3D environments over the Internet.

As we move toward this singularity, the "immernet" will enable the diffusion of social production oriented platforms, providing unimaginable opportunities for inhabitants of those virtual worlds to create new mechanisms of commerce and structures for enabling them. This will also require new ways of learning and interacting among the netizens.

## Convergence Point 1: Immediate Networked Virtual Spaces

Here, 2D synchronous learning platforms such as WebEx and Live Meeting will integrate with knowledge sharing repositories such as SharePoint and Ning, resulting in networked virtual spaces. These spaces will integrate synchronous sharing with asynchronous storage, yielding a one-stop-shop for storage and sharing of content.

**Figure 1.3.** The Immernet Singularity

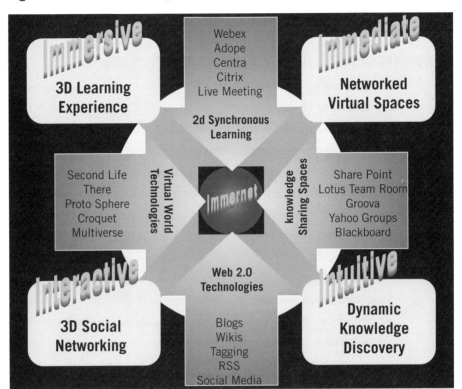

## Convergence Point 2: Intuitive Dynamic Knowledge Discovery

Here, Web 2.0 technologies integrate with knowledge sharing spaces. The impact of blogs, wikis, and social media as engines of user-generated content is well established. However, the primary transformation lever in the Web 2.0 constellation of tools is the one least discussed: social tagging. Most content created and stored in the Web 2.0 domain is tagged with keywords by both creators and users. User-generated tags activate the flows of human connectivity between stocks of content housed in blogs, wikis, and social media sites. More tagging means more knowledge accidents of both the people-to-people and people-to-information kind. The mash-up between real-time tagging and networked virtual spaces allows for immediacy of access to key information and interaction with key people around a given task or activity. In this emerging virtually afforded, contextually relevant, matchmaking world, knowledge discovery and real-time interaction with experts on the topic become the norm on a platform that allows the network itself to become more intuitive.

## Convergence Point 3: Integrated 3D Social Networking

With the infusion of three-dimensional (3D) technology platforms, it is only a matter of time before 3D social networking takes off. When this happens, MySpace truly will become MySPACE. This social movement into the 3D domain will prompt corporate information officers (CIOs) to develop enterprise-grade 3D social networking applications for their corporate citizens, just as they did in the past with applications such as instant messaging. Today enterprise vendors such as Forterra (Olive) and Proton Media (ProtoSphere) are integrating Web 2.0 tools into their 3D interfaces.

## Convergence Point 4: Immersive 3D Learning Experiences

In similar fashion to 3D social networking, synchronous 2D learning and collaboration platforms will enter the third dimension. While current learning and collaboration platforms do allow for virtual interactivity, they do not afford the immersive experience that drives sustained engagement. As a result most web conferences or lectures are sub-optimized in their ability to transfer knowledge in a compelling way. By adding immersion to the equation, organizations can allow for higher quality learning interactions between employees who work at a distance.

The Immersive Internet will become a worldwide virtual platform that allows people to immediately exercise their skills and abilities around endeavors that matter most to them. This next-generation Internet will function like an eBay for trading work activity instead of second-hand products. No one will work for the immernet. Instead the immernet will work for them. Providing its netizens with the opportunity to find both work and people to work with. The Immersive Internet becomes the ultimate netWORK.

Immersive Internet technology makes rich personal exchanges possible without the need for formal structures. The nonlinear dynamics of this new information ecosystem are challenging the traditional structures of enterprise. In fact, a recent study from IBM's Global Innovation Outlook suggests, "The future might consist of a billion one-person enterprises—people who act as free agents moving freely and frequently from project to project as their skills, focus, and passion shift."[32] eBay allowed people to sell their personal items in a world-wide yard sale; the Immersive Internet will allow people to sell their personal skills and abilities in much the same way.

As the webvolution continues to pervade society and industry, we move from "business-as-usual" to "business unusual." Corporations, academic institutions, and government agencies that wish to remain vital and viable in this increasingly interconnected and complex economic landscape will need to determine how to integrate the power of social production into the very fabric of their enterprises.

# Business Unusual

An apple falling on Newton's head leads to the creation of the laws of physics, which leads to the invention of the internal combustion engine, that is followed by the growth of the automobile industry, culminating in Alfred Sloan's creation of the modern-day bureaucracy and Henry Ford's assembly line.

History has taught us that market economies are typically characterized by extended periods of stability that are occasionally punctuated by short periods of high instability that forever alter the status-quo. In similar fashion, throughout history, the diffusion of innovation has typically followed a predictable path: A scientific discovery informs the creation of a new technology, which ushers in a new set of business opportunities that end up reshaping the structure of industries and organizations.[33]

In the past, disruptive technologies such as the printing press and the steam engine were catalysts in creating step-changes in the social and economic landscapes of their respective eras. Today, the transformational effects of the Internet on business are readily apparent. We now live in a service-driven, knowledge-based economy in which product and service lifecycles are shrinking and the work environment is increasing in complexity and velocity. Today's increasingly digital economy places a premium on innovation, customization, new business models, and new ways of organizing work to maximize efficiency.

Broadly speaking, innovation is the process of converting corporate knowledge into value. Alfred Sloan and Henry Ford capitalized on new opportunities and redefined the factory structure and infrastructure for the emergent automotive industry. Successful Immersive Internet enterprises will be those that consistently create new knowledge, share it widely throughout the organization, and rapidly embody it in new differentiated market offerings or more effective workflow approaches. Immersive Internet pioneers are leading the charge in redefining how commerce can be capitalized upon in new and different ways based on social production. Learning and development organizations need to catch up and help their organizations adapt to the new social production methods of doing business.

In this economy fraught with uncertainty, organizations that can't change as fast as the environment within which they operate are destined to regress to mediocrity. Think of the business environment as a pressure chamber and imagine an organization as a balloon within that chamber. If the molecules within the balloon are not moving as fast as the molecules in the chamber, the balloon will shrink. The relentless pace and acceleration of web technology is ratcheting up the pressure in the business environment, requiring that enterprises take on the qualities of adaptive organisms rather than rigid hierarchies. The same is true of academic institutions that must prepare future workers to be productive within these new paradigms.

Today, insights drive innovation, and innovation drives profitable growth. These insights are generated from serendipitous knowledge accidents—the magic moment wherein expertise collides with opportunity and whole new industries are born. At the heart of the capacity to innovate is the ability to learn. An organization simply cannot innovate without learning something new. As has always been the case, a bright future for any enterprise depends on having access to bright people. As a result, the ability to instantly coalesce capability around an increasingly unpredictable set of market opportunities is the pre-eminent challenge of the 21st century organization.

In many ways the organizations that have enjoyed success in a pre-webvolution era face the largest challenge of all. These businesses and academies are built on a rigid core—both structural and infrastructural—that is optimized around a hierarchical command-and-control-based economic model.

As web-based social production pervades and the Immersive Internet takes hold, these organizations will be challenged to rethink their business and academic models from the ground up, requiring significant and sweeping transformation throughout the organization.

For change to occur it is a precondition that learning take place. An old dog becomes an older dog unless it learns a new trick. In the case of centralized hierarchies, the old dog must unlearn all that brought it success in the pre-webvolution era and quickly learn how to leverage the Immersive Internet to reconfigure its resources and capabilities to achieve sustainable competitive advantage in a world gone web.

In the webvolution brains have surpassed brawn as the engine of enterprise. The perennial challenge of the learning function within the enterprise is to ensure that human capital investment yields a workforce capable of innovating faster than the competition and work processes that allow the organization to adapt to changes with minimal disruption. This suggests that the learning function should become increasingly strategic to the enterprise.

The remainder of this book explores how the enterprise learning function must reinvent itself to enable the organization it serves to transform, survive, and thrive in the Immersive Internet era.

# Learning to Change

The SMITH FAMILY was excited about their visit to the Lost Colony in Manteo, North Carolina. Megan, just turning seven, had learned all about how 120 brave men, women, and children established the first English settlement on Roanoke Island in 1587. Three years later, when Governor John White returned, the colony had vanished leaving only one clue as to their whereabouts: The word "Croatoan" carved on a post.

As they entered the Lost Colony, Megan was eager to solve the mystery of how they had vanished. In visiting the first building, brimming with curiosity, Megan asked *"Mommy, Mommy what did they do in here?" "This is a blacksmith's shop,"* answered her mother. *"This is where he made tools and horseshoes. That is called an anvil, and the blacksmith used it to shape the hot metal from the fire over there."*

*"What did horses need shoes for, Mommy?* asked Megan. *"Well back then people used horses to get around. . . . They did not have cars back then,"* answered Mom. *"But Mommy, horses poop and they go very slow, it must have been hard to get around back*

*then. . . . I am glad we have our minivan with a DVD player in it so
I can watch movies when we travel."*

They strolled into the next building. Mom braced herself for the
next barrage of questions. *"Mommy, Mommy, what did they do in
here?* asked Megan. *"Well this is where they made clothes Megan. . . .
Daddy will explain it to you, I need to change Connor's diaper."*

*"Well Megan, over here is where they sheared the sheep to get
wool to make clothes,"* said Dad. *"Ouch. Did that hurt the sheep,
Daddy?"* asked Megan, quite concerned. *"Not at all"* said Dad.
*"Then they took the wool and put it into this spinner to make yarn,
they then took the yarn and put it on this machine called a loom
to make cloth, which they used to make clothes using this sewing
machine over here."* *"Wow,"* said Megan, *"that looks like a lot of
work just to get some clothes. I am glad that all we have to do is hop
in the minivan and go to Wal-Mart when I need a new Dora t-shirt."*

As they went into the next building, Dad was prepared. Before
she even asked, he began, *"Now, Megan, this is a bakery. Over here
is where they blended ingredients to make the dough. Over here is
where they rolled the dough into loaves that they then put into this
oven to cook."* Looking very concerned, Megan asked, *"Wait a minute. Dad, don't tell me they didn't have Wonder bread back then?. . .
No wonder this became a Lost Colony. . . . How can anyone go a day
without Wonder bread? Wait, I figured out the mystery, Dad! Maybe
Croatoan is olde English for 'We Need Wonder bread!'"*

As they waited for Mommy and Connor to come back from the
restroom, Megan and her dad chatted about how things have really
changed for the better over the last four centuries. Then they all
headed toward a larger building over by the chapel. This time Megan
didn't need to ask a single question: *"Mommy, Daddy, don't tell
me, don't tell me. . . . I know what this is!. It is a CLASSROOM!"*

## Challenging Classroom Captivation

The printing press and the steam engine are often cited as disruptive technologies that forever altered the world's social and economic landscape (as

mentioned in Chapter 1). What is not often mentioned is that both of these technologies did not achieve their full disruptive impact until at least a half-century after their invention.

For the first fifty years the printing press was used to automate the manual process of monks transcribing Latin bibles. It was not until Luther applied this invention to print his version of the bible in the local vernacular that the true disruptive impact of the technology was fully realized. Access to Luther's bible in the German language ushered in Protestantism, a new form of Christianity that revolutionized both politics and economics in 14th century Europe.

Similarly, in the 17th century, James Watt's steam engine was originally used to automate existing manufacturing processes such as spinning cotton. It took over fifty years before the steam engine was applied to create the first railroad steam engines or locomotives. To this day, many economists and historians credit the steam engine as the technology that caused the most change in our social, economic, and political systems.

In both of these cases we observe a similar pattern Peter Drucker calls "routinization," a phenomenon whereby existing industries initially apply radically new technology to automate and accelerate age-old processes and methods.[1] This was done when early filmmakers set up a moving picture camera and merely filmed theatrical plays.

Today, the Internet is being heralded as the preeminent disruptive technology of our time. Bill Gates, founder of Microsoft, is credited with noting that the danger with the information revolution is that we will overestimate the short-term implications and underestimate the long-term impact.[2] As the webvolution continues to pervade both society and business, as indicated in Chapter 1, we are witnessing first-hand how industries and enterprises are undergoing significant and sweeping transformation as they adapt to the new-normal in a world gone web.

Furthermore, unlike past disruptive events, the application of web technologies to business endeavors has not simply routinized existing processes to become digital clones of their analog forms. Instead, in less than twenty years, industries such as retail, music, information technology, software development, and entertainment have been fundamentally redefined by the web. In short, it appears that as the webvolution extends its range and reach, the lag time between technological invention and industry transformation is shorter than during previous disruptive eras.

As outlined in the vignette that opens this chapter, the Megans of this world have high expectations. Companies that cannot sense and continually adapt to meet rapidly changing and increasingly challenging customer expectations are destined to suffer the fate of the Lost Colony.

Today, business has moved well beyond the routinization of traditional industrial approaches to bring fundamental changes in structure and infrastructure of industry and enterprise to remain competitive in an increasingly interconnected, turbulent, and complex business environment.

Gutenberg's disruptive invention was not only pivotal in transforming both society and business, but also played a significant role in transforming learning. As printing presses pervaded Europe, the predominant "master apprentice" on-the-job learning model was replaced with the "teacher-student" classroom-centric model. The ability for knowledge to be widely disseminated in a portable format (a book) enabled teachers to increase their reach. Books also provided students with access to insights from masters they previously could only obtain through direct interaction.

The Smith family visit to the Lost Colony is testament to the fact that today's corporate schoolhouse continues to be captivated by the classroom-centric model. While traditional industrial processes in manufacturing, transportation, textiles, apparel, and food processing have been transformed so dramatically by technological disruption that Megan could not recognize their analog forms, she was instantly able to recognize the classroom. Similarly, if we had the ability to teleport an ancient Greek to the present time, showing him a classroom would cause very little dissonance. However, if you were to show this same Hellenic time-traveler a Wal-Mart store, an interstate highway, or a Boeing 747 jet, he would not comprehend what he was seeing.

To date, learning professionals have not paused to heed the lessons learned from the monks, the industrialists, or the webvolutionaries. As a result, they have fallen prey to the routinization trap. Trainers appear to be wrapped up in some strange form of unconscious collusion wherein their dogged adherence to the classroom paradigm has rendered them oblivious to the incredible potential that the webvolution holds to revolutionize learning for both businesses and educational institutions.

The enterprise learning function is responsible for developing the talent that drives sustainable competitive advantage for the firm. In remaining bound to the formal classroom as the primary learning modality, the learning function is significantly limiting its ability to deliver strategic value to the enterprise at precisely the time when the ability to learn and adapt in perpetuity is becoming a core capability required by all firms. Just as businesses have had to change their strategies, structures, and infrastructures to remain competitive in increasingly dynamic market environments, the learning function must also adapt to meet the dynamic needs of the enterprise it serves. Ironically, while business has clearly learned to change, the learning function itself has not. To address this issue, learning leaders would do well to pay heed to Gloria Gery's assertion that: "We don't need new technology, we just need new thinking."[3]

The Immersive Internet is going to have at least as profound an impact on society and business as its read-only grandfather, and perhaps a lot more. The learning profession has already missed the opportunity to transform itself during the first two waves of the webvolution; if it wants to remain relevant to the enterprise, it simply cannot afford to miss the third. In business, as in baseball, it could be a matter of "Three strikes and you're out" for the learning function.

Instead of positioning the Immersive Internet as a next step in "how" classroom-based learning will be delivered, learning leaders should be asking "what" kind of learning this new technology can enable. To avoid yet another round of routinization that builds further rigidities around automating and accelerating the classroom paradigm, learning leaders must begin to focus on how to leverage the participatory web to unleash the latent innovative energy that lies dormant within the existing structure of enterprise.

In times of disruptive change, moving forward by looking into the rear-view mirror can result in driving off a cliff. To avoid this undesirable outcome, business people are often challenged to think outside of the box. Today, the primary challenge for the learning function is to "think outside of the classroom." Not doing so could result in the learning function becoming captive to its own limiting paradigms and marginalizing its value to the enterprise to the point of its own extinction.

The next section of this chapter explores how adhering to the status quo, one that is preoccupied with productivity, will increasingly marginalize the learning function's value to the enterprise.

# A Preoccupation with Productivity

Since the invention of the printing press, step changes in technology have been limited to optimizing or accelerating how formal learning is delivered and consumed. For over four hundred years there has been no significant change in the dominant design paradigm of how training is developed and delivered. In the next wave of the webvolution, learning professionals would do well to eschew their preoccupation with applying technology to do that which they have always done and, instead, focus on leveraging technology to enable new forms of learning that meet the dynamic needs of the digital enterprise.

Furthermore, at the strategic level, trainers need a similar evolution in their thinking about the kind of learning they should be providing. At the most general level, learning can be broken into two primary form-factors: (1) teaching people how to do things we already know how to do and (2) creating collaborative environments that allow people to develop new ideas and concepts to address unanticipated opportunities or challenges.

The first form-factor focuses on productivity. It seeks to drive efficiencies and maintain the status quo. The goal of productive learning is to get everyone in the organization to regress to the mean of optimal productivity in performing work activity.

The second form-factor focuses on growth. Growth comes from innovation and generating collective insight into the market that competitors have not yet seen. This insight emerges from connecting networks of individuals and helping them develop a collective point of view on the future that none of them could have come up with individually. It is social, it is emergent, and it is delicate. Most importantly, it is very different. Generative learning that is centered on innovation has a very different form and theoretical underpinning than does productive learning.

Productive learning focuses mostly on the individual and on helping that individual to adopt a pattern of behavior that improves productivity. Generative learning, by contrast, is a collaborative endeavor. Shared meaning and insights are developed at the group level, and these insights drive enterprise transformation to ensure growth and sustainability. Today, the learning function is focused primarily on productive learning. As a result, it appears that trainers are more likely to want to maintain the status quo, rather than challenge it.

Adhering to the status quo raises seven scary problems that, if not addressed, could result in significant marginalization for the learning function. These problems need to be understood and addressed if the training function is to move into the future and fully leverage the power of the Immersive Internet.

## Seven Scary Problems with the Status Quo

For over hundreds of years, trainers have been captivated by a shared perspective that assumes the classroom is the optimal design for delivering learning. Today, the webvolution is challenging this long-held assumption on a number of fronts (see Figure 2.1). These challenges can be summarized into seven scary problems that the training industry must address if it wishes to remain robust and relevant.

### The Autonomous Learner Problem

The autonomous learner problem has two core issues: (1) where the need for learning typically arises and (2) how web technologies make it increasingly easy for people to become on-demand learners.[4]

Most of what a person needs to know to do his or her job is actually learned on the job. This is because the job activity itself allows employees to recognize that they need to learn something new to do their work. In essence, the motivation to learn—or the teachable moment—emerges from the process of doing the work itself. As a result, it is not surprising that many organizations report 85 to 95 percent of a person's job knowledge is learned on the job.[5]

**Figure 2.1.** Seven Scary Problems with Training's Status Quo

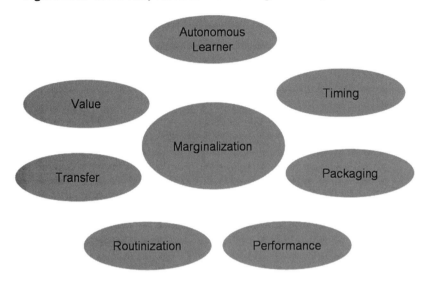

Given this backdrop, it becomes increasingly clear that enterprise learning simply cannot be limited to the classroom context. Despite this, the learning profession routinely distances itself from learning that is not formal or classroom based. Instead, they leave employees to fend for themselves when it comes to addressing the significant and pressing learning needs that arise within the context of carrying out daily work activities.

Fortunately for the employees, the webvolution has brought with it a number of tools that allow them to find for their own answers. For employees operating in a work context that is more confusing today than it was yesterday, the web provides them with the autonomy to address their unanticipated learning needs in real time. Unlike the learning function that refuses to address their immediate and informal needs, these free-range learners are no longer captive to the classroom.

From a tactical perspective, the learning function appears to be allocating the majority of the effort in the area of least impact. From a strategic perspective, it begs the question that if the majority of learning needs arise in the informal context, what is the business risk associated with leaving informal learning to chance?

## The Timing Problem

The timing problem has two core issues associated with work and learning. The time sensitivity of the learning needed in the digital enterprise is at odds with the time needed to analyze, design, develop, and deliver formal learning programs.

Today, business is conducted at the speed of thought, and unforeseen learning needs emerge in the blink of an eye. In a world in which market demand shifts overnight, the need to sense a change at the edge of the enterprise and react to it in real time becomes a source of sustainable competitive advantage.

The rapid pace of business almost guarantees that most formal learning programs will be outdated shortly after launch. Without modification, the current instructional systems design model is simply too slow to accommodate many emergent learning needs within the digital enterprise. Bringing knowledge from the edge of the firm, designing it around learning objectives, packaging it into learning modules, and pushing it back out to the edge takes too much time. Today employees need immediate insights into unforeseen needs. They cleverly leverage web technologies to learn in real time rather than waiting for a course that will be offered some time in the future.

From a tactical perspective, the learning function appears to be adhering to a formal learning process that is incapable of addressing the time sensitivity of most learning needs within the enterprise. From a strategic perspective, it begs the question that, if the majority of learning needs are being identified and addressed at the edge of the enterprise in real-time by free- range learners leveraging web-based tools, what strategic value does the central learning function provide?

## The Packaging Problem

The packaging problem also has two core issues: The format of a "course" is not aligned with the needs of today's time-starved workforce, and courses tend to be organized around topics as opposed to tasks.

Given the time, most anyone would take the opportunity to enjoy a leisurely five-course meal. Today's reality, however, is that most people only have time to go through a fast-food drive-thru window. The traditional packaging of formal learning is not aligned with the time-sensitive needs of today's employees.

Furthermore, courses are organized around topics as opposed to tasks. People's need and motivation to learn emerges largely from their inability to complete a task in the work context. Learning content that is not organized around the context within which the learning need arises causes unnecessary overhead for the learner. Often, workers with a pressing need would prefer instructions to instruction. In the webvolution era, information in context (a Google search on negotiation) often trumps instruction out of context (signing up for a Getting to "Yes" course).

From a tactical perspective, the learning function appears to have built a set of rigid procedures around the formal course development process that run counter to the needs of the employees and enterprises that they serve. From a strategic perspective this begs the question—as futurist Alvin Toffler postulated—now that we are moving from place-based factory work to any time, any place knowledge work, don't we also need an any time any place educational parallel?[6]

## The Performance Problem

The performance problem has only one core issue, but it is significant: Most enterprise performance problems are multi-causal. They have more than one underlying root cause.

Contrary to popular opinion, lack of knowledge or skill is only a small part of the reason that organizations don't perform as desired. Performance discrepancies can come from the wrong set of input data, poor tooling and processes, sub-optimized intrinsic motivation (job fit) or extrinsic motivation (compensation), or simply from asking people working at full capacity to do more than they are capable of doing.[7] Given this backdrop, it becomes clear that training alone cannot address the multiple root causes of poor performance within the enterprise.

Studies suggest that lack of skill or knowledge typically accounts for only 10 percent of enterprise performance issues.[8] From a tactical perspective, the learning function appears to be being asked by the enterprise to address more of the performance issues than it has jurisdiction over. From a strategic perspective, this begs the question as to whether there may be more strategic leverage in repositioning the value-add of the learning function around maximizing organization performance as opposed to maximizing classroom or e-learning throughput.

## The Routinization Problem

We have already identified that the routinization problem is at the core of the learning function's increasingly marginalized value to today's digital organization.

To date, the learning function has largely applied technology to create e-training content and automate the existing training and development process for formal learning. Given the scary problems outlined above, it is increasingly clear that accelerating the process for formal learning delivery will merely serve to more rapidly render its inherent inadequacies in meeting the dynamic and time-sensitive learning needs of the digital enterprise.

## The Transfer Problem

The transfer problem has one core issue, but it is an issue that has been around since the dawn of time. It is the fact that just because you know something doesn't mean you act on that knowledge. One author's mother knows that smoking is bad for her, she tells him so every time she lights a cigarette.

Even the best courses have a transfer issue—not necessarily because the learning did not stick, but because the resulting desired behavior did not become manifest in the workplace. Studies show that as much as 80 to 90 percent of investments in training programs fail to result in behavior change on the job.[9]

From a tactical perspective, it appears that the learning function is putting self-imposed limits on itself to draw the line on learning transfer when what every organization needs is behavior change. From a strategic perspective, this begs the question as to whether or not the learning function can develop interventions that improve transfer, change behavior, and impact performance.

## The Value Problem

The value problem has two core issues. The learning function has very little understanding as to what executives expect from the learning function, and as a result it often defaults to justifying its existence based on learning throughput as opposed to performance outcome.

A recent ASTD study[10] suggests that there are many different reasons why stakeholders choose to invest in learning: from developing leadership capability and employee skills at the individual level, to driving business performance or overseeing the talent management process at the business-unit level, to implementing strategy, driving transformation, expanding globalization, and enabling innovation at the enterprise level, there are numerous discrete reasons why learning is perceived to add value within the enterprise.

Unfortunately, the study shows that there is considerable misalignment between what executives expect from learning and what learning leaders believe it should be delivering. While the majority of learning activity and investment is focused on capability building at the individual level, industry executives want learning to take a role in driving strategic transformation, globalization, and innovation at the enterprise.

Instead of spending more time understanding how their stakeholders perceive the strategic value of learning within their enterprise, learning leaders are defaulting to justifying their existence by demonstrating how they are increasing the efficiency with which they deliver formal learning. Unfortunately, some quick analysis suggests that this approach to demonstrating value leads to the ultimate demise of the corporate schoolhouse.

Let's do the numbers. According to ASTD's *State of the Industry Report*, training budgets are about 2 percent of payroll or .44 percent of revenue on average.[11] If we assume a 100 percent improvement in training throughput productivity as a result of routinization, we can either double our training throughput or half our costs. If we go with the latter, a flawless implementation of technology and tools to streamline the design, development, and delivery process for formal learning yields a whopping .22 percent of revenue back to the business. This is not the kind of return that is going to have the CEO doing summersaults down the executive corridors. Once again the self-imposed preoccupation with productivity is hampering the learning function from delivering strategic value to the enterprise.

From a tactical perspective, the learning function's obsession with measuring its value in terms of training throughput as opposed to business outcome appears to be further marginalizing its perceived value to the business. At the end of the day, executives do not want productive learning processes—they want productive employees. From a strategic perspective, this begs the question as to whether the learning function might be better positioned should it shift its focus from the return on the learning investment for training throughput to the return on value expected from stakeholders.

In the next section, we'll examine how these seven scary problems have a compounding effect in creating further distance between the dynamic learning needs of the business and the rigid learning practices of the training function.

## Compounded Marginalization

Each of the issues identified above: classroom captivation, a preoccupation with productivity, and the seven scary problems, when layered on top of each other, have a compounding effect that is marginalizing the value-add of the learning function to the digital organization to a point where it could well be nearing extinction (see Figure 2.2).

We begin by identifying the opportunity space for the learning function within the enterprise. This space is bound by two key axes: performance and learning.

Within an enterprise, learning extends from the most formal curriculum to the most informal—from classroom lectures to an instant message call for assistance. It is not only focused on content and curriculum, but it includes the long tail for learning whereby learners leverage web technologies to learn from each other in times of need.

Similarly, in terms of performance, the enterprise itself needs to manage both the top line and the bottom line. While cutting expenses is certainly important, successful companies cannot simply shrink their way to greatness. To survive and thrive today, organizations must be ambidextrous.

**Figure 2.2.** Compounded Marginalization of the Training Function

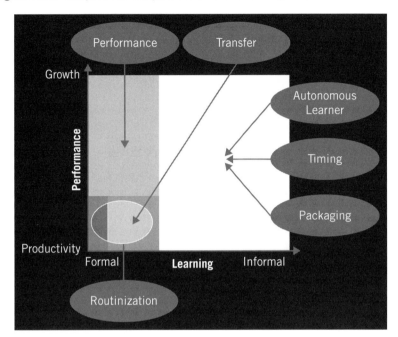

They have to be able to simultaneously anticipate and capitalize on growth opportunities while all the time optimizing the cost structure of the enterprise for maximum efficiency.

Given this backdrop, the opportunity space for the learning function to deliver strategic value to the enterprise extends from productivity to growth from a performance perspective and extends from formal to informal from a learning perspective. It is increasingly clear that maintaining the educational status quo is no longer a tenable strategic alternative.

## Rejecting Informality

The biggest loss in opportunity for the learning function lies in the fact that it has, consciously or not, rejected informal learning. Simply put, if the majority of learning happens informally within the context of work and the course paradigm is ill-suited to the time-sensitivity or task orientation of the modern-day digital enterprise employee, it does not stand to reason that the learning function should continue to focus almost exclusively on formal learning.

Collectively, the autonomous learner, timing, and packaging problems that are not being addressed by the learning function account for the de-selection of at least 80 percent of the addressable opportunity space for learning.

## Performance Predicaments

The next tranche of losses in the opportunity space come from two different performance predicaments. First, as the performance problem highlights, at the individual level, learning itself only has jurisdiction over about 10 percent of enterprise performance issues where the root-cause is due to a lack of knowledge or skill. Second, as the preoccupation with productivity has taught us, the learning function is focused primarily on maintaining the status quo for both the function itself and the enterprise that it serves by focusing on productive learning over generative learning.

Taken together, on the performance axis, the fact that the preoccupation with productivity drives most activity within the training function results in the de-selection of at least 90 percent of the addressable opportunity space for performance.

## Painted into a Corner

The compounding effect of rejecting informal learning and being preoccupied with productivity has painted the learning function into a corner. Ironically, instead of seeking innovative ways to open the aperture in opportunity space, Training remains under the spell of routinization as it allocates the majority of its time and energy to automate the formal learning process. As Figure 2.2 clearly shows, this approach merely increases the speed with which the training function delivers formal learning focused on driving enterprise productivity.

The value problem has already highlighted that an increase in learning throughput yields less than 1 percent of revenue for the firm. The transfer problem has highlighted that only 10 percent of training investment results in changed workplace behavior. Put these together and automate them via the application of technology and you merely increase the efficiency with which you train poorly.

In synthesizing the problem space associated with the status quo, it is appropriate to ask how the learning function must reinvent itself to add strategic value for the digital enterprise. Next we'll explore how focusing on networked, generative learning approaches would be a significant first step.

# Networked Learning

In the webvolution era, a networked ecosystem enables a new vision for learning: one in which individuals and organizations fundamentally change the way they talk about, work with, and act on what is known and what needs to be known to adapt, survive, and thrive. Jay Cross puts it best this way: "Schooling has confused us into thinking learning was equivalent to pouring content into people's heads. It's more practical to think of learning as optimizing our networks."[12]

Human networks create a meaningful context within which content can be consumed and digested to create new value. In the past, content was king; today context is the kingdom. The enterprise that is able to network and tap into resource nodes to address a surfaced need within another part of the network will be able to successfully conduct business within a digital ecosystem that is tuned to optimize learning and growth.

How would our concept of learning in organizations change if learning professionals began to view themselves as facilitators of generative learning? If they oversaw a process in which the full collaborative force of the Internet was wielded to build relationships and foster innovation among people within and across the enterprise?

To achieve this vision, the learning function's focus and value proposition must migrate from being preoccupied with productive learning (that is, teaching people how to do things we know how to do to cut costs), to nurturing generative learning (that is, enabling human capital to develop ideas and concepts that grow revenue). Generative learning is socially constructed. It feeds on context and social interaction to channel human intuition toward rapid collective sense-making around a given opportunity or issue.

In the enterprise of the future, work and learning become synonymous. Without the ability to innovate and adapt in perpetuity, enterprises will regress to a mean of mediocrity. Consequently, the primary challenge for learning leadership over the next few years will be to fundamentally recreate the function to drive the innovation agenda, for both the enterprise and the function, without falling prey to the routinization trap. Attempting to address the innovation agenda with more efficient productivity-focused training strategies and technologies is akin to attempting to play tennis with a golf club. The tool is not suited to the reality of the challenge at hand and must be avoided at all costs.

The pre-eminent challenge for the learning function in the 21st century is ability to allow the enterprise to coalesce its capabilities around unanticipated market opportunity. Often, past successes institutionalize rigid processes that hamper future transformation and growth. For the learning function this has been true for four centuries. Today, unlearning those strategies may be the only way to ensure that the organizational learning function successfully meets this challenge.

## Learning to Change

Technology has revolutionized business; now it must do the same for learning. Successful learning functions of the webvolution era will be the ones that learn how to blend people, processes, and technology to drive collective insight and intuition. To spark innovation and create an adaptive enterprise, work structures will have to be revisited and work processes will have to be redesigned to cultivate learning. Similarly, work practices and policies must reflect the changing needs of the organization and of knowledge workers within it.

Learning is a far more complicated phenomenon than can ever be limited to the classroom context. If we convey knowledge about tasks we already know how to do, we call it *productive learning*. If we share knowledge about tasks that are new and different, we call it *generative learning*. Productive learning serves largely to maintain the status quo within an enterprise by conveying what is already known, while generative learning involves not only absorbing existing information but also creating new solutions to unanticipated problems. Information age learning requires that individuals and organizations change the way they think about and act on what is known and what needs to be known in order to innovate, change, and win.

In short, just as business has had to change dramatically as a result of dynamic market economics, so too must the learning function. Critical to successfully navigating this change is recognizing that the path to strategic leverage within the firm lies in cultivating a generative learning culture. Creating a true learning organization will require significant and systemic changes to the learning function practice, not merely the automation of training processes and the digitization of training content, but a wholesale redefinition of how learning adds value to organizations.

# 3

# Escaping Flatland

"**G**O!" SHOUTED the Challenge Master. Team Bravo, along with the four competing teams, sprinted to the shore. David looked across the water to the little island. It did not look that far away. But given the ominous triangle fins swimming around in the shallow water, this team challenge promised to be the biggest one yet. The team gathered around the items lying on the ground.

*"Listen up,"* said Michael, *"first team to get across to the island wins. I suggest we start designing and building a bridge ASAP."* *"Hold on,"* responded Brett, *"can we take a few minutes to explore options? I know time is tight, but there may be a unique way to overcome this challenge."* *"Negative,"* said Michael. *"We agreed that I am to lead this challenge and time is of the essence. We need to start getting our team working on a bridge immediately."*

The team sparked into action deciding on what kind of structure would make best use of the materials on hand. Under Michael's firm direction, a design was quickly agreed on and sub-teams set to work building bridge sections. Brett quickly scanned the shore to see how the other teams were doing. Most teams were busily engaged in putting together structures. Team Alpha, however, seemed to be much more relaxed and engaged in deep conversation. *"What are they up to?"* Brett wondered.

The minutes ticked by. *"Almost there,"* said Michael. *"Two more sections and we are home free. Our design made the best use of materials. Time is our only enemy now."* Another quick scan from Brett revealed that Teams Gamma and Delta had run out of materials. Team Epsilon had enough materials but they were not as far along. As for Team Alpha, they appeared to have passed on this challenge. He didn't see them anywhere. *"Great,"* thought Brett, *"With Alpha passing on this challenge we will be back within striking distance of the lead."*

Just then, the two-minute warning sounded. Michael started barking orders more rapidly as the team worked feverishly to put the final section in place. As victory neared, Brett glanced toward the island. To his great surprise, he saw a jubilant team Alpha standing in the center of the island.

*"Hold on, how did you get over there?"* Brett asked. *"We flew,"* Team Alpha's captain said smugly. *"In this virtual environment there is no gravity, so we chose to take an unconventional approach to addressing this challenge. We took advantage of the environmental factors to find a more effective way to win,"* he said, pretending he was trying not to gloat.

*"That's not fair,"* objected Michael. *"It is MORE than fair,"* responded the Challenge Master,. *"The whole point of this exercise was to ensure that each team explored all options in an unfamiliar environment before taking familiar action . . . . Alpha was the only team to think outside the box. The rest of you went straight into bridge-building mode. The lesson here is that unconventional environments require unconventional responses. Now log off, put away your headphones, and meet in the conference room in five. "*

The teams knew better than to argue with the Challenge Master. *"I should have pushed harder on Michael at the beginning of this challenge,"* thought Brett to himself. *"I'm glad it's my turn to lead next. I'll be sure we don't fall into that trap again."*

# A Brave New Learning World

Avatars, virtually mediated team interaction, flying students defying gravity: it's enough to make a learning professional experience vertigo. Unfortunately, for those not on the bleeding edge of game-based technologies, all this talk of avatars, virtual social worlds (VSWs), massively multiplayer online role play games (MMORPGs), and metaverses, seems right out of some science fiction novel (and, in some cases, it is.)[1]

As outlined in Figure 3.1, we have crafted the term "virtual immersive environments (VIEs)'" pronounced *vees.* This term was chosen to highlight the immersive nature of these environments and to clearly differentiate the social

**Figure 3.1.** VIE Technology Enables 3DLE Outcomes

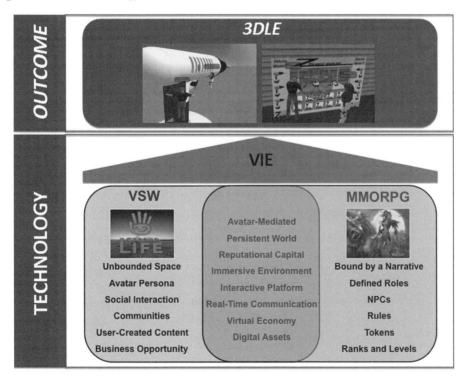

(VSW) and game (MMORPG) uses of similar spaces from the corporate and academic uses of these types of immersive environments. All three environments share similar characteristics, but the focus of each is dramatically different.

Let's look at the two more well-known forms of virtual worlds. While VSWs and MMORPGs share common attributes such as avatar-mediated interaction, persistent virtual worlds, reputational capital, immersive and interactive social contexts, broadcast and narrowcast communication channels, and a virtual economy within which virtual digital assets are bought and sold, they also have many differences.

*BusinessWeek* has described the virtual social world (VSW) of Second Life as some unholy offspring of the Matrix, eBay, and MySpace.[2] In fact, this description is quite accurate. Second Life and other social virtual spaces combine the ability to conduct transactions like eBay, promote rich social interactions like MySpace, and have a strange surreal and compelling feeling like the Matrix. VSW members in Second Life prefer to be called residents and they are free to do as they choose. VSWs foster the creation and development of communities of practice, commerce, and socialization. MMORPG players, by contrast, are more focused on achieving the goals of the game. The players have defined roles, associate with a guild or a clan, and purposefully work through a series of quests or challenges to move to higher levels of achievement within a tightly bound game-based narrative.

VSWs and MMORPGs share many attributes and can be considered kin, but they certainly are not twins. Affordances from both of these technologies can be combined to form a VIE where elements of both technologies can be leveraged to create immersive and engaging 3D learning experience (3DLE) outcomes. The VIE is the technology and the 3DLE is the experience that is designed within the VIE to foster learning.

Despite the obscure, tortuous, tongue-twisting acronyms, the Immersive Internet is now upon us. The transformation of the web from a static, one-way conduit of information into a three-dimensional world where people, as avatars, interact, work, and collaborate virtually has undoubtedly arrived. Those who embrace the Immersive Internet to transform the learning experience will survive and thrive, while those who ignore it will become increasingly marginalized by the businesses or students they serve.

Web 2.0 and Immersive Internet technologies are enabling on-demand networked learning between peers where information in context trumps instruction out of context. Unshackled from the rigidities imposed by the classroom environment and course construct, learning has been set free within and outside the enterprise and university. Learners are no longer captives of the training function or their professors. They have a treasure trove of technological affordance at their disposal to address their informal learning needs in real-time.

One of the best ways to understand those technology affordances and the advantages of learning in a 3DLEs is to travel inside a virtual world, exploring it with a seasoned guide. This guide could describe the nuances of 3DLE design, demonstrate the advantages of certain activities within 3DLEs, and point out the obstacles and limitations that still must be overcome with the application of VIE technology to learning.

Since a guided tour in a 3D virtual world is not possible within the 2D and linear format of this book, the next-best option is for us to provide you with a scenario comparing learning within a typical 2D online learning environment and a 3DLE. To that end, we introduce our discussion of 3DLEs with a tale of two learners: Jane and Jack. These two stories originally appeared in an eLearning Guild publication called "360 Synchronous Learning Report" and we'd like to acknowledge the eLearning Guild for granting permission to republish the stories in this chapter.[3]

## Learning in Flatland: Jane's 2D Learning Experience

It is 9:50 A.M. as Jane sits down at her desk to get ready for her 2D synchronous learning session. She logs into the website. After a few moments of loading, a welcome slide appears on her screen beside a list of other students who are attending the session. Some of the names are familiar, some she thinks she recognizes but can't be sure, and some are completely unfamiliar.(See Figure 3.2.)

The welcome slide invites students to use the whiteboard tools to mark their locations on the world map. It looks to Jane as if half of the participants have already tagged their locations either with a checkmark or a smiley-face. Jane goes ahead and places a checkmark on her hometown. There is also a pre-class text chat taking place, but she decides not to enter into the

**Figure 3.2.** Typical 2D Synchronous Learning Environment

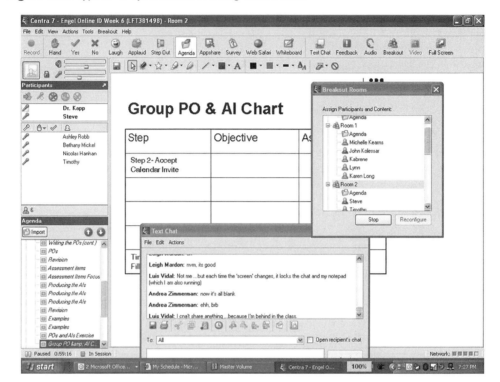

discussion as she has some real work to do and it is clear that the chat is just filling time until the instructor formally launches the session.

In another window, Jane opens up her e-mail and checks a few messages. A few minutes later, a disembodied voice begins the session, "Today we are going to discuss the features and placement of the new Model Z power drill. At the end of this session you will be able to. . . ."

Half listening, Jane continues to review her e-mail and send a few instant messages to work colleagues as the instructor addresses the session preliminaries. She then quickly previews the forty-page course presentation to determine how much attention she will need to spend during the session. Satisfied that she can comfortably multitask while participating in this synchronous session, she opens a word processing document to finalize work on an important sales proposal that is due at the end of the week.

Ten minutes later, Jane's focus returns to the synchronous learning session when the instructor begins discussing the features of the Model Z. On the screen is a 2D image of the new Model Z. The image of the drill contains a number of arrows that highlight the new features of the Model Z and the benefits it has over competitive drills. At this point, the instructor prompts the audience for questions. One of the learners, Sam Jones, raises a virtual hand to ask a question about the positioning of the Model Z on store shelves and at trade shows. The instructor explains how to place it on the shelf and group it with other products from the brand and how to fasten the drill to the display.

Jane does not quite understand the instructor's explanation and asks for some more detail. The instructor pulls up a picture of a sample display from a popular hardware store to further clarify his point. The instructor then sends out a poll asking everyone to describe his or her level of understanding on the placement and promotion of the new Model Z. Jane feels she gets the gist of what the instructor is talking about and doesn't want to waste everyone's time by asking for a more detailed answer, so she goes along with the crowd and votes that she "completely" understands the features, benefits, placement, and promotion material presented in the session and gets back to working on her report.

Following the positive response from the polling question, the instructor tells the class that it is now time for a breakout lesson. The class is broken into groups and asked to create a one-slide presentation of how they would place the drill in a specialty store.

After a half-hour, the instructor asks each group to show the slides of the arrangement and then critiques their presentations. One student indicates, "You can't really tell because of the slide, but this one drill is really much closer to the customer on the shelf than this other one."

The session ends with the instructor providing positive and constructive feedback on the team presentations. He uses drawing tools to point out some flaws in the suggested layout and uses chat to document his feedback for each team. He then closes out the session by wishing the participants the best of luck in driving revenue in the upcoming quarter with the Model Z power drill and provides them with a link to a website that includes all the session materials and additional resources that they might find useful.

It is now 11A.M. Jane logs off and saves the updates to her sales proposal. She bookmarks the URL for the Model Z resource site, and gets ready for her next call.

## Escaping Flatland: Jack's 3D Learning Experience

It is 9:50 A.M. Jack sits down at this desk and logs into the virtual immersive environment (VIE). As the VIE loads, Jack gets an urgent in-world instant message from a few of his learning colleagues, "Jack as soon as you log in, teleport over and help us out. There are learning bucks to be had here for the team." Jack immediately hits the teleport button and is taken to a lobby area outside of the 3D learning facility.

The scene was a familiar one. The facilitator had set up an early-bird learning bucks challenge: "The first team to correctly identify ten new Model Z features earns 20,000 learning bucks." There were four teams hovered around four virtual Model Z drill podiums. Each was working quickly and collaboratively to determine what features to add to their virtual scoreboard. The team to the right of Jack appeared to be in the lead with six new features correctly identified. Jack's team was not far behind with five.

Jack's teammates, Abbott and Heather, were already in full swing. Abbott had fired up the product web page that highlighted the new Model Z features. Heather had a 3D version of the Model Y in one hand and the Model Z in the other. She was comparing them to see how they differed. (See Figure 3.3.)

"Jack, so glad you got here," said Heather. "Start inputting the features that Abbott barks out for us on the scoreboard, will you?" As Jack runs over to the scoreboard keyboard, he thinks he hears the familiar e-mail beep beckoning from the Flatland, but he is too busy to deal with it. After all, there are learning bucks available, and his team is in second place company-wide. "Fire away, Abbott," says Jack from the scoreboard console, nervously eying the team to the right, who were now up to seven correct features.

There was no response. Jack looks over at Abbott and sees that he is snoozing. Jack quickly sends Abbott an instant message. "Abbott, where the heck are you? Get back in here and focus. The other team is about to beat us." From Flatland, Abbott replies, "Sorry, got an urgent text message from my boss. I will be right back in."

**Figure 3.3.** Abbott Looks for Features on the Model Z Drill in a Pre-Class Exercise

Back in the VIE, Jack calls out to Heather, "You got anything for me?" She replies "Yes, how about 'vibration resistant thermoplastic grips.' It looks to me like the Z really has the Y beat on that one." Jack quickly enters the feature into the scoreboard and it is accepted. They are right back in the hunt! Right on the heels of Heather's input, Abbott, back from his Flatland interaction, rattles off four more features from his exploration of the Model Z drill podium. Jack enters them double-speed.

The alarm bell above their scoreboard goes off and the whole lobby area fills with confetti and flying fish. "We did it!" Abbott said, as they high-five each other and hit the pose balls to do their obnoxious victory dance. "Sorry about having to duck out," says Abbott, "So glad you dialed in early Jack; otherwise we would not have made it. This puts our team one step closer to first place in the learning bucks challenge. That trip to Hawaii is within our grasp."

The facilitator comes up to Jack's team and congratulates them. He then asks everyone to follow him so that they can start the formal session. Jack's avatar follows the crowd. As they walk, it appears as though he and his fellow learners are shrinking to the size of ants. Suddenly the whole class finds itself comfortably seated on the butt of the handle of the new Model Z.

The facilitator briefly reviews the twenty top features by teleporting the class from feature to feature. He then challenges each team to run around the drill and pick up the flags located on the features they did not already cover on their learning bucks challenge prior to the formal session. "First team back here with all the remaining flags wins. On your marks, get set, go." Jack, Abbott, and Heather scurry down the handle toward the front of the drill. They only have ten flags to pick up. (See Figure 3.4.)

They part ways at the power switch and Jack picks up the three flags toward the front of the drill. Unfortunately, their team planning was not

---

**Figure 3.4.** Hunting for Flags on a Giant Model Z Drill

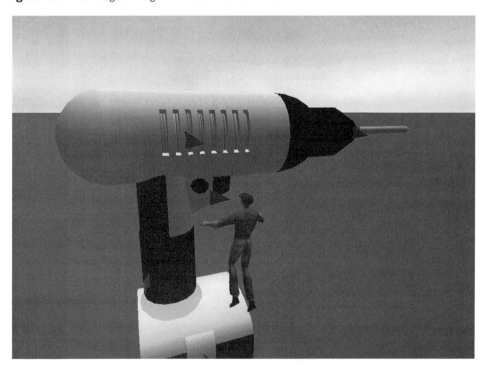

up to par with another team, and when they arrived back at the butt of the Model Z with all ten flags they were five seconds behind the winner.

Following the orienteering challenge, the facilitator leads the class over to a standard product display and goes over the key placement considerations for the Model Z. Sam Jones, a fellow learner who is wearing a shirt and tie with a Mets baseball cap (Jack wondered if he had any other clothes in his virtual closet), raises his hand to ask a question about the positioning of the product on store shelves and in trade shows. The facilitator says, "Good question, let's go look at some examples" and then he disappears.

Jack receives a message asking him to teleport to the facilitator's location. He clicks and is teleported into a small hardware store. He is directly in front of a shelf that is displaying the Model Z, among other drills. The facilitator highlights the key points on placement of the drill within this context and asks the group whether they have any questions. Given that all of them are nodding their heads, the facilitator again disappears and Jack receives another teleport message. This time he and his learning colleagues find themselves on a trade show floor. On the floor, the facilitator reviews the various methods of displaying the Model Z and Jack can see how the product is grouped with other products. Jack walks around the display and notices how the drills are fastened to the display. He marks this spot as a place he wants to return to later to learn more about the construction of the display. (See Figure 3.5.)

Once again the facilitator asks the group whether there are any questions. The chorus of nodding heads suggests that the students are getting the picture quite clearly. He decides to move on to one of the two application sessions of the learning experience.

The instructor asks for a volunteer and Jack quickly raises his hand. The instructor informs him that he is going to role play the process of selling a Model Z drill to a construction supervisor. He asks Jack to put on his sales uniform, which consists of a bright yellow shirt with the company logo and khaki pants. In real life, Jack gets a little warm and starts to sweat just like he does on real sales calls. The instructor dons a hardhat, a bright yellow vest, and a dusty pair of jeans. The two teleport to a construction site. It's loud and busy, just like the dozens of sites Jack has visited in the physical world.

**Figure 3.5.** Trade Show Product Display for the Model Z Drill

Jack doesn't have a script and neither does the instructor, but Jack doesn't hesitate. He knows he can make the sale and secure more learning bucks. Jack begins his three-part sales message by first engaging the customer, linking the product to expressed needs, and finally closing the sale. The conversation takes many twists and turns, catching Jack a little off guard a couple of times, but in the end, he makes the sale and earns some more learning bucks. His colleagues congratulate him and give him virtual high-fives.

Next, Jack and his colleagues receive another teleport message and they end up in a learning application area. Jack smiles, as he knows that there will be more learning bucks in the offing. The facilitator outlines the application challenge to the teams. Each team has a 14-foot by 14-foot area with the same signage, shelving, and product mix. Their task is to create the most

**Figure 3.6.** Abbott Works to Build a Display for the Model Z Drill as a Class Exercise

compelling display that highlights the most important benefits of the Model Z. They have twenty minutes to complete their task. (See Figure 3.6.)

Twenty minutes later, a group of product managers teleport into the learning application space. The entire class walks through each team display and listens to the feedback from the product managers. The facilitator captures the feedback in the chat function and assigns an overall score based on the feedback. Avenging their loss on the orienteering challenge, Jack's well-oiled team once again emerges victorious.

Jack saves a recording of this entire session so that he can review in detail the specific actions that his team took to emerge as victors in the learning bucks challenges.

It is now 11 A.M., time to finish that important proposal due next week.

# From Interactivity to Engagement

Jack and Jane's different learning experiences clearly illustrate how the Immersive Internet is impacting the landscape of online learning and will have an even greater impact within the next few years. In fact, Steve Prentice of Gartner has predicted that, in the near future, 80 percent of active Internet users (and Fortune 500 enterprises) will have presence in a 3D virtual world.[4] He is not alone; futurist William Halal, founder of techcast.org and author of *Technology's Promise*, writes that virtual worlds are growing at 33 percent per year. He predicts that by 2015 virtual worlds will dominate the Internet.[5]

Understanding the Immersive Internet and the implications on society, business, and learning will not be easy. Corporations, academic institutions, and government agencies need to consider the ramifications of the Immersive Internet and what it will do to knowledge transfer, work transactions, and existing learning paradigms.

Virtual worlds provide the opportunities for learners to be online in the same place at the same time looking and interacting with one another. This is far different than simply being logged into the same screen looking at the same slide. The 3DLE provides a sense of "being there" which, again, ties to visual and mental cues that make the recall and application of the learning that occurs in a VIE more effective.

A 3D learning experience (3DLE) is a highly immersive virtual environment in which the learners act and interact in real-time with each other and with the instructor to accomplish a challenge or task. Designed effectively, 3DLEs create the proper conditions for rich human interaction around a task where peer-to-peer or group learning is enabled and appropriate guidance is provided as learners journey through a series of activities designed to synthesize conceptual learning through immersive and interactive activity.

In 2D learning environments (or Flatland), a number of interactive tools are employed. Floor controls (emoticons, raising hands, etc.), whiteboarding tools, breakout rooms, chat, application sharing, polling, and Q&A are all designed to help drive interactivity. Unfortunately, as is clearly demonstrated in Jane's experience, engagement in 2D synchronous learning suffers, not because of a lack of interactive tools but because of a lack of a sense of immersion in the activity itself. By contrast, as illustrated in Jack's vignette, the first-person interface, or 3D avatar-mediated interaction, brings with it all the elements of interactivity from Flatland applications while adding the immersive qualities that truly drive an engaging experience for the learner.

A 3DLE has at its core the notion of leveraging both interactivity (I) and immersion (I) to achieve a level of engagement (E) that creates the motivation to learn as a by-product of engaging in an activity.

Here is an "equation" that breaks down the components of a 3DLE:

$$I * I = E$$

In a 3DLE, the learner becomes an actor in a virtual world in which the technology creates the spatial, temporal, and material conditions for both immersion and interactivity, driving a multiplier effect on learner engagement. Learners see themselves in relationship to the challenge at hand and experience the consequences of their actions related to the accomplishment of a given activity or challenge. In a 3DLE, because of its truly immersive qualities, interaction is not disembodied and transactional: it is embodied and experiential.

Given this backdrop, 3DLE can be defined as "the process of being immersed into a 3D virtual environment in which a learner acts through an avatar to engage with other avatars for the explicit purpose of learning, while being guided through a series of experiences that facilitate comprehension and application of formal learning objectives as well as enabling informal peer-to-peer learning."

From an instructional design perspective, the addition of the immersive component brings with it the opportunity to move beyond having learners interact around content. It also provides the opportunity to immerse learners in a context that allows them to synthesize the learning content in a personally engaging and experiential manner. The learnings that occur within the 3DLE are surfaced at the moment when the lack of knowledge or capability intersects with the need to have that knowledge or capability to execute the challenge at hand. Just as is the case within the actual work context, the motivation to learn that originates from the inability to complete a task within the 3DLE is part and parcel of the experience itself.

3DLEs require not only providing learners with the right content, but also creating the right context within which this content can be consumed and synthesized through thoughtfully designed activities. These activity-based learning contexts must be engineered so that teachable moments are surfaced at every turn. These teachable moments will not be encountered the same way for every learner. Instead, the areas being covered within the learning context are encountered, consumed, and applied based on the experiences of the learner—not the mandate of the instructor.

3DLEs allow instructional designers to come full circle in their learning approaches by applying this new technology to move back to a learning model by which content and context no longer have to be decoupled. The instructional methods employed to design effective 3DLEs are closer to an apprenticeship in which learning in and through interactions with others while collectively engaged in work activity becomes a core design principle.

Done right, 3DLEs provide the opportunity for instructional designers to overcome their captivation with the classroom and move in a direction that is more congruent with the needs of the increasingly digitized and virtualized enterprise. Done wrong, 3DLEs will remain the domain of digital avatars in digital classrooms discussing content on digitally rendered PowerPoint slides. The journey to make the swift and sweeping change needed to bring learning back in strategic alignment with the dynamic needs of the enterprise it serves will require a fundamental understanding of how this technology affords the opportunity to fundamentally redefine the structure and infrastructure of the modern-day learning function.

## The Seven Sensibilities of VIEs

The first step to avoiding the routinization trap is to distance oneself from existing processes and practices and examine a newly emerging technology on its own merits.

Our initial analysis of 3DLEs designed within VIEs has surfaced seven sensibilities that, when woven together, can create a powerful contextual learning experience that truly differentiates the first-person interface from its Flatland predecessor. (See Figure 3.7.)

---

**Figure 3.7.** The Seven Sensibilities of VIEs

The Sense of Self

The Death of Distance

The Power of Presence

The Sense of Space

The Capability to Co-Create

The Pervasiveness of Practice

The Enrichment of Experience

## The Sense of Self: From Emoticon to Avatar

The Sanskrit word avatar is often translated into English as "incarnation." In reality, it literally means *descent* and usually implies a deliberate descent from higher spiritual realms to lower realms of existence such as the embodiment of a god in the physical world.[6] In today's virtual world environment, your virtual character becomes an avatar that is embodied and immersed within the 3DLE context.

The recognition of an avatar as an extension of self is a differentiating sensibility of VIEs. Just as is the case in the real world, we can infer much from how people choose to represent themselves as avatars within the virtual world. Many virtual world platforms allow the users to craft their avatars any way they want. The learners can change hair styles, body type, skin tone, and other elements of the avatar to create just the right look for their virtual extension of their physical selves. Some virtual-world residents enjoy spending time creating their digital sock puppets to match their real-life personas.

Research has shown that people behave in a similar fashion within the virtual world as they do in the physical world. Researchers at California State University in Los Angeles found that "people don't go online to leave their bodies behind and find new selves, but instead seem to be taking their offline selves, including their biological selves, with them." In the study, published in the *Journal of Applied Developmental Psychology*, the classic sex differences in play preferences of fifth-graders, characterized by rough-and-tumble games among boys and intimate conversations among girls, existed even after youngsters adopted a range of personas for virtual encounters.[7] In fact, only 13 percent of the participants decided to switch genders. The vast majority stayed true to their physical world behavior, even when they changed genders of their avatar.

In another study, researcher Paul W. Eastwich at Northwestern University found that "interactions among strangers within the virtual world are very similar to interactions between strangers in the real world," even in the area of racial bias. Eastwich goes on to say, "You would think when you're wandering around this fantasyland . . . that you might behave differently, but people exhibited the same type of behavior—and the same type of racial bias—that they show in the real world all the time."[8] The sense of who a person is and what he or she represents is clearly reflected in the online behaviors of his or her avatar. The sense of self is merely extended into the virtual space.

The overarching differentiating sensibility that avatar-mediated inter-action brings to the learning equation is engaging embodied interaction. In the earlier learning vignettes, Jane's disembodied virtual representation is a largely emotionless emoticon that is limited to giving a thumbs-up, a clap of the hands, an animated laugh, or a simple smiley face. In the 3DLE context, however, Jack's avatar is clearly a digital extension of his physical self—one that his fellow avatars recognize and interact with on an ongoing basis, whether in a learning or a work context (see Figure 3.8).

## The Death of Distance: Where Geography Becomes History

While time zones still present a problem for connecting people around the globe, in virtual worlds the barriers of geography have essentially become history. Virtual worlds afford a third place—cyberspace—within which avatars can connect, collaborate, and co-create, irrespective of their actual physical locations.

In a virtual world context there is no home and away. The neutrality of the virtual world context dissolves the feeling of distance or isolation that remote geographies often feel relative to the home country of the enterprise or individual. A person from the United Kingdom can drop in on a class in Asia with the touch of a teleport button. There is no travel required,

**Figure 3.8.** The Evolution from Emoticons to Avatars

no paperwork, and no advanced notice necessary. In this respect the virtual world may perhaps be even more flat than the real world.[9]

In the earlier vignette when Jack joins his colleagues, it does not matter where they are physically. What matters is that they are together virtually in the same place. The avatars meet in the same 3D virtual space, where they engage in a challenge. They take cues from their virtual surroundings, and this drives their in-world behavior. Jane's experience, on the other hand, is quite the opposite. While everyone is connected to a website at the same time, the primary use of the whiteboard activity serves to highlight just how physically distant each participant in the session is from the others.

## The Power of Presence: Being Virtually There

One can argue that there is no substitute for real-time person-to-person interaction. This is what makes apprenticeships and mentorships so powerful. In business and college classrooms, as in life, half the battle is won just by showing up. In short, presence matters. Virtual-world contexts provide rich presence and reputation management affordances that make being virtually there almost as good as being physically there. The mode of interaction mimics that of real life, and the sense of self and death of distance help create a powerful virtual context in which the presence of avatars feels genuine to those who interact with each other.

In the vignettes above it is clear that Jack is more "present" in his session than Jane is in hers. Jane can hide behind her emotionless emoticon and work on her report. However, if Abbott tries to drop into Flatland to attend to an instant message, Jack is onto him immediately.

## The Sense of Space and Scale: A Matter of Perspective

While geography is history in virtual worlds, space and scale are virtually unlimited. While most avatars are anthropomorphized in some way, shape, or form, it is important to recognize that it is just as easy to become a white blood cell traveling through the body as it is to become a moon in orbit around a planet in 3DLEs. Unlimited space and scale integrated with new 3D visualization mechanisms for rendering complex data sets provide a significant opportunity for collaborative generative learning.

In covering the features and benefits of the Model Z, Jane chose not to subject herself to "death by PowerPoint." Instead, she bookmarked the URL so she could go back to the content when she needed it later and went about working on her sales proposal, all the time hiding behind her disembodied login name. By contrast, Jack's team had no time to do anything but hurtle themselves headlong down the handle of the Model Z to secure the ten flags. They literally knew every inch of the virtual drill by heart by the time they completed the 3DLE challenge.

## The Capability to Co-Create: Making Meaning Together

The ability to co-create on a global basis regardless of distance is an important new opportunity for generative learning and work in general. Far beyond the notion of Flatland screen sharing, true co-creation brings people into a shared virtual context in which they can actively participate in achieving a commonly held desired outcome.

In Jane's scenario, the team was to engage in an activity that culminated in a PowerPoint presentation that highlighted their plans for optimal placement of the Model Z. Clearly, in this instance, the deliverable was less than ideal given the session's learning objectives. The challenge Jack's team faced within the 3DLE was much more on-target. The team actually co-created a display that product managers critiqued and that could be viewed in three dimensions.

## The Pervasiveness of Practice: Learning While Doing

Virtual worlds can be designed to simulate real-world situations that allow the learner to practice as much as desired in advance of the real-world activity. Most successful 3DLEs are devised as a series of tasks or challenges that allow the learners to learn while doing, rather than instructing them on what they need to know before doing. The notion of practice, simulation, and learning through trial and error is central to the design of engaging 3DLEs.

From the moment he joined the session, Jack was fully engaged in learning via multiple engaging activities designed to hone his knowledge and skills with regard to the features and placement of the Model Z. Jane, on the other hand, had only to engage in one activity.

## The Enrichment of Experience: Watching, Thinking, Feeling, and Doing

Done right, 3DLEs create compelling, visceral, and memorable experiences. In his book *Experiential Learning*, David Kolb describes learning as a four-step process: (1) watching, (2) thinking (mind), (3) feeling (emotion), and (4) doing (muscle). 3DLEs by virtue of their differentiating sensibilities lend themselves very well to creating compelling learning experiences that activate this process.[10]

3DLEs employ elaborate contextual design elements whereby the timing and layering of reward mechanisms are carefully tuned to maintain a flow state (the ever-elusive high-performance zone that resides between stress and boredom). The three challenges, coupled with the tokening system of learning bucks, resulted in a 3DLE within which Jack and his team learned, first-hand, the twenty features of the Model Z and how to best present it in different contexts. Jane, on the other hand, left with an URL she could refer back to at a later date when she needed to know the features of the Model Z and how to place it.

# Synthesizing the Sensibilities

When woven together, these VIE sensibilities create immersive and interactive 3DLEs that drive learner engagement to levels previously unattainable in the Flatland. Table 3.1 summarizes the differences between traditional 2D learning and 3DLEs.

Additionally, the 3D, or first-person-interface, mirrors the context with which our visual minds are wired to operate. We naturally encounter and make sense of our surroundings in a physical 3D context. The fact that this particular 3D interaction is in digital form seems to make little difference to the synapses that fire in our brains. Many of the same visual and spatial cues, sense-making, and decision-making processes we have honed to outwit predators are brought to bear in the digital-based 3D interface.

Beyond alignment with our brain's wiring, there are also some very practical reasons that 3DLEs can be advantageous.

## More Focused Presence

It is much harder to multitask in 3DLE. While multitasking may seem like a good idea in many work situations, in a learning context, it dilutes an

**Table 3.1.** Differences Between Traditional 2D Learning and 3DLEs

| Sensibility | 2D Synchronous Learning | 3D Synchronous Learning |
|---|---|---|
| Sense of Self | Emoticon | Avatar |
| Death of Distance | Same Time, Same Website | Same Time, Same Virtual Space |
| Power of Presence | Disembodied | Embodied |
| Sense of Space | Website and Slides | Virtual Space |
| Power to Co-Create | Document Presentation | Display Building |
| Power of Practice | Exercises | Exercises and Activities |
| Enrichment of Experience | Interaction | Interaction Immersion |

individual's attention and prevents him or her from truly understanding the information being taught, as well as inhibits retention and later recall.

This is a primary argument against 2D synchronous learning. The learners aren't always fully "present." On the other hand, Jack is so engaged in helping his team that he chooses to ignore the all-too-familiar e-mail alarm. Abbott is "busted" for going back to Flatland to IM with his boss during a challenge. The immersive context that 3DLEs provide is very sticky and demands more attention than its Flatland cousin.

## More Authentic Learning Contexts

3DLEs are much more effective at rendering real-world work situations than a classroom or an online whiteboard or slide show. 3DLEs enable learners to become immersed in a learning context as close to the actual performance environment as the learner can get without actually being there. These worlds can be highly realistic, such as the building the product displays for the Model Z drill. Furthermore, the product manager avatars critiquing the Model Z displays were "walking" around the displays co-created by the learning teams, not looking at a 2D representation of what they intended to do.

## Congruent Contextual Cues Facilitate Recall

When immersed in a 3D environment, a person is cognitively encoding the sounds, sights, and spatial relationships of the environment and is behaviorally engaged. The person becomes emotionally involved and behaves and acts as he or she would in the actual situation. When this happens, it allows the learner to more effectively encode the learning for future recall and provides the cues needed to apply the experience from the 3D world to actual on-the-job performance. In short, 3DLEs are the ultimate "learning by doing" platform.

They can provide a "fun" environment for working together, as well as an environment filled with stress and surprises. 3DLEs can mimic the actual work situation and cause real physical reactions from participants such as increased heartbeat, laughter, and perspiration.

## Embedded Peer-to-Peer Learning

Collaboration and peer-to-peer learning emerge naturally in a 3DLE context, while they must be specifically engineered into a 2D context. Given the immersive nature of the 3D environment, many of the challenges outlined in Jack's story allow the power of peer-to-peer collaboration to take hold once the challenge is set in motion.

3DLEs take advantage of the interactive and immersive affordances that are baked into the infrastructure to enable and encourage spontaneous and serendipitous avatar-mediated networked learning.

In short, by enabling immersion and interactivity around a contextually relevant and realistic set of activities, 3DLEs enable learners and facilitators to escape Flatland and enjoy engaging, first-person-interface-enabled learning episodes.

# Implications for Trainers and Educators

The current trainer-centric classroom-based model for learning is being challenged by society and technology on all fronts. 3DLEs are accelerating that process even more as enterprises begin to adapt structures and infrastructures to keep pace with the webvolution. As more and more businesses deploy virtual immersive environments, employees are going to need to know how to work and complete transactions within this context. Many of the activities will be the same as in the physical world in terms of business, but other activities will be dramatically different in a virtual world because of the flexibility these worlds provide. Employees will need to know how to conduct various types of virtual-world transactions and move seamlessly back and forth between the Flatland and 3DLEs.

In a three-dimensional generative learning environment such as a VIE, the role of the traditional training function becomes increasingly marginalized, and speeding it up with technology merely accelerates the visibility of its shortcomings to drive generative learning and, by association, enterprise profitability. New methods, training techniques, and learning environments have to be created for organizations to be successful.

This, in turn, will require that the learning function adopt new learning paradigms that enable them to meet the dynamic needs of the enterprises they serve. More importantly, to avoid further marginalization, learning professionals should lead the Immersive Internet charge so that they can prepare both enterprises and employees to function effectively in a world gone web.

To ensure success, schools must revamp their online distance programs, recruiting practices, and educational efforts to include spaces within VIEs. These spaces will be visited by alumni, current students, and prospective students. They can provide an excellent opportunity for current and past students to interact, learn, and even interview one another for potential work, both in the physical world and within virtual worlds. The dynamics of 3D worlds will change the student/faculty/alumni relationships, allowing freer access to explore worlds and locations not previously able to be explored.

# Part Two

**Building a Blueprint**

4

# Architecting Learning Experiences

## Avoiding the Buggy-Whip Experience

Virtual immersive environments (VIEs) provide instructional designers with a new technology platform upon which to create compelling 3D learning experiences (3DLEs).

With the advent of VIE technology, the learning profession finds itself in a similar position to the buggy-whip manufacturing industry in the mid-1800's when internal-combustion engine technology arrived on the scene. At that time, the buggy-whip manufacturers' paradigm of transportation (the horse and buggy) clouded their ability to recognize how this technology would revolutionize the transportation industry (the motor car). By the mid-1890s, as consumers left their horses and buggies in droves for a more efficient transportation alternative, the market for buggy whips had withered into insignificance.

To avoid the fate of the buggy-whip manufacturers while simultaneously achieving the fullest potential that VIE technology has to offer to transform learning, instructional designers must avoid falling prey to the routinization trap introduced in Chapter 2. This will require a fundamental and permanent transformation in how learning professionals perceive learning and how they approach the design of 3DLEs within VIEs. In fact, 3DLEs require a set of wholly new design principles that are unshackled from the classroom delivery paradigm and grounded in the affordances that VIE technology can lend to the learning experience.

# 3D Learning Experience Design Principles

3DLEs must be designed to create engaging episodic interactions that lead the learner along an optimal flow state of challenge and reward as they rapidly—but often not consciously—assimilate new learnings along the way.

The learning that occurs within a 3DLE surfaces at the moment when the lack of knowledge or capability of the participant intersects with the need to have that knowledge or capability to overcome a challenge or complete a specific task. The learning experience is engineered so that teachable moments surface at every turn. Those teachable moments are not the same for each participant. Instead, the content covered is encountered, applied, and reflected upon based on the experience of the learner, rather than the mandate of the teacher.

In designing 3DLEs, content is king, but context is the kingdom. Context helps bring definitions, concepts, topics, procedures, and principles to life by rendering them actionable to the participant within the 3DLE. The true value of 3DLEs will never be achieved by attempting to mimic the classroom context. Instead, the true potential of 3DLEs will be realized in demonstrating how purposeful they can be in allowing participants to act and interact toward a common goal, fail, try again in a different way, and eventually (but much more rapidly and safely than in real life), achieve the desired learning objectives.

In essence, the optimal goal of a 3DLE is to blur the lines between learning and doing to where the distinction between the two is unrecognizable.

As was the case in the age of apprenticeship, learning and doing become fused and situated in a context where action and execution synthesize concept and content in real time.

To achieve these desired design outcomes, our proposed model outlines eight design principles to guide instructional designers in their quest to create immersive and engaging 3DLEs. This model is a result of the collaborative effort between the authors and some of the most respected and recognized 3DLE designers in the field: Chuck Hamilton, Christopher Keesey, Randy Hinrichs, Ken Hudson, Steve Mahaley, and Sarah Robbins.[1] Thanks to their input and insights, we believe we have synthesized the key design principles that have emerged to date (see Figure 4.1).

The 3DLE Design Principles Model is broken into two primary components. The grounding principles and the experiential principles.

**Figure 4.1.** 3DLE Design Principles

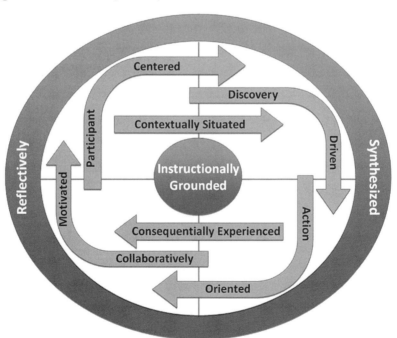

# The Grounding Principles

All 3DLEs should be grounded in solid instructional design approaches and require reflective synthesis at the individual and team level. These two principles form the core and the perimeter within which the other principles are applied to develop immersive and engaging 3DLEs.

**Instructionally Grounded.** Irrespective of whether the 3DLE is a part of a larger blended intervention or a stand-alone entity, it is essential to ensure that the learning intervention is addressing a vetted business need and that the learning objectives within the intervention are optimally tuned to address that business need. Furthermore, it is also critical to ensure the 3DLE approach is the most effective and efficient mechanism to transfer the learning objectives to on-the-job performance.

In essence, adherence to this principle requires that all of the formative evaluation work that is required to develop a traditional learning program must still be conducted. Furthermore, as an overlay to this front-end analysis, a clear and compelling case must be made that there is significant and differentiated business value to be derived from developing a 3DLE solution when compared to traditional approaches.

**Reflectively Synthesized.** Given the experiential and collaborative nature of 3DLEs, the need for self-reflection and group-based synthesis of the experience should also be an integral element in the design. The design of 3DLEs should allot time for both instructor review of the application of the skills taught and peer-to-peer review of actions taken and results achieved.

In 3DLE design, structured reflection at the individual and group level is not optional. The placement of the reflectively synthesized principle at the perimeter of the model implies that participants cannot leave the experience without passing through a reflection gate.

**The Experiential Principles.** Once it is confirmed that there is a clear set of learning objectives that address a business or academic need and that the learning required is best transferred via a 3DLE intervention, the next challenge is to design a context that is optimally suited to allow the participants to experience and internalize the learning objectives in a visceral way.

The six remaining design principles are specifically geared toward informing and guiding the 3DLE design process itself.

**Participant Centered.** The first design principle proposes that the participant (not the teacher) should be positioned at the center of the learning experience. Unlike the classroom-based "sage on the stage" model by which the teacher imparts knowledge upon the passive learning consumer, in a 3DLE the participants have agency. Their actions and interactions have consequential outcomes within the learning experience itself.

In 3DLEs, the locus of control moves from the teacher to the learner, and the contextual design must accommodate the actions and interactions that participants have within the immersive environment. Learning objectives are not covered conversationally, but experienced viscerally. In 3DLEs, participants become a component in the design of the learning experience itself.

In a typical classroom setting, objectives are introduced, explained via illustration or example, and processed via conversation. In a 3DLE situations are encountered, are experienced, and learning is synthesized as a part of the experience itself. Content and process are fused to the point where the distinction between learning and doing becomes almost imperceptible.

In placing the learner at the center of the 3DLE design and in exploring how to bring the learning objectives to life via participant agency, instructional designers can discover new possibilities and approaches to improve and enrich the participants' learning experience.

The participant-centered design principle is demonstrated in Jack's 3DLE when, upon his avatar's arrival, he is immediately engaged by his virtual teammates in the early-bird learning bucks challenge to identify the new Model Z features (see Chapter 3).

**Contextually Situated.** In a traditional classroom setting, the learning context is pre-established. The participants are faced with an instructor, a projector, and a whiteboard. There is very little contextual variation from classroom to classroom. The content itself may change, but the classroom context and its associated technological affordances are relatively static.

The second design principle requires that instructional designers move beyond the realm of classroom content delivery into the realm of situated context. All 3DLEs require the creation of a specific context within which the learning occurs. The more authentic and engaging the challenge, issue, or task context, the more powerful the learning experience becomes for the participant. This 3DLE situational context must accommodate how participants will learn from the facilitator, from each other, and from the environment itself.

The primary challenge for instructional designers in adhering to this principle revolves around creating the optimal situational context to accommodate the learning experience. The context must be authentic and action oriented, but it must also be bounded in such a way that it ensures all of the learning objectives are encountered by the participant without it being too obvious or onerous. Striking the right balance between contextual authenticity and learning objective coverage is essential in setting the appropriate context within which to situate the learning experience.

The contextually situated design principle is demonstrated throughout Jack's 3DLE. In the course of the 3DLE, Jack and his colleagues were exposed to multiple situated contexts. When the learners first arrived, they were engaged in a competitive context searching for Model Z features. Next they were engaged in a challenge flying around a giant drill to find new feature flags. They were then teleported from store display to store display, participated in a role play, and finally were placed into a workspace to create their own displays (see Chapter 3).

**Discovery Driven.** Once the appropriate situational context and participant roles and agency have been defined, the next instructional challenge is to establish motivation for sustained and engaged interaction within the 3DLE.

In a traditional classroom setting, the establishment of motivation is something that is often left to the instructor. In a 3DLE, since the instructor is not central to the design, the motivation must be built into the flow of participant action and interaction within the 3DLE.

To help establish a sense of engagement and flow for participants, instructional designers should create 3DLEs that selectively reveal information and incentives over time. Providing the right level of strategic ambiguity or ill-structured problems within the situational context incents participants to become more engaged in the flow of the 3DLE. By establishing a set of minimal guidelines and allowing participants to become actively engaged, discovering cues and clues along the way, instructional designers can sustain participant motivation within the 3DLE.

In essence, the third design principle acknowledges that, as we move from an educational paradigm where instructors explain content to students within a classroom context to one where learners explore a context within which learning content is independently discovered, instructional designers must be mindful about how to motivate and engage participants throughout the discovery process.

The discovery-driven design principle is demonstrated throughout Jack's 3DLE in the first two activities where teams are incented to discover the new Model Z features first in a competitive, game-show context and second in a virtual treasure-hunt activity around the giant drill (see Chapter 3).

**Action Oriented.** At its core, experience is rooted in action. As Randy Hinrichs astutely points out in his essay in this chapter, "It is not about being there, it is about doing there."

The success or failure of a 3DLE hinges upon the actions and interactions of participants as they engage in a series of episodic activities designed to surface teachable moments that synthesize the learning objectives associated with the intervention.

3DLEs are situational and problem-centered, as opposed to being objective-centered. They revolve around tasks not topics. They are designed so that the learning objectives are embedded within the experiential activity. In 3DLEs, the learning is not separated from the doing. In 3DLEs, learning is a natural outcome of having engaged in an activity. This is a stark contrast to traditional classroom training, which is usually positioned as a pre-condition to doing.

The action-oriented design principle is demonstrated throughout Jack's 3DLE. From the moment that Jack logs into the 3DLE, he is fully engaged in a series of activities that demand his full attention. In fact, when Abbott drops out of the 3DLE to tend to a real-world business matter, Jack goes after him to pull him back into the action (see Chapter 3).

**Consequentially Experienced.**  Learning is an iterative process. Trial and error is core to the development of professional competence. The old adage "If at first you don't succeed, try and try again" is foundational in instructional design, academic growth, and professional development. In mastering any profession or subject matter, novices move back and forth between action and reflection as they develop from unconscious incompetence to conscious incompetence, to conscious competence, ultimately achieving the mastery level of unconscious competence.

The fifth design principle requires that trial and error be embedded into the 3DLE. Practically speaking, this means that the participants should be required to demonstrate their ability to perform a given task or challenge, that they experience the consequence of their actions in carrying out that task, and that they are provided feedback related to the task to allow them to improve their performance on subsequent iterations.

More importantly, by viscerally experiencing the outcome of actions within the 3DLE, participants are more apt to internalize the underlying learning objective. As learners are required to move beyond proving the acquisition of knowledge on a test to actually experiencing the consequence of an activity that applies knowledge in an authentic context, the desire and willingness to learn are increased. Immediate constructive feedback on the heels of failure is one of the most profound and powerful teachable moments. It is also an affordance that is easily applied within the 3DLE context.

The consequentially experienced design principle is demonstrated in Jack's 3DLE when his team receives real-time feedback from experienced product managers on the effectiveness of the Model Z product display constructed by his team (see Chapter 3).

**Collaboratively Motivated.**  Learning is often a team sport. 3DLEs naturally enable participants to work together to achieve goals and learn from one another through collaboration. The sixth design principle proposes that the instructional design approach migrate from enabling individual information acquisition to affording collective experiential sense-making.

In 3DLEs learning shifts from structured teaching to social and situated peer-to-peer learning. Participants are simultaneously consumers of, and contributors to, the learning experience. Their collective action and collaborative co-creation drive generative insights that cannot be individually derived by any single member of the group. In designing 3DLEs, collaboration should be encouraged and incented as frequently as possible.

The collaboratively motivated principle is demonstrated throughout Jack's 3DLE. The potential to win team "learning bucks" drove much of the team-based engagement in the specific challenge and discovery-based activities (see Chapter 3).

# Synthesizing the Principles

Table 4.1 synthesizes the key questions instructional designers should ask as they work to ensure adherence to the 3DLE Design Principles:

**Table 4.1.** Key Questions an Instructional Designer Should Ask

| Design Principle | Key Questions to Consider |
|---|---|
| **Instructionally Grounded** | Is the learning intervention addressing a vetted business or educational need?<br>Are the learning objectives optimized to address the business or educational need?<br>Is a 3DLE the most efficient and effective mechanism for transferring the learning? |
| **Participant Centered** | Does the design place the participants in the center of the experience?<br>What role(s) do the participants play in the experience?<br>What actions and interactions can the participants take to encounter teachable moments within the experience? |
| **Contextually Situated** | What situational contexts best accommodate the learning objectives of the intervention?<br>What is the role of the facilitator, other participants, and the environment itself in creating an authentic situational context for learning? |
| **Discovery Driven** | What is the minimum set of guidelines that need to be established to catalyze action within the learning experience?<br>What information or incentives can be selectively revealed within the learning experience to motivate engagement and collaborative action within the experience? |

*(Continued)*

**Table 4.1.** *(Continued)*

| Design Principle | Key Questions to Consider |
|---|---|
| **Activity Oriented** | What is the set of episodic activities that will immerse the participants in the learning experience? <br> What are the key actions and interactions within these episodes that trigger teachable moments for the participants? |
| **Consequentially Experienced** | How will participants be required to demonstrate their ability to perform? <br> How is iterative trial and error and feedback built into the learning experience? <br> What are the consequences of failure for the participant? |
| **Collaboratively Motivated** | How will collaborative and co-creative action on the part of the teams be incented and rewarded? Is the reward intrinsic or extrinsic? <br> How is collaboration encouraged by the design? |
| **Reflectively Synthesized** | How is personal reflection accommodated in the design? <br> How are team after-action reviews accommodated in the design? |

# From Principles to Macrostructures

Determining the best method of applying the principles to create a compelling 3DLE requires an architectural blueprint. As an instructional designer begins to design a 3DLE, following a specific architectural approach makes the process more effective.

Since VIE technologies and the 3DLEs that they enable are emergent methods of instruction with academic and corporate settings, a comprehensive learning architecture is needed to guide individuals in the process of creating immersive and engaging 3DLEs.

The previously defined 3DLE principles fit logically into four larger macrostructures: Agency, Exploration, Experience, and Connectedness, as shown in Figure 4.2.[2]

These macrostructures can be applied as a coverage model in the design of 3DLEs. To achieve coverage, instructional designers should ensure that each macrostructure is activated within the 3DLE design. Each 3DLE, based on its specific desired learning outcomes, will lean more heavily toward one or two of the macrostructures, but all four should be engaged at some level.

**Figure 4.2.** 3DLE Macrostructures: Agency, Exploration, Experience, Connectedness

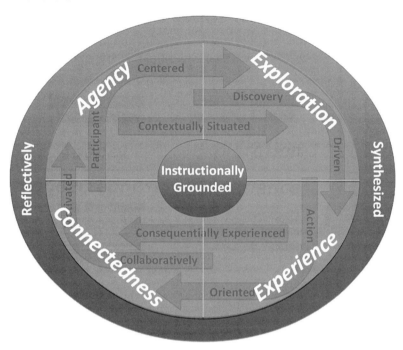

The descriptions of each macrostructure, outlined below, provide a definition and articulation of how to ensure that the macrostructure is activated within the design.

## Agency

Agency is the ability of the person operating the avatar within the 3DLE to take action. Placing the participant in the center of the experience and allowing him or her to take independent action within the 3DLE assures that the agency macrostructure is activated.

## Exploration

Exploration is the ability to navigate the environment and examine it to gain knowledge. Situating avatars in authentic contexts and allowing them to discover teachable moments while navigating the 3DLE assures that the exploration macrostructure is activated.

## Experience

Experience is the ability to engage in activities, have meaningful interactions, and encounter the consequences of those actions and interactions within the environment. Ensuring that the consequences of actions and interactions within the 3DLE are encountered by the avatar assures that the experience macrostructure is activated.

## Connectedness

Connectedness is the ability to interact with each other to create and build knowledge and understanding. Motivating collaborative action around a given endeavor and affording that collaboration with incentives ensures that the connectedness macrostructure is activated.

The next section of this chapter will discuss how these macrostructures provide a framework within which 3D learning archetypes and the seven sensibilities of VIEs can be organized.

# From Macrostructures to Archetypes and Sensibilities

The four macrostructures serve as an organizing framework for specific 3DLE archetypes. As shown in Figure 4.3, each macrostructure houses a specific set of 3DLE archetypes.

Archetypes are the basic building blocks of 3DLEs. Each archetype achieves a specific set of learning outcomes and activates a specific macrostructure. Currently, eleven 3DLE archetypes have been identified. These archetypes and examples of their applications within 3DLEs will be described in detail in the Chapter 5.

It is anticipated that, as experience in leveraging VIEs to create 3DLEs matures, more archetypes will be identified. The open-ended nature of macrostructures is purposely designed to accommodate these additional archetypes as they are discovered.

Once the archetypes are overlaid on the macrostructures, it is easily observed how each archetype fits with a specific macrostructure. While

**Figure 4.3.** The Eleven 3DLE Archetypes Mapped to the Four 3DLE Macrostructures

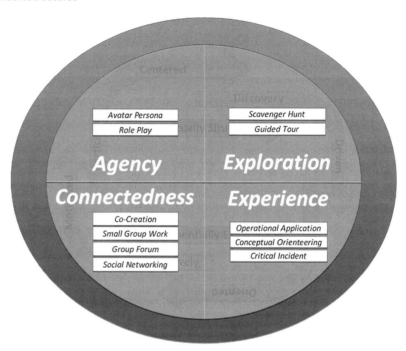

overlaps and cross-over will and should occur in 3DLE design decisions, the four macrostructures provide a useful way of discussing and thinking about creating 3DLEs to effectively meet the desired learning outcomes. The macrostructure/archetype model provides a framework that instructional designers and others can share with stakeholders to help them understand the opportunities and challenges associated with 3DLE design.

Finally, to round out the development of a comprehensive 3D learning architecture, it is also possible to house the seven sensibilities identified in Chapter 3 within the same four macrostructures (see Figure 4.4).

The next section outlines how the principles, macrostructures, archetypes, and sensibilities can be organized into a comprehensive 3D learning architecture.

**Figure 4.4.** The Seven VIE Sensibilities Mapped to the Four 3DLE Macrostructures

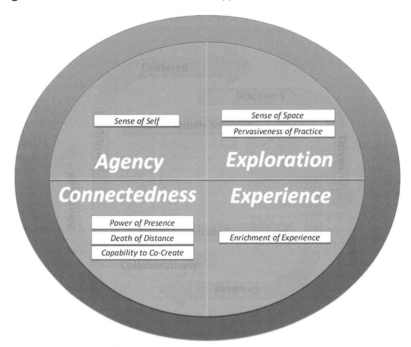

# Achieving Architectural Alignment

Jack and his co-workers became immersed and engaged in the 3DLE because it optimally leveraged the seven VIE sensibilities and the activity adhered to the eight design principles outlined earlier in this chapter. The 3DLE design successfully aligned the sensibilities with the principles and achieved the desired learning outcomes because the designers were employing a comprehensive learning architecture that provided clear direction for the creation of the 3DLE.

The use of a 3DLE architecture helps the instructional designer ensure that all the structural levels of the design are in alignment and appropriately balanced (see Figure 4.5).

A core element of the 3DLE architecture is that it aligns at every level. This alignment is what makes the architecture so valuable when considering the development of 3DLEs.

**Figure 4.5.** Alignment of Model Elements

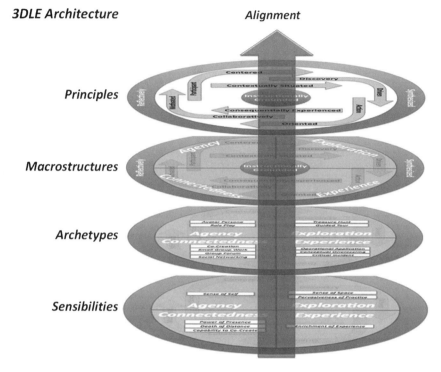

Table 4.2 synthesizes the key questions instructional designers should ask as they work through each layer of the architecture to develop a 3DLE.

# Implications for Learning Professionals

The value of the 3DLE architecture is that instructional designers creating 3DLEs now have a foundation upon which to make informed judgments about what design principles, macrostructures, archetypes, and sensibilities are most appropriate to achieve the desired learning outcomes in an aligned and balanced way.

Learning professionals who are new to this field should leverage the architecture as a "guide on the side" as they work to develop 3DLEs.

**Table 4.2.** Key Questions to Ask at Each Level of the Architecture

| Architecture Level | Key Questions to Consider |
|---|---|
| **Principles** | Do the desired learning outcomes absolutely require the application of a 3DLE? <br> Is the design instructionally grounded and does it incorporate reflective synthesis following the immersive activities? <br> Has every effort been made to ensure that the eight experiential design principles have been adhered to in 3DLE design? |
| **Macrostructures** | What are the primary macrostructures that are activated by the desired learning outcomes? <br> What design principles are most aligned with these macrostructures, and do they receive appropriate emphasis within the 3DLE design? <br> Is the 3DLE design balanced? Have all macrostructures been activated to some degree? <br> Is there alignment with the learning goals? |
| **Archetypes** | Which archetypes are most aligned with the primary macrostructures and emphasized design principles? <br> Is the 3DLE design streamlined? <br> Do the archetypes fit together seamlessly into a narrative or set of activities that engage the learner? |
| **Sensibilities** | Which sensibilities are most aligned with the primary macrostructures, emphasized design principles, and archetypes? <br> How can these sensibilities be leveraged to create a more immersive and engaging 3DLE? |

## Insights from Innovators
### Randy Hinrichs, CEO of 2b3d

Outlined below are Randy Hinrichs' top-ten 3DLE design principles. Randy originally shared these principles at the 3DTLC conference in Washington, D.C.

### 1. It's Not About Me, It's About We

People naturally clan together to learn. We start with inner knowledge that we begin sharing externally to validate our premises and ensure that what we know is useful to the greatest majority of us in our environment. Blogging, twittering, and virtual world interactions are all outgrowths of the intrinsic need we have to augment our collective insights and consciousness.

When designing 3DLEs, think about "we" as much as you think about "me."

## 2. It's Not About the Technology, It's About the Neurology

Virtual immersion reduces the reliance on mere 2D text and imagery. A visual active and contextual environment can contain embedded rules that are not obvious, but appeal to our visual sense of what's right and what's wrong. Within such an environment, an individual must adapt to the environment using existing knowledge schemas, seeking information rapidly and rejecting non-relevant information, and cataloguing other information that could be useful later. This process of environmental adaptation creates a neurological change in the brain. It forces the person to find resources in the environment and compete to survive.

When designing 3DLEs, think about how to change the participants' neurology.

## 3. It's Not About Revolution, It's About Evolution

Dramatic changes to one's environment can be uncomfortable and non-productive. People embrace small changes in their environment in which learning processes pass from one generation to the next. Storytelling, narration, learning by doing, guilds, sharing in groups, presentation, and testing are all part of our learning processes.

The similarities in the instructional design coupled with the new affordances allows for natural, gradual divergence in learning modalities. The new interfaces of simulation, role playing, and immersive 3D visualization must reinforce learning styles, not threaten them or make the learner uncomfortable. The basis of continuity creates inherited traits and enables each generation to evolve into the next without resistance. What we know about sound instructional design should not change; how 3D better enables or activates the learning experience is what we should be focusing on.

When designing 3DLEs, think about introducing 3DLEs as a natural evolution, not a big-bang revolution.

### 4. It's Not About Being There, It's About Doing There

Adapting to the environment at a slow pace, assessing the environment through accumulated experiences and relationships, identifying resources, prioritizing the events, and exercising activities creates a culture of doing. Design for creation and recreation in virtual worlds. Seek interactivity so decisions have to be made and consequences experienced. Without engagement and feedback, the learners tend to diminish their experience, lose energy and motivation. Keep them making decisions and responding to the environment.

When designing 3DLEs, think about what people will be doing there.

### 5. It's Not About the Electrons, It's About the Physics

There is much focus on bandwidth, graphic card compatibility, networks, and security associated with virtual worlds as barriers to implementing virtual worlds. All of these issues will be addressed in due course. Others create educational hurdles by seeking to leverage virtual worlds to create spaces in which they can see physical structures that look like the world they recognize.

Adaptive learning requires experiencing the environment. Think about the physics in the environment, gravity, and the various properties of matter in their solid, liquid, and gaseous forms. Think about light and its intensity, frequency, and polarization. Anything can be programmed in a virtual world to simulate physical interactions. It is the exploration and constraints of these physical properties that can be leveraged to teach complex concepts in virtual worlds.

When designing 3DLEs, use real-world physics instead of creating classrooms, stages, and lecterns. Get people pulling apart atoms, immersing a lead weight in oil versus water—use real-world physics to test hypotheses, rather than presentation screens to inform about hypotheses.

### 6. It's Not About Theory, It's About Rapid Feedback

Design scenarios should encourage people to research information, synthesize it into a plan, formulate it into an action, then conduct activities in the environment that allow users to test their plans and receive immediate feedback from the environment. Do I need to pull that box down from that shelf way up there to check to see whether it has physical contents that I should include in my inventory audit? How do I get it down from the top shelf? Do I call a plant manager, or get it myself? These are the kinds of scenario-based reflections that utilize rule-based systems for self-evaluation and accumulation of expertise. Also, make sure there are rewards for advancing to the next level of difficulty. When they get the box down, make sure they count the contents inside and the results are stored and used for another activity. The student must form his or her own hypothesis, test it, and draw a conclusion from his or her own actions.

When designing 3DLEs, think about building feedback and reflection into every activity.

### 7. It's Not About the Application, It's About the Integration

It's much less about getting 2D into virtual worlds than it is about using the 3D affordances of virtual worlds. The experiences we design for learners in virtual worlds need to help people integrate their work processes together. They must be experiences that help participants learn how to collaborate.

The affordances for learning in a virtual world are effectively tools for managing information: writing tools, synthesis tools, process tools. The strength in bringing communities together to integrate their ideas into actionable steps, consensus, and collective execution across multiple companies, multiple populations, and multiple platforms provide the best design choices. Let the integration of the environment and the tools for decision making merge in virtual spaces.

When designing 3DLEs, think about how to integrate 2D tools with 3D affordances to create memorable experiences.

### 8. It's Not About the Database, It's About the Human Race

While artificial intelligence shows some promise, connecting real people over dynamic networks is the secret sauce of virtual world and social networking technology. Tapping into the spontaneity, the collective insight, the desire for the team to conquer a challenge is what makes communicating with people over the network so compelling. Human beings are incredibly malleable and can reduce data to action in the blink of an eye.

When designing 3DLEs, think about encouraging increased human interaction.

### 9. It's Not About Instructional Design, It Is About Experiential Design

Yes, we must gain the learners' attention, inform them of learning objectives, stimulate recall, present new material, provide learning guidance, elicit performance, provide feedback and correctness, assess performance, and enhance retention and recall. But with today's carnival of content, mixed media, and unlimited access to new information, we must also create a story for the learner in which he or she is the main character.

Virtual worlds are about theater, character development, relationships with other characters, plot, conflict, denouement, catharsis, and conclusion. We need to design for the full immersive experience in which the users must adapt to the environment, survive in the environment, and fail if they haven't learned well enough. Adults are goal oriented and they want to relate information and experience to the direction they are moving in. If they are enabled by experimentation, discovery, and self-reflection, they grow rapidly.

When designing 3DLEs, think about the learning experience more than the learning objectives.

## 10. It's Not About Globalization, It's About Localization

Communities are developed in a virtual world by creating a place that embeds the culture, expectations, and appropriate behaviors within the environment. Think of a hospital, a vision of 21st century health care, a financial trading floor, a restaurant kitchen. People come to these places identifying what looks right, what feels right. In community development, ideas form around like minds. Globalization is a phenomenon that suggests our markets are opening to partners around the world. Communities in virtual worlds are a phenomenon that suggests that our partners come together in shared spaces to concentrate their efforts, processes, values, and goals, creating solutions for the customer. Communities are a place in which collections of life experiences and knowledge come to the forefront and connect people and activities into a learning environment.

When designing 3DLEs, think about the cultivation of connections and communities.

5

# Designing by Archetype

## Introduction

The 3D learning architecture described in the previous chapter is critical to aligning the sensibilities of virtual immersive environment (VIE) technologies to the principles required for effective 3DLEs and critical elements in that architecture are the learning archetypes. The archetypes provide the practical and actionable learning designs that enable the creation of effective 3DLEs. This chapter explores the learning architectures introduced in Chapter 4 and describes them in more detail.

As the discussion of the archetypes begins, it is important to note that some well-known learning designs cut across archetypes. For example, you can add game elements like a timer and competition to almost any of the archetypes. You can time a scavenger hunt or the length of time it takes a learner or group of learners to solve a problem in a critical incident learning event. So no specific archetype of "game" is identified. Additionally, you can use any of the archetypes as an assessment. You can have a learner give a guided tour of an area he or she has studied as an assessment or have the person set up a scavenger hunt to determine knowledge or assess his or her ability in a role play. So we chose not to have a specific archetype of "assessment."[1]

It is also possible to add the concept of micro and macro environments to almost any of the archetypes. You can conduct a tour, for example, as either a regularly sized avatar or one seemingly shrunken to the size of an ant or a molecule. You can apply the same idea to a critical incident or even to social networking (network as a bee to learn how hive-based communities interact). You can also be a giant and walk among tiny buildings to get a view of how the various structures should be laid out on a college campus or in a newly developed town or community.

While the use of VIEs for instruction is still relatively new, we have identified eleven archetypes that can be used as foundational building blocks in creating successful 3DLEs. It is our belief that, as the technology matures and more people begin to use VIES, more archetypes will be developed. The eleven archetypes are:

- Avatar Persona
- Role Play
- Scavenger Hunt
- Guided Tour
- Operational Application
- Conceptual Orienteering
- Critical Incident
- Co-Creation
- Small Group Work
- Group Forums
- Social Networking

# Creation of the Archetypes

The concept of the archetypes was originally created in an essay the authors wrote for The eLearning Guild 360-degree report on Synchronous Learning

Systems titled "Escaping Flatland: The Emergence of 3D Synchronous Learning."[2] The essay outlined the seven sensibilities and the archetypes and described how the archetypes could be used to create learning in a VIE. Since that time Lesley Scopes, a successful master's candidate at the University of Southampton, UK, expanded the concept of the archetypes and created formal definitions. She also introduced what the authors have defined as the macrostructure concept. Scopes' macrostructures were divided by learning domains. She called them Cognitive Domain, Dextrous Domain, Social Domain, and Emotional Domain. She then created frames and subframes, which she called Role Play, Peregrination, Simulation, Meshed, and Assessment and Evaluation. In an effort to simplify the detailed work created by Scopes, the authors have modified the domain terminology and renamed them: Agency, Exploration, Experience, and Connectedness. This was in an effort to both broaden and simplify the extensive and detailed work of Scopes.[3]

Listed below are the learning archetypes originally described in that first essay with modifications based on subsequent experiences of the authors as well as insightful additions by Scopes, who is credited with formalizing the definitions. It is suggested that her dissertation, "Learning Archetypes as Tools of Cybergogy for 3D Educational Landscape: A Structure for eTeaching in Second Life" be read by anyone wishing to explore the archetypes and the concept of a cybergogy (a digital-based rethinking of pedagogy) in more detail.

In this chapter, the discussion is limited to the archetypes and how they can be applied through examples and specific references to the learning experience of Jack, Abbott, and Heather as they learned about the Model Z drill in the scenario described in Chapter 3.

# Defining the Archetypes

The following is a description of the eleven archetypes first introduced in the 3D learning architecture. Typically, a 3DLE incorporates more than one of the archetypes in its instructional design.[4]

## Avatar Persona

*Formal Definition:* Ability of people to act and observe themselves acting within the environment as an avatar. Acting and navigating within the virtual world as the avatar. (See Figure 5.1.)

While this is not a specific method for designing instruction, under-standing the impact being an avatar has on an individual and how it impacts and influences learning is important. Experience has shown that, when new participants enter a VIE as an avatar, they need time to test drive it to make sure it operates and looks how they want it to look.

This is because of the emotional and intellectual investment people make in their avatars. The avatar experiences the environment and the learning and

**Figure 5.1.** Customizing an Avatar Is an Important Element in the Avatar Persona Archetype

the participant is a bit of a voyeur on the process, but a highly vested voyeur. This means that observational learning is a large part of the participant's experience within a 3DLE. Additionally, it seems from some related research that the third-person perspective, the most common view in VIEs, has some educational benefits over a first-person perspective typically experienced in a classroom or during an online virtual classroom session.

As reported in a *New York Times* article titled "This Is Your Life (and How You Tell It)," there was an experiment at Ohio University in which researchers had college students who described themselves as "socially awkward" in high school recall one of their most embarrassing moments.[5] They asked half of the students to re-imagine the humiliation in the first person, and the other half to re-imagine it in the third person.

Students who imagined acting in third person rated themselves as having changed significantly since the incident first occurred, while those who re-imagined the incident in first person did not indicate that they had changed significantly. It appears that the third-person perspective allowed the students to reflect on the meaning of their social miscues and then actually grow and change psychologically, while the first-person perspective did not cause a similar change.

Not only did the ratings of themselves change, but the students' behavior changed as well. According to the article, "a subsequent experiment showed that members of the third-person group were much more sociable than the others. 'They were more likely to initiate a conversation, after having perceived themselves as more changed,' said Lisa Libby, the lead author [of the study] and a psychologist at Ohio State University." In addition, Dr. Libby and fellow researchers hypothesize that projecting future actions in the third person may affect how people behave in the future. In another study, students who envisioned voting for president in the 2004 election from a third-person perspective were more likely to actually travel to the polls than those imagining themselves casting votes in the first person.[6]

With this in mind, if a person is asked to perform an activity in the three-dimensional VIE where one of the most frequently used "modes" is the third-person perspective, it seems reasonable that the person's behavior would change as a result of viewing him- or herself performing that behavior in third person. While more studies are definitely needed to confirm this connection, Dr. Libby's research indicates that real and lasting behavioral changes could occur as a result of learners performing desired behaviors and activities in a virtual world using the third-person perspective.

Therefore, the avatar persona is a large part of the learning experience and process and needs to be understood as one method of helping to facilitate learning within 3DLEs. The avatar persona is evidenced by how Jack interacts within the VIE and is best seen in the avatar for Sam Jones, who always wears his Mets cap. Jones identified with his avatar and ensures that the avatar is dressed appropriately to represent the persona he wants to portray (see Figure 5.2).

**Figure 5.2.** The Avatar for Sam Jones with the Ever-Present Mets Cap

# Role Play

*Formal Definition:* To assume a role in an alternative form (living or inanimate) with the objective of understanding aspects of action and interaction to learn how to perform that role or gain a better understanding of the person typically serving within that role.[7] (See Figure 5.3.)

The in-world role-play archetype provides a realistic environment in which two or more people act out a scenario. For example, an experienced copier sales manager can play the role of a potential customer in a virtual store with virtual products. A new trainee can play the role of a sales representative and engage the potential customer in a discussion in an attempt to sell him a copier.

---

**Figure 5.3.** Role Playing a Salesman and a Customer in a Virtual Retail Store

Role playing is valuable for immersing a trainee in a job she would actually be doing, as shown in Figure 5.2, where a person is role playing the part of a salesman in a large retail store. This type of environment is flexible. No matter what direction a learner takes, the experienced person playing the other role can provide the right feedback and act appropriately for the role.

In a VIE, the role-play archetype removes some of the traditional obstacles and barriers of conducting face-to-face role plays. For one, online role plays are easier to take on because the learner can get closer to the role. She can dress the avatar in the right clothes, put it in the right environment, and obtain the right tools just as on the job. The environment can be realistic and immersive and literally place the learner into the role she is assuming.

Participating in a virtual world role play helps crystallize the learner's knowledge because the learner is forced to apply all his or her skills and abilities to the role. This is evidenced by the role plays that Jack participated in when trying to sell the Model Z to a construction supervisor. When Jack put on his "sales uniform" (yellow logo shirt and kaki pants), he was focused on the task at hand and even became nervous and anxious as he began to engage in the mock sales call. The result is that Jack, after the role play, had a much better understanding of the nuances and pressure of the job.

A good design for this type of role-play event is to provide a minimal script with a few guidelines and specific objectives and then let the learner role play with a more experienced peer or facilitator. Once the event is over, hold a debriefing to further educate both the participants and the learner observing the role play.

In addition to taking on prospective roles, a role play can also allow a learner to experience a role she does not normally fill, such as allowing a person to experience a different gender or a different race. This provides the learner with a new perspective. This can also be done by having a doctor take on the role of a patient to observe the sights and sounds from a completely different point of view or having a salesperson take on the role of a customer. The instruction can place the learner into many different situations in which she can participate in different roles within the same activity.

One distinct advantage a role play has over a pre-programmed simulation or branching story is that it is open-ended from the learner's perspective.

In a pre-programmed simulation, the designer of the instruction needs to consider as many of the possible branches of the simulation as possible to cover the broad spectrum of learners and their possible responses. The designer, because of limited resources, must then choose only those branching scenarios the learner is most likely to encounter or create. The instructional designer must keep exceptions or variations to a minimum, since the branching can grow quite large with just a few choices.

For example, if an experienced sales trainer assumes the role of a potential customer, as in the scenario with Jack, and an employee assumes the role of a salesperson, the sales trainer can role play almost any approach the employee decides to take. The experienced trainer can react instantly to the questions and inquiries of the sales trainee and modify his or her answers according to the exact technique and approach used by the trainee. The learner can receive customized feedback based on his or her approach, and even try it over and over again.

A disadvantage of role playing is that both the learner and the instructor need to be in the virtual world at the same time. Additionally, given the current state of avatars, the ability to read facial expressions and subtle body language cues does not exist. Virtual worlds are, at this point, simply not complex enough to convey those nuances. Although this is one of many aspects of virtual worlds being worked on by developers and that be overcome eventually.[8]

## Scavenger Hunt

*Formal Definition:* The interaction of individuals or groups in either freeform or prescribed environments with the intent of developing knowledge based on simple inanimate or pre-programmed interaction with the environment.[9] (See Figure 5.4.)

This archetype is effective for teaching basic facts and declarative knowledge. In the scavenger hunt archetype, the learner or learners move through an environment looking for specific information. One version of this is

**Figure 5.4.** Scavenger Hunt Looking for Attributes of a Green Building. Clicking on the potted plant reveals one of the items that must be found during the scavenger hunt.

when Jack and his team looked around the four virtual Model Z drills to identify the new features. Another variation occurred when the team was placed onto the large Model Z drill and asked to collect the red flags located on the features of the drill. Still another variation involves moving from virtual place to place collecting information or clues. Learners can also be asked to "take a snapshot" of a particular place to indicate that they have indeed found the location.

These scavenger hunts are also a good method of introducing new employees to an organization. You can conduct virtual scavenger hunts with new employees from all over the world, providing an engaging mechanism to learn facts and information about the company while simultaneously encouraging them to learn more about their fellow employees.

Use scavenger hunts to orient learners to a new environment or space in which they will be operating. For example, you could establish a scavenger hunt in a virtual factory to provide the learners with an opportunity to learn the location of certain machines or safety stations. Another use is to orient employees to a new city, town, or building layout prior to their actual physical arrival at that location.

Scavenger hunts can be timed and/or rewarded to add an edge of competition or to enhance the sense of playfulness and can be useful for forging communication and collaboration skills within a team.[10] They are a good way to open an educational session and a good method of engaging learners with the VIE in which they are operating. A good design is to meet the learners before the scavenger hunt, give them a designated time for the hunt, let them hunt, and then have them meet in a general location and debrief as a group.

An advantage of scavenger hunts is that an instructor or facilitator does not have to be present. The scavenger hunt can be established ahead of time with the required items placed appropriately in the VIE for the learners to find. The learner simply obtains instructions on what he or she should be looking for as the scavenger hunt begins.

A disadvantage is that a scavenger hunt usually takes a while to plan and set up, and sometimes learners do not find all the items they are required to locate. Learners become frustrated with scavenger hunts if they feel they are too difficult.

## Guided Tour

*Formal Definition:* A guided tour is a formalized, escorted situation based on constructs designed to facilitate interaction of individuals or groups with various environments. These tours take learners to areas of pertinent or general interest while the tour guide/device speaks with authority on the subject matter at hand.[11] (See Figure 5.5.)

**Figure 5.5.** Self-Guided Tour with the Use of an Info Fez in Virtual Morocco

You can use a guided tour to show learners the location of items and/or help the learners understand the relationships between locations and features within an area or product. During the tour, facilitators point out various items to the learners. This is good for basic facts and declarative knowledge such as the names of items and associated jargon. For example, a cardiovascular surgeon may want to take his students for a walk down a patient's blocked aorta and have them squeeze through the area where plaque has built up to highlight the names of the specific locations of the heart and to show the path blood travels through the body. Similarly, a NASA scientist may want to take her interns on a trip through the solar system, or a chemist may want to do a similar guided tour of a complex chemical compound.

An alternative method to a guided tour is a self-guided tour. Self-guided tours take place with the aid of pre-programmed heads-up displays or some sort of virtual device carried by the avatar—or even a map that guides the participant to the right places. In these types of tours, the participant carries a pre-programmed item providing information in the form of audio or visual cues as the learner arrives at specific locations.

In the virtual world of Second Life, visitors to virtual Morocco can obtain an "Info Fez." When a visitor dons the fez and walks around virtual Morocco, he receives information on the bottom of the screen about the history and culture of the land whenever the fez nears a certain information point in the VIE. The learner receives a tour of virtual Morocco through the information provided by the fez in much the same way as a person touring an historical site in the physical world with an MP3 player to guide him, as happens at such tourist attractions as Alcatraz in San Francisco, California.

In the Model Z scenario, the instructor used the guided tour approach several times, once as he led the learners around the drill showing them features and again when he teleported the avatars from one display location to another. Jack and his colleagues were guided around different displays of the Model Z so they could see how to group the drill with similar products and how placement maximizes the sales potential of the drill. The guided tour approach can be planned or spontaneous, based on learner questions.

A virtual world tour can be handy for studying the design of buildings, and many architectural programs provide virtual tours to their students. Tours can include public buildings, private spaces, historical buildings, or other types of places that could be used to provide architectural design examples. Tours can be used for training security guards where to look for unusual or suspicious items in bus and train stations.

Guided tours can even take place in unreal places, such as the inside of an extremely large network router, the human nervous system, or a city sewer system. Learners can be in an environment in which they are shrunk to a size small enough to experience areas in which they could not otherwise travel. In other situations, the learner could fly from stop to stop on the tour, examining areas from a bird's eye view.

Advantages of this type of design are that items or buildings not normally close to each other can be placed into a small space to be toured in a short period of time or the learner simply teleports from one location to another. Having the tour led by a facilitator provides the opportunity for additional questions to be answered. It also allows learners to explore areas that may otherwise be off limits because of safety or space constraints in the physical world.

Disadvantages of a facilitator-guided tour include the necessity for all learners to participate at the same time. The pre-programmed tour option doesn't have that caveat, but does take a while to develop and program. In general, creating the appropriate environment and ensuring its accuracy take time to develop properly.

## Operational Application

*Formal Definition:* Interaction and manipulation of objects for the purpose of gaining proficiency in functionality and performance.[12]

The key to this archetype is that the learners are challenged to apply physical world rules to objects in the VIE. This is similar to a flight simulator. In this archetype, you ask the learners to apply rule-based and procedural knowledge to a situation. The learners may move from location to location to apply skills, or apply the skills in one virtual location.

In an operational application the learners are challenged to apply their knowledge. This is "learning by doing" in the VIE. The learner, or team of learners, must follow the rules and parameters of the physical world to achieve a goal. The facilitator observes the learners and then makes comments or recommendations. Learning outcomes can include learning to drive a truck or operate a specific piece of equipment. This design provides practice for what happens on the job.

In the Model Z scenario, this is when Jack and his team where given the 14-foot by 14-foot area with signage, shelving, and product mix and had to develop a compelling display. Another possibility is asking learners to properly load an airplane with cargo and then for it to virtually fly and to observe the results of their actions in loading the plane. (Does it stay aloft or come crashing down because it was improperly loaded?) Other examples include repairing a piece of equipment, troubleshooting a computer network, conducting a virtual experiment, or fixing a car.

Given the graphic capabilities of most virtual worlds, it is possible to reproduce almost any item in the virtual world that is in the physical world. This includes simulating pieces of equipment and machinery from automobiles and helicopters to forklifts and bulldozers. Figure 5.6 shows the controls of a helicopter in a VIE.

The advantage of this design is that learners can practice the proper steps and procedures for operating equipment. Additionally, the graphic capabilities of VIEs allow for extremely realistic replication of instrument and control panels.

The disadvantage is that learners receive no tactical feedback (although some groups have hooked up virtual devices in virtual worlds to physical

**Figure 5.6.** VIEs Can Be Used to Provide Training on the Operation of Complicated Equipment

devices like the controller for Nintendo's Wii). Another disadvantage is that the designer must be familiar with manipulating graphics, with enough skill to place them in the proper position within a virtual vehicle or piece of machinery.

## Conceptual Orienteering

*Formal Definition:* Activities or situations in which learners are presented with examples and non-examples of environmental or situational conditions for the purpose of discrimination and creating an understanding of key concepts.[13] (See Figure 5.7.)

**Figure 5.7.** Avatar Checking Out the Damage on a Virtual Truck in the Environment of ProtoSphere

Teaching concepts involves providing the learner with examples and non-examples of the concept and then allowing the learner to determine the attributes that describe the concept. This allows the learner to recognize and apply the concept in a variety of different environments. In the archetype of conceptual orienteering, learners are shown a number of different items, examples, or situations that they can mentally compare. Then the facilitator asks the learners to identify the similarities and differences.

The process of side-by-side comparison allows learners to recognize and apply concepts in a variety of different environments. Learners studying to be government medical inspectors could be teleported from one manufacturing line to another to see the difference between inspecting a plant that creates medical devices and one that creates ingestible drugs.

The goal is to provide a visualization of the differences to the learner, who can then determine what attributes apply to the concept and what attributes do not. The learners can visually see attributes and do a mental comparison through the ability to instantly move from one location to another. These do not always need to be physical attributes. For example, you could create a 3D environment to resemble what it looks like to someone who is legally drunk and provide a frame of reference for the person attempting to understand the impairment that occurs when a person has too much to drink. The learner can then get behind the wheel of a virtual car and see and feel the effects of trying to drive while "drunk."

In the Model Z scenario, Jack's facilitator used this practice when he took the learners from the small hardware store to the tradeshow. The learners could visually see attributes of large and small displays and do a mental comparison through the ability to instantly move from one location to another.

Another example is the use of Proton Media's ProtoSphere to teach insurance agents what type of damage different collisions cause—what a side impact does to a car as compared to a frontal impact. A virtual representative can walk around a car or truck, lift it into the air, turn it and examine the damage, and understand the concept with a facilitator close by to both ask and answer questions.

You can take this concept beyond physical items into the mental arena. For example, there is a location in Second Life that shows what the world looks like from the view of a schizophrenic. The idea is to give the learner a conceptual orientation of what it would be like to have the condition. The learner can then better understand the implications of the event or the condition. You can use the same concept to display what it would be like to work in a dimly lit coal mine, a confined space, or other unfamiliar environment.

Additionally, conceptual orienteering can involve data visualization. This is a VIE in which actual, real-time data or even more static data are converted to graphical images and the participant interacts with those images through an avatar. This might be a virtual stock market where stocks are indicated by different colors, red for losing and green for gaining, or it might be a VIE where weather data is translated into the VIE and the avatar experiences what the weather is like half a world away. Or an avatar can see spreadsheet data and observe trends as three-dimensional data points. The possibilities of orienting a learner to a certain concept based on the visualization of data are just now beginning to be explored on a wide basis.

In other types of conceptual orienteering, a participant can participate at both the macro and micro levels. You can shrink learners to the size of blood cells and propel them through the blood stream to observe a drug's interaction with a virus. Or a person can fly over a proposed subdivision to observe the layout and intersection of roads and sidewalks. Or be transported to another time and place to observe customs of the people. Or shrunk to the size of an ant and be placed on the handle of the Model Z drill.

One advantage is that learners can experience a concept that is not otherwise possible because of time and space limitations or because of potential danger. They can stand in the middle of a tsunami or fly around a molecule. The VIE can also allow the learners to repeat the experience over and over again so they can really grasp a concept.

Disadvantages include the time it takes to create the environment necessary to convey the concept. It is also sometimes difficult to determine the best environment to create to effectively immerse the learner into the concept. If the design is not established properly, the possibility that the learner may not learn the concept from the environment does exist. (See the example in Figure 5.8.)

**Figure 5.8.** Author Tony O'Driscoll/Wada Tripp Sitting on a Molecule

## Critical Incident

*Formal Definition:* Plan for, react to, or conduct activities that are unexpected, infrequent, or considered to be dangerous when practiced in the real world.[14]

The critical incident archetype is when the learner is placed into an environment or situation similar to the real event in which he or she must use prior knowledge to solve a problem. This could involve placing the learner into the middle of a disaster like a chemical spill or the aftermath of a hurricane, or into a more benign environment like a retail store where a shoplifting incident is occurring or a street corner during a drug buy. It could even be dealing with a crisis as part of a typical job, like what to do if, during surgery, a patient has a heart attack.

Jack and his colleagues were not involved with a critical incident, since it wasn't required as part of their training. However, a critical incident could have occurred if they needed to respond to a sudden accident at the construction site they were visiting. It could have been possible for the instructor to create an event where a safety violation occurred that resulted in a serious problem and Jack and his fellow teammates may have been asked to implement emergency actions to save a life.

As an example of how effective a 3DLE can be for teaching how to respond to a critical incident, witness the lifesaving heroics of a gentleman named Paxton Galvanek. Galvanek, then only twenty-eight years old, received "medical training" while playing the MMORPG *America's Army*. In the 3D learning space, he learned to evaluate and prioritize casualties, control bleeding, recognize and treat shock, and administer aid when victims were not breathing (see Figure 5.9).

Galvanek helped rescue two victims from an overturned SUV on the shoulder of a North Carolina interstate. He was the first one on the scene and was able to safely remove both individuals from the smoking vehicle. He then properly assessed and treated their wounds, which included bruises, scrapes, head trauma, and the loss of two fingers.

"Because of the training he received in America's Army's virtual classroom, Mr. Galvanek had mastered the basics of first aid and had the confidence to take appropriate action when others might do nothing. He took the initiative to assess the situation, prioritize actions, and apply the correct procedures," said Colonel Casey Wardynski, *America's Army* Project Director.[15]

In the critical incident archetype, the learner must respond to the situation properly by applying what she has previously learned. The facilitator can serve as part of the incident or as an external observer who monitors and records the actions of the learner.

The three-dimensional aspect of this learning adds to the realism of the event. If multiple people are involved, the instruction can incorporate aspects of teamwork, collaboration, and co-creation into the learning outcomes of the critical incident.

**Figure 5.9.** VIEs Allow Learners to Rehearse Dealing with a Critical Incident During Surgery

For example, one critical incident might be the introduction of a virus or disease into a virtual world. Medical workers could then track results and view the actions of the avatars to gage how real people react. The learner would then be forced to make decisions. Do I stay away from other avatars? How will the medical staff react? What is the proper triage for this type of outbreak?

These types of critical incidents are already happening in virtual worlds at several levels. On a level aimed at teaching kids about epidemics, the virtual world of Whyville, every year has a Whypox outbreak. Whyville is a VIE geared toward children between eight and sixteen. Whypox is a virus that is a cross between a cold and chicken pox. It causes red pimples to appear on the avatar and disrupts online chats by sneezes in the form of the user's typed text being replaced with the word "achoo" from time to time.[16]

In an exercise designed to teach first responders how to deal with a critical incident of an outbreak, members of the California Department of Health Services received extensive training on how to administer antibiotics from the Strategic National Stockpile in the event of an anthrax attack in a VIE.

The setting, patients, and buildings were all virtual. A model of the California Exposition and State Fair was set up for the first responders to practice their skills during the critical incident exercise. This was cost-effective because full-scale exercises take a lot of advanced preparation and require day-long drills, which are expensive, time-consuming, and potentially dangerous to mock patients and healthcare workers because of the movement of equipment, number of people, and the difficulty in coordinating all the activities.[17]

The critical incident archetype places learners into an environment or situation similar to the real event, where they must use their prior knowledge to solve a problem. This use of a virtual world challenges team members to respond together to resolve an issue, incident, or problem. The individuals must act and react as they would during the actual incident. Immersion in a virtual world and then being forced to solve an unexpected problem provides learning in both the affective and cognitive domains. Figure 5.10

**Figure 5.10.** VIEs Can Teach First Responders How to React to Unexpected Situations

shows one of the authors, dressed as a fireman, preparing to extinguish a virtual fire caused by a sudden car accident in a VIE.

An advantage of this design is that learners are immersed in a dangerous situation, but are not actually in danger. This design captures the learners' attention and provides them with a realistic environment in which they are forced to work together to solve an issue and are forced to think rapidly, as they would in the actual situation. It also provides an advantage over a simulation of a dangerous situation in that the VIE involves multiple participants and, in addition to learning how to react to the incident, the participants must learn to work together as they would in the event of the actual incident.

One disadvantage is that it takes a while to program and develop explosions, spills, and similar disasters. It also takes time to program the various mechanisms such as fire hoses and other instruments to deal with the disaster. It can also be difficult for a facilitator to view all of a participant's actions when many different activities are occurring at one time.

## Co-Creation

*Formal Definition:* Social facilitation enabling two or more individuals to work together with a goal of contributing to the formation of something new.[18] (See Figure 5.11.)

This archetype involves two or more learners working together to create a new item or items within a 3D space, as shown in Figure 5.11. The idea is for the learners to follow broad guidelines to develop their creation and for them to work together to accomplish the goal. The outcome can be the creation of a new object, idea, or design. Roles of the learners within the co-creation team can be allocated by a facilitator or be allowed to evolve organically based on an individual's personality traits, strengths, and skill sets.[19]

The learners could be working together to create a landscaped garden for a landscaping class or be asked to develop a prototype for an automobile, building, or even an office layout. The key is to have the learners work

**Figure 5.11.** Avatars Working Together to Create a Block for the Cornerstone of a Building

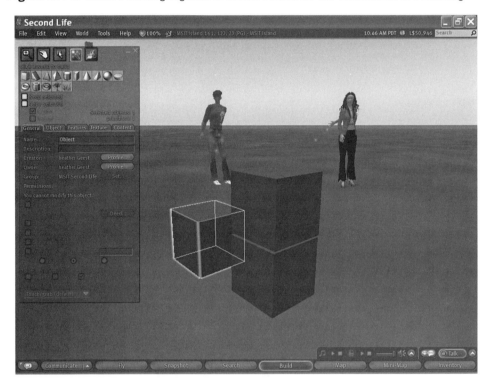

together on the creative process. Each contributes and creates value in the completion of the final product.

This archetype was demonstrated when Jack and his team were tasked with developing a 14-foot by 14-foot Model Z display that product line managers subsequently evaluated. Together the teams had to create the display.

One of the advantages of co-creation is the collapsing of time and the minimal need for specialized skills. If a learner can use the digital tools in the virtual world, he or she doesn't need to know how to lay brick or wire electricity to create a building, so development is faster than creating a real-life building or even an actual balsa wood 3D model. Teaching learners the in-world building tools is enough for them to be able to create machines, cars, or buildings. Also, because buildings and cars can be rapidly built, time is minimized, as opposed to creating a real-life model or object.

One of the disadvantages of co-creation is that one learner may dominate the creation process and not truly engage in co-creation. Another disadvantage occurs when one person has in-world building skills and another does not. The instructor needs to be careful to ensure the learners are co-creating during the process and that work is evenly distributed.

## Small Group Work

*Formal Definition:* The congregation (by design) of small numbers of participants into one cohesive group for the purpose of sharing, contributing to the body of knowledge, or presenting or soliciting information.[20] (See Figure 5.12.)

**Figure 5.12.** Small Group Meeting in ProtoSphere

These are small group sessions; they can be a grouping of chairs or even cubes hovering in the air. The learners gather together and then exchange ideas and chat either through voice or text-based channels. A facilitator who monitors the discussion and ensures all learners participate and are contributing to the group leads the breakout session. You can use different modalities to facilitate breakouts: text chat-only or text chat-plus-voice. Depending on the nature of the breakout and the makeup of the audience, text chat-only may provide some advantages when there is brainstorming work to be done or when there are participants from cultures that are not as fluent in the primary language being spoken.

Small group work was evident when the Model Z of Jack, Abbott, and Heather were assigned the task of creating an appropriate display. Each of the class members was assigned a team, and team members had to work together in a small group. The small Model Z groups worked independently from each other while the instructors and others went from group to group to evaluate the effectiveness of the display each group had created.

## Group Forums

*Formal Definition:* The congregation (by design) of large numbers of participants into one cohesive group for the purpose of sharing, contributing to the body of knowledge, or presenting or soliciting information.[21] (See Figure 5.13.)

This archetype is a large group meeting in which a large number of learners gather together to receive a learning message. Typically, the message is delivered by one or two individuals who are providing the training. This is good for general learning for a short period of time and leverages the death of distance and the power of presence where avatars feel that they are really interacting with the large group forum presenter. Within some virtual worlds the group size can range into the hundreds. Other times, the group forum is considerably less, such as twelve to twenty.

When the instructor in the Model Z scenario addresses the entire class and provides information to the group, whether it is instruction or logistics for an exercise, that is an example of the group forum.

**Figure 5.13.** A Large Forum Meeting Space

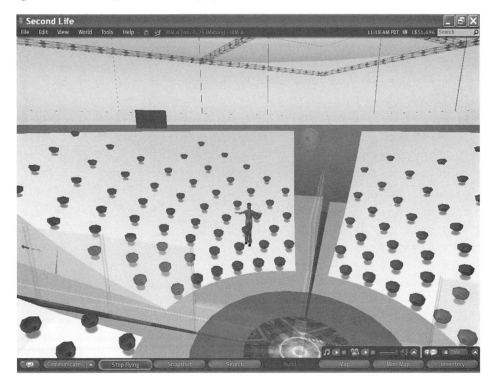

## Social Networking

*Formal Definition:* Creation of time and space to allow participants within an environment to connect with one another on an informal basis for the purpose of sharing knowledge and information and creating new knowledge and information. (See Figure 5.14.)

An important archetype to understand when conducting 3DLE is social networking. This archetype requires the designer of the learning event to specially build time into the event for the learners to exchange information and ideas, place the learners into an environment in which they work and purposefully ask broad or general questions, or simply allow the learners to loiter in a specific environment.

**Figure 5.14.** Socializing in the VIE of ProtoSphere Before an Educational Session

The proximity to the work environment and the fact that they have specific goals creates an environment in which the learners will naturally share information; in fact, this works especially well when the group is a mix of experts and novice learners. To accelerate the natural tendency to share knowledge, instructors can create teams and ask them questions to foster cooperation.

The social networking archetype permeated the interactions of Jack and his fellow learners. They networked with each other prior to class in an exercise established specifically to allow learners time to discuss and interact before the formal instruction. Additionally, the exercise of flying around the giant Model Z provided chances for the learners to speak with each other and learn from each other's discoveries. Finally, the opportunity to work together on the project of creating the displays for review provided time for networking and discussion among the members of the team.

# Instructional Goals

The learning archetypes are based on sound instructional fundamentals based on teaching specific types of knowledge. Each of the archetypes can be used to teach one or more types of knowledge within a VIE. When creating instruction, it is helpful to match the type of knowledge being taught with the appropriate archetype, as shown in Table 5.1.

# Implications for Learning Professionals

Understanding the learning archetypes and how they align with the macro-structures, principles, and sensibilities of the learning architecture will lead

**Table 5.1.** Different Types of Knowledge and the Matching Learning Archetypes

| Type of Learning | Description | Archetype |
|---|---|---|
| **Facts, Jargon, Labels** | An association between two or more items or objects | Guided Tour; Scavenger Hunt; Large Group Forum; Avatar Persona |
| **Concepts** | Categories used for grouping similar or related ideas, events, or objects | Conceptual Orienteering; Role Play; Small Group Discussion; Social Networking; Avatar Persona |
| **Rules/Procedures** | Ordered sequence of rules or steps a learner must complete to perform a task | Role Play; Operational Application; Social Networking; Avatar Persona |
| **Principles** | Guidelines for behavior or actions that are not sequential | Role Play; Social Networking; Avatar Persona |
| **Problem Solving** | Learner confronts a novel situation and must use previous knowledge to solve the problem | Critical Incident; Role Play; Co-Creation; Social Networking; Avatar Persona |
| **Affective Domain** | Impacting the emotion of the learner, such as influencing a person's attitude toward something like quality, safety, or diversity | Conceptual Orienteering; Role Play; Small Group Discussion; Co-Creation; Social Networking; Avatar Persona |
| **Psychomotor Practice** | Mimicking the physical actions and reactions that would occur within the actual work environment | Operational Application; Avatar Persona |

to effectively developing 3DLEs and leverage the affordances of VIE to provide the best possible learning outcomes for participants.

Learning professionals in corporations and academic institutions need to focus on creating 3DLEs for participants that are built around the learning architecture so the experiences are worthwhile for the learners and achieve the desired outcome. The best approach is to understand the model and how it aligns with the aspects of designing instruction and use the architecture as a guide for applying the archetypes to the appropriate learning method.

# Learning from Experience

## Follow the Leaders

In any newly emergent field there are always pioneers who innovate and set the example for others. This chapter is dedicated to sharing case study examples from those who are blazing a new course for learning in the third dimension. Figure 6.1 summarizes the case studies in this chapter.

Figure 6.1 also summarizes the macrostructures and 3DLE archetypes used in each case study. This figure should be used as a guide to help readers identify a case study that best aligns with their current project. The case studies in this chapter follow the order outlined in this figure.

## Case Study Format and Questions

See the outline below for the case study format and questions asked during the interviews. The remaining sections of this chapter cover each case study

**Figure 6.1.** Summary of Case Studies

| Case Title | Coverage Model |
|---|---|
| **Virtual Global Inclusion Summit** (Microsoft/Sodexo) | 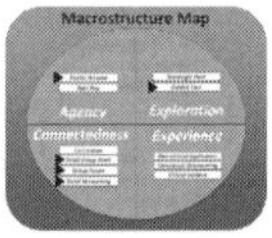 |
| **Diversity and Inclusion with Virtual Worlds** (Cisco) | 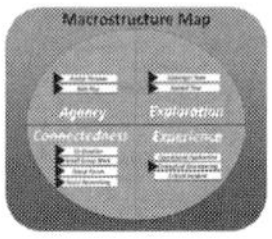 |
| **Experiencing an Inventory Observation** (Ernst & Young) | 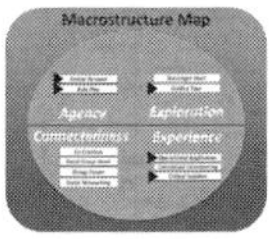 |
| **Witnessing History in Virtual Worlds: Kristallnacht** (U.S. Holocaust Museum) | 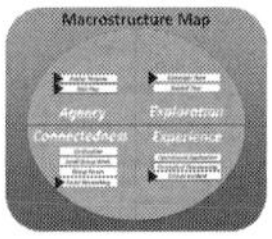 |
| **Virtual First-Responder Learning Experience** (Catt Laboratory) | 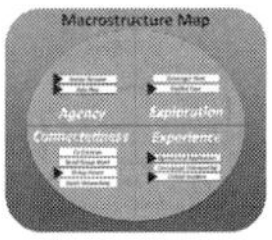 |
| **Virtual Border Service Officer Training** (Loyalist College) | 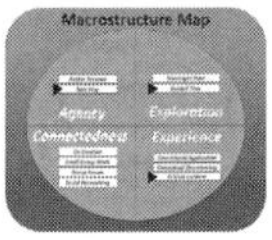 |
| **Teaching Rhetoric in a Virtual Environment** (Ball State University) | 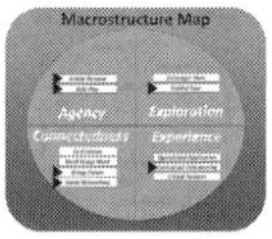 |
| **Environmental Science in a Virtual Green Home** (Penn State University) | 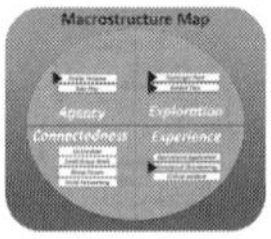 |
| **Creating a Virtual Challenge for Global Graduates** (BD) | 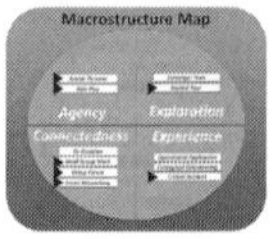 |
| **Hosting Virtual Academy of Technology Events** (IBM) | 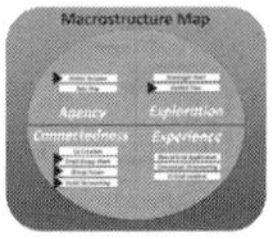 |

in detail. Instructional designers, faculty members, managers, and executives can use this guide to hone in on key questions they need to address within a specific project or for general information.

**Case Study Format and Interview Questions**

Organization Background

- Please provide some brief background on your organization.

The Challenge

- What was the primary business challenge to be addressed with this project?
- What key learning objectives were you seeking to accomplish by implementing this project?

Why 3D?

- What led you to explore the application of 3D to address the business and learning challenge?

Making the Case

- How did you convince the organization to adopt 3D approach?
- What was the most important element to securing sponsorship for the project?

The Solution

- What did the solution look like?
- How was the solution designed and deployed?
- How was the solution experienced by the participants?

The Benefits

- What benefits were achieved from applying 3D to address the business issue?

The Results

- What evidence do you have to suggest that this 3D solution was successful?

Lessons Learned

- What two to three pieces of advice would you have for others seeking to implement 3D learning solutions within their organization?

# Case 1: Diversity and Inclusion with Virtual Worlds
## Organization Background

The FutureWork Institute, Inc.®(FWI) is a global diversity consulting firm that interprets and analyses future workplace trends to help transform organizations. Using its research and consulting expertise, FWI works with clients to help them build more inclusive environments in their organizations. The Institute was recently featured in *BusinessWeek* for its innovative approach to work, and it was also recently awarded the Promise of Diversity Innovation Award by The American Institute for Managing Diversity. This case study chronicles how FWI developed two separate 3DLE solutions to address specific diversity and inclusion-related client requirement sets.

## Challenge 1: Virtual Global Inclusion Summit

For Microsoft and Sodexo, a leading provider of integrated food and facilities management in the United States, Canada, and Mexico, the declining economy caused both organizations to consider new ways to align with their firms' sustainability mandates and fiscal stewardship by attempting to reduce or eliminate travel and hotel expenses. Both organizations decided to explore the implications of using an alternative method to holding a physical global inclusion summit.

The primary challenge for Sodexo and Microsoft was to develop a 3DLE solution that:

- Developed executive understanding of their firms' diversity and inclusion strategy;

- Educated participants on how micro-inequities at work can negatively impact a person's career and cause people to disengage;

- Increased participant knowledge and communication around specific aspects of diversity: gender, race/ethnicity; generational diversity, disability, sexual orientation; and

- Encouraged networking around best diversity and inclusion practices from around the world.

## Why 3D?

More than on any other topic, education on issues surrounding diversity and inclusion relies heavily on the synthesis of personal experience. In the physical world, the use of carefully crafted activities during which employees play specific roles in a narrative that is designed to elicit a specific response are staged by expert facilitators. These kinds of learning experiences are labor intensive and present significant challenges to deploy on a global scale.

In a VIE, individuals could take on different avatar-based personas in executing the different activities; they could experience how it felt to be perceived differently. For instance, a middle-aged Caucasian male could take on the role of a teenage Hispanic female in a given inclusion activity and have a completely different experience. This virtual world affordance presented learning opportunities that were not possible in the physical world.

## Making the Case

FWI developed a compelling cost analysis demonstrating the positive ROI associated with hosting a virtual meeting for one thousand managers, versus bringing them together for a physical Global Inclusion Summit.

Based on this analysis and the primary requirements associated with running a virtual summit, FWI chose the Unisfair platform to host the meeting for the following reasons:

- It could simultaneously accommodate the 1500+ participants the Virtual Global Inclusion Summit attracted;

- It had the lowest barrier to entry in terms of technology requirements and ease of use;

- Having hosted over five hundred events, the Unisfair team had significant experience in running these types of large-scale virtual events; and

- Unisfair's platform supported a three-month on-demand period where 1,500 people per day could go through the same experience of the Virtual Global Inclusion Summit.

## The Solution

Upon arrival at the Summit pavilion, participants were welcomed by Margaret Regan (FWI president)'s "avatar"—an actual projection that materialized and dematerialized. Regan oriented participants to the space and outlined the program agenda for the virtual conference (see Figure 6.2).

Following this introduction, participants teleported to the main conference hall, where they viewed video welcomes from Sodexo and Microsoft executives who outlined their global diversity and inclusion strategies. This was followed by a global dialogue on diversity and inclusion with live Q&A from participants.

---

**Figure 6.2.** FWI President Margaret Regan's Avatar Welcomes Participants

After the panel, participants were invited to teleport to an interactive theater to experience the topic of micro-inequities. Upon arrival, they were given an introduction to micro-inequities and shown short video segments depicting the primary micro-inequities that had been identified via a poll prior to the conference (see Figure 6.3).

Following each scene, participants had the opportunity to ask questions of the actors, who stayed in role to explore how they felt about the various micro-inequities that were portrayed.

After the formal session, participants were encouraged to visit exhibit booths and a networking lounge, where they could join one of twenty facilitated discussion topic sessions or just mingle informally.

Finally, participants also had the ability to stop by a resource center, where they could review and download materials associated with the conference to their personal briefcases.

## The Benefits

The key benefit for Microsoft and Sodexo was that they were able to successfully host a Virtual Global Inclusion Summit while simultaneously achieving

**Figure 6.3.** Conference Attendees Exploring Micro-Inequities at Work

cost savings and aligning with the organizations' desire to be more sustainable in their operations.

Sodexo was able to quickly compute the ROI from the session:

Travel/Lodging Cost Avoidance by hosting a virtual event: $1,617,000

Environmental Impact Avoidance by hosting a virtual event: 450,000 pounds of Carbon Dioxide Equivalent (CO2e)

Negative Productivity Avoidance: 900 missed office days due to travel; 7,200 missed office hours due to travel

Another benefit was the scale and reach that the platform allowed for the company's diversity and inclusion strategies to be more effectively and efficiently deployed, discussed, and applied across the world. The ability to roll 1,500 participants through the activity each day allowed for a very rapid diffusion of the strategy and learning.

## The Macrostructure Map

The macrostructure map outlined on the next page provide a quick visual summary of the archetype coverage of the 3DLE design for the Virtual Global Inclusion Summit. (See Figure 6.4.)

## Challenge 2: Global Women's Action Network

Cisco wanted to bring its Global Women's Action Networks (WAN) together virtually for training, learning, and collaboration and, in so doing, have employees and clients experience the capabilities of VIE technology.

The primary challenge for Cisco was to develop a 3DLE that:

- Enabled women from all parts of the world to learn from and network with each other—and eventually with clients—in a virtual environment

- Create an environment that showcased the special features of Second Life around their four areas of focus: work/life flexibility, professional development, IT development, and sustainability.

**Figure 6.4.** Macrostructure Map for the Virtual Global Inclusion Summit

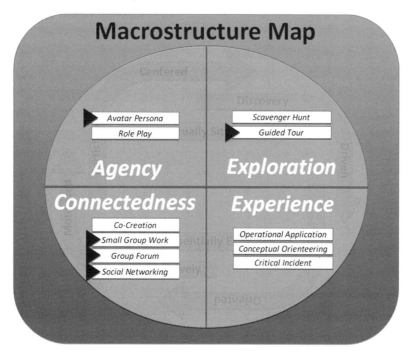

## Why 3D?

One of the primary differentiating characteristics of VIEs is that they are avatar-mediated. Participants embody an avatar that has the ability to act within a virtual environment. The potential to leverage this differentiating affordance to re-create the educational activities known to be effective in the physical world was very compelling.

## Making the Case

Cisco was keen to test the boundaries of VIE technology as it related to addressing diversity and inclusion issues for women. They had already begun to experiment in Second Life and had identified a launch date for a virtual Global Women's Action Network meeting. Since time was of the essence and since FWI had already developed a comprehensive set of diversity and inclusion activities on FutureWork Island in Second Life, Cisco opted to

partner with FWI and transfer a number of these activities over to the Cisco
Women's Network Second Life venue.

## The Solution

To help their clients understand the range of possibilities that VIE technology
brings to diversity and inclusion education, FWI created FutureWork Island in
Second Life. FutureWork Island is a showcase for many innovative approaches
to provide diversity simulations and educational experiences. Upon arrival,
visitors are presented with an interactive map (see Figure 6.5). The interactive
map has nine signs directing avatars to different sites where learning takes
place. Each learning space has its own unique activity and design.

The diversity and inclusion simulations on FutureWork Island provide
interactive ways to experience the rich diversity of the global workforce,

**Figure 6.5.** Participants Exploring the Interactive Map on FutureWork Island

navigating gender, race, culture, ethnicity, religion, sexual orientation, and the four generations at work.

Participants from around the world can test their generational attitudes, compete in a global diversity quiz game, discuss work/life balance as they create their own personal and professional balance scale (see Figure 6.6), or talk about gender differences while collecting chips that increase or decrease their status based on responses (see Figure 6.7).

Generational bingo is another example of how much fun visitors can have as they compete against colleagues and use their generational experience to select historical markers and fill out their bingo boards. Another activity, Generational Rooms, allows teams to identify key values, attitudes, and work preferences associated with each of the four generations in the workplace: Veterans, Boomers, Gen Xers, or Millennials. As they select generational markers and iconic items of importance to each of these generations,

**Figure 6.6.** Participants Creating Their Personal/Professional Balance Scales

**Figure 6.7.** Participants Gather Chips That Increase Status in Responding to Gender-Related Statements

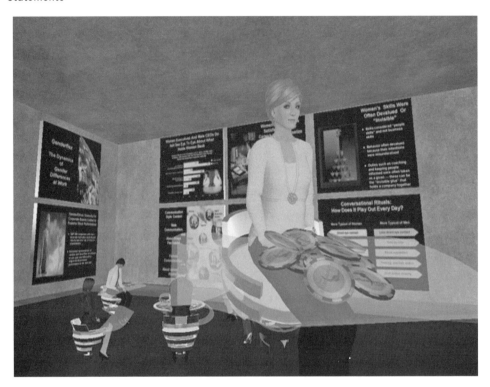

the items appear ("rez") in the generational rooms. Completing the activity even allows participants to download tips on working with each generation.

In addition to the activities themselves, participants have the ability to choose from one of twenty avatars representing a cross-section of the rich diversity in the global workplace. By assuming an identity that is very different from their own, visitors can walk in someone else's shoes (see Figure 6.8).

In examining these options, Cisco quickly honed in on a set of experiences that included having participants pair up by the pool to work with the work/life balance scales and discuss their personal and professional time balance, moving in large groups to the quiz pavilion to take part in a gender and work/life global quiz competition, and socializing by learning dances from different cultures in a dance pavilion (see Figure 6.9).

**Figure 6.8.** The Various Avatar Personas That Participants Can Assume

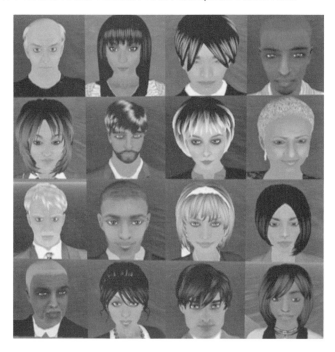

**Figure 6.9.** Learning Dances from Different Cultures as a Social Networking Activity

## The Macrostructure Map

The macrostructure map outlined below provide a quick visual summary of the archetype coverage of the 3DLE design for the Global Women's Action Network. (See Figure 6.10.)

## Benefits

The key benefit for Cisco was the ability to quickly pull together a compelling set of activities that both educated the Cisco Woman's Network on diversity and inclusion issues while simultaneously exposing them to the next-generation collaborative technologies.

## Combined Lessons Learned

Combining lessons learned from both projects, here are three key pieces of advice for those considering embarking on 3D learning experience projects such as the two outlined above:

---

**Figure 6.10.** Macrostructure Map for FutureWork Island/Cisco Women's Action Network

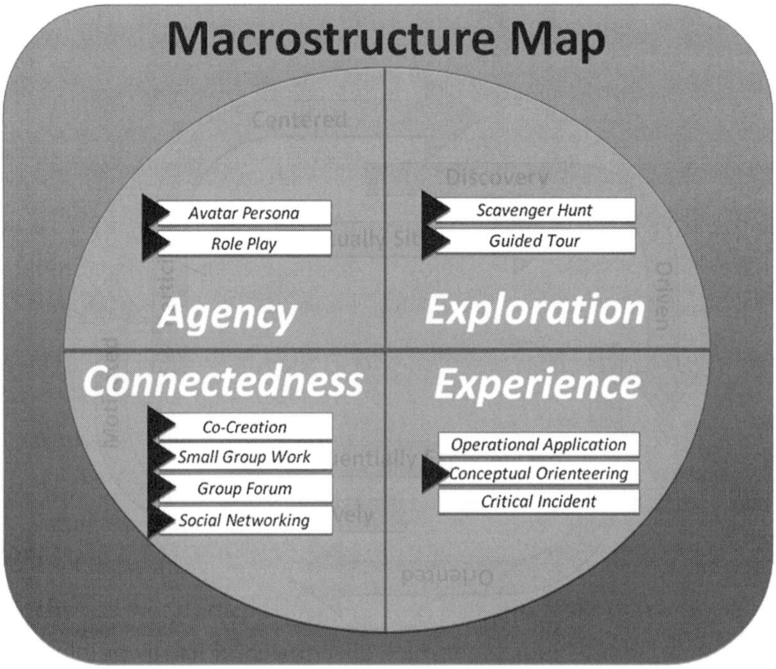

**Lesson 1.** Understand the client's learning needs, participant volume requirements, technology access and security requirements, and participant appetite for working with new technologies. Use all of this information to select the right platform to meet the client's needs at that point in time. As clients mature in their use of and experience with VIEs, you can move them from less sophisticated platforms to more elaborate ones.

**Lesson 2.** Whatever platform you choose, it is critical to provide participants with an on-ramp to help them become comfortable with the VIE technology. Time must be allocated in advance of the instructional program to provide basic instruction on VIE navigation, and mentoring must be made available.

It is important to separate the learning associated with coming up-to-speed on the VIE platform from the learning that will be delivered within the instructional program. If participants have to learn both at the same time, it usually results in frustration.

**Lesson 3.** Don't assume that what works in the classroom or in traditional events translates to the virtual environment. Learning in virtual worlds is more experiential, action-oriented, and social. Focus must be placed on function and interactivity in designing 3DLEs. Also be sure to allow plenty of time for unstructured interaction. In the Microsoft/Sodexo case, there was little formal interaction around the pre-planned facilitation topics, but lots of informal social interaction. Create purposeful space and time for informal and serendipitous interactivity in your design.

# Case 2: Experiencing an Inventory Observation
## Organization Background

Recognized around the world, Ernst & Young (EY) is one of the "big four" accounting firms. As a services organization, EY recognizes that the firm's value is most effectively conveyed to clients through the preparedness and professionalism of its people. As a result, EY takes training and development very seriously.

This case study chronicles how EY's Americas Learning and Development organization partnered with the Assurance division to develop a 3D learning environment (3DLE) to teach new hires to effectively conduct an inventory observation.

## The Challenge

Most accountants remember their first inventory observation (IO)—that tangible moment at the outset of their careers when all the terms and protocols covered during months of training finally were exercised on a client site.

Some have fond memories of the experience, being reminded of a kind mentor who patiently showed them the ropes. Others remember the uncertainty they felt about how to act in conducting their first IO, despite having done well on all the tests. Either way, it is clear that the IO is a rite of passage for most accountants, and success or failure in this career can hinge on how quickly young accountants can turn theory into practice in a way that adds value to the client.

As a big-four firm, EY welcomes many new recruits each year. On average, a new hire will take in excess of 130 hours of formal learning in the first year. Much of this formal learning is conducted in a classroom.

As a result, EY's chief learning and development officer for the Americas, Mike Hamilton, wanted to understand whether a 3DLE solution might be more efficient in transferring IO knowledge requirements and more effective in preparing the participants to successfully execute an IO.

## Why 3D?

Inventory observations are very situational in nature. While the terminology and protocols are largely standardized, the application of these approaches varies considerably based on the situation on the ground. In the process of conducting an IO, unanticipated situations often surface that require quick decisions to ensure that the observation is completed as accurately and expediently as possible.

Given the situational and experiential nature of the IO work activity, Hamilton hypothesized that a 3D learning experience might have some advantages over the traditional instructor-led, case-based approach.

## Making the Case

To test his hypothesis, Hamilton convened a conference during which he invited subject-matter experts to explore the area of 3DLE design and delivery with his team. Hamilton and his team spent two days exploring examples and probing the experts to determine whether or not their hypothesis had merit.

In the end, it was determined that a pilot should be conducted wherein the traditional approach would be compared to the immersive learning experience (ILE) approach.

The two primary questions to be answered in the pilot evaluation were

1. Can participants learn and retain as much knowledge via an individual ILE approach as they do in a traditional instructor-led training (ILT) approach?

2. Does completing an ILE more effectively prepare participants to conduct a physical inventory observation than a traditional ILT approach?

## The Solution

Because there already existed an inventory observation ILT course, the first task was to create an ILE alternative based on this content. The existing ILT course consisted of a traditional lecture, where terminology and procedures were covered, followed by a case study exercise and debriefing activity. It was decided for evaluation purposes that the ILE should also have separate theory and practice portions so that knowledge transfer efficiency on theory and perceived preparedness on practice could be independently evaluated.

The EY Assurance/learning team worked with external design firm 2b3d to create the inventory observation 3DLE in Second Life. Upon arrival, participants were first brought to a customized orientation to familiarize them with the platform.

Once that was completed, the participants were teleported to Theory Plaza, an area in front of "Grandma's Gourmet Cookies" production facility (see Figure 6.11). In Theory Plaza, participants were exposed to all of

**Figure 6.11.** Participant Is Oriented to the 3D Auditing Inventory Tour

the content from the ILT lecture materials via video snippets, information kiosks, and interactive games.

Here, participants were instructed to check in at the front desk (see Figure 6.12) to get instructions, then to find Plant Manager Parx, who introduced them to their personalized Tour Bot (see Figure 6.13).

The Tour Bot led the learners around the plant, familiarizing them with the various sections of the warehouse. This allowed the students to look around and prepare for their audit observation. Following the tour, the participants meet with the plant manager again, who asks them to begin their work in the finished goods area.

As participants begin to work to identify tagged boxes. Authentic challenges such as the need to reach boxes via forklift (see Figure 6.14), convert units of measure, determine obsolescence, and determine how to inventory

**Figure 6.12.** Participant Received Instructions on How to Begin Inventory Observation Task

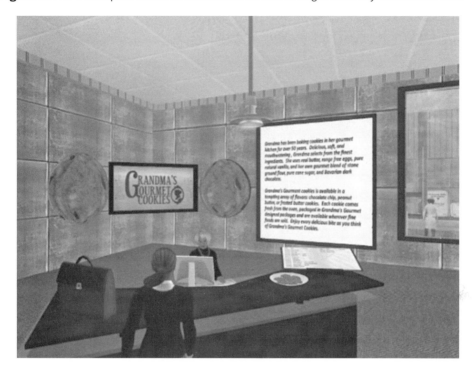

**Figure 6.13.** Plant Manager Parx Introduces the Participants to Their Personalized Tour Bot

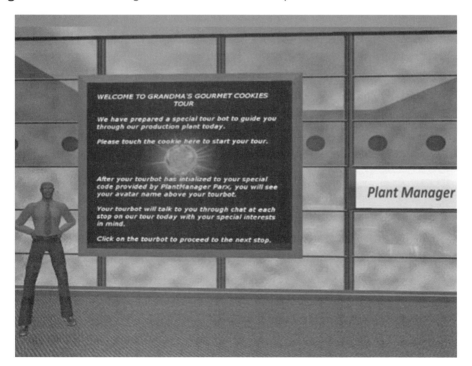

**Figure 6.14.** Participants Asking Forklift Operator to Access Inventory on Top Shelf

water-damaged boxes and materials that have been paid for but not yet shipped are introduced.

In the receiving area, participants had to deal with inconsistencies in how incoming materials were counted. Some had tags, while others used count sheets. As they progressed further into the inventory observation activity, participants were met with authentic situational challenges at every turn: deciding what needs to be test counted, determining the most appropriate way to conduct unit conversions, determining what materials should be tagged as obsolete (see Figure 6.15).

Finally, at the end of the inventory observation, participants were required to reconcile a compilation for the inventory observation (see Figure 6.16). For those who made it all the way through the warehouse, the experience truly was the lesson.

**Figure 6.15.** Participant Deciding What Needs to Be Test Counted

**Figure 6.16.** Participant Begins Final Compilation Activity

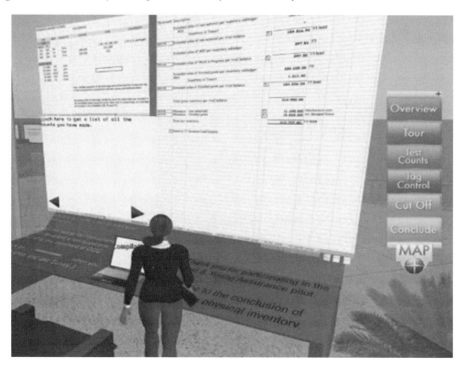

## The Macrostructure Map

The macrostructure map in Figure 6.17 provides a quick visual summary of the archetype coverage of this 3DLE design.

## The Results

The comparative evaluation between the instructor-led training (ILT) and the immersive learning experience (ILE) yielded three key findings:

1. ILE participants learned and retained as much as their ILT counterparts. Furthermore, they did so via a more cost-effective self-paced discovery learning approach in Theory Plaza that took less time to complete than the ILT theory module.

2. ILE participants who completed the warehouse activity felt less confident in their ability to conduct an inventory observation than their ILT counterparts. This suggests that the ILE participants

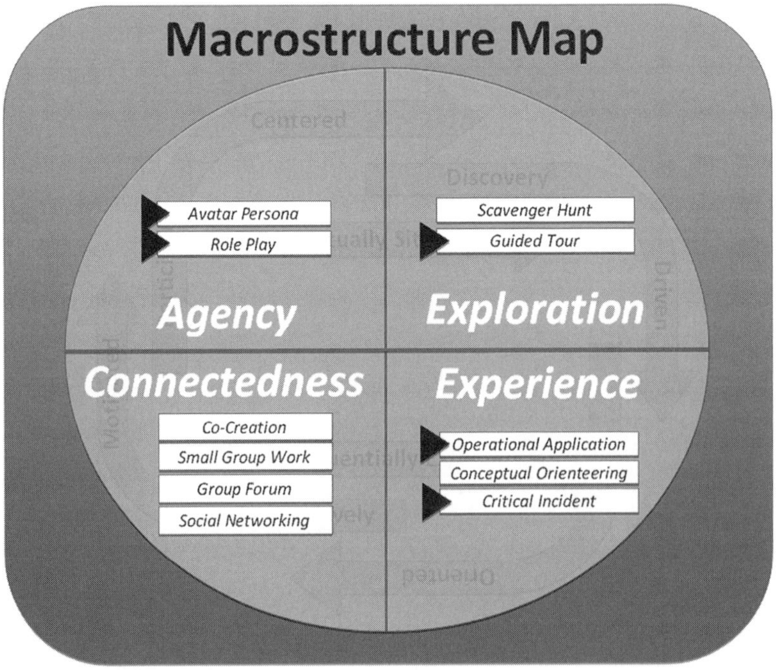

**Figure 6.17.** EY Virtual Inventory Observation Macrostructure Map

developed a more authentic understanding of what was required to successfully complete an inventory observation than those who discussed the case study in the ILT.

3. Unanticipated issues with technology, platform, and logistics negatively impacted ILE participant perceptions of intervention effectiveness and experience. Technical issues with hardware and network access, platform issues with the ability to navigate, logistical issues with pilot timing, and time requirements to complete the intervention contributed to a lower satisfaction score for the ILE when compared to the ILT.

## Lessons Learned

The EY team broke the lessons they learned from the pilot into two categories: design and implementation.

**Design Lessons.** **Lesson 1:** Having an existing course to build from actually proved to be a negative. Not enough time was dedicated to design activity. Approaching this project as a "clean sheet" would have been more effective and would have allowed the team to better apply the full capabilities that the Second Life platform had to offer. Instead, too much emphasis was placed on repurposing existing 2D content for consumption in Theory Plaza.

Also, while it was acknowledged and agreed on by the team that independent comparative evaluation of the theory and practice components of the ILE and the ILE was central to the pilot, it quickly became clear that this evaluative objective placed significant constraints on the creativity of the design process itself.

**Lesson 2:** Don't approach design with a set of preconceived notions. The development of effective 3DLEs is not simply a matter of porting existing 2D content over to a VIE. Be open to new and different ways to leverage VIEs to achieve the desired learning objectives. One of the design concepts called for the learning module entirely in the production plant and wanted to make content available on a just-in-time basis when the students encountered obstacles in their inventory audit observations. In the end, the Theory Plaza approach was taken to make sure that the assessment results would provide the students with a tested and predictable set of results. In short, the assessment requirement defined a routinized, traditional approach to learning for the sake of evaluation purposes.

**Lesson 3:** Finally, as with all learning design, the technology should not drive the design, the learning objectives should. In this case it was hypothesized that the sensibilities associated with virtual world technologies would lend themselves well to the learning objectives associated with conducting an inventory observation. While the pilot evaluation results suggest that this argument might have merit, the team members cautioned that, while VIEs provide many opportunities to enable experiential learning, the use of VIEs should be supported and viewed as but one tool in the toolkit, the use of which should not be mandated.

**Implementation Lessons. Lesson 1:** Don't underestimate the technical challenges associated with getting the software to run on participants' computers and enabling participants to gain network access to run the software. Hardware and firewall issues should be dealt with as early as possible in the deployment process.

**Lesson 2:** Don't assume that the younger generation is facile with virtual world environments. Allow plenty of time for them to familiarize themselves with the platform and make sure they are sufficiently capable of navigating the environment before introducing any programmatic activities.

**Lesson 3**: 3DLE program logistics should be managed very tightly with a tendency toward over-communication and parsing the steps required to bring the participants along a learning curve in appropriately sized parcels of activity. Hardware setup and network access testing, platform training, and avatar customization and environment navigation are all key building blocks that need to be accomplished before the participants engage in the 3DLE experience itself.

# Case 3: Witnessing History in Virtual Worlds: Kristallnacht—The November 1938 Pogroms
## Organization Background

A living memorial to the Holocaust, the United States Holocaust Memorial Museum stimulates leaders and citizens to confront hatred, prevent genocide, promote human dignity, and strengthen democracy. A public-private partnership, federal support guarantees the Museum's permanence, and donors nationwide make possible its educational activities and global outreach.[1]

Since opening in 1993, the museum has received more than twenty-nine million visitors, including eighty-eight heads of state and more than 3,500 foreign officials from over 132 countries. In 2008, the Holocaust Museum website received twenty-five million visits. More than one hundred countries visit the Museum's website daily and, overall, 35 percent of the visits are international.[2]

This case study chronicles the development of an installation in Second Life to commemorate the 70th anniversary of Kristallnacht—the "Night of Broken Glass"—a turning point that marked the intensification of Nazi anti-Jewish policy that would culminate in the Holocaust.

## The Challenge

The original driver behind the exploration of the application of virtual world technologies came from the organization's chief information officer. Specifically, he wanted to explore the applicability of this emerging technology for staging virtual exhibitions and finding new ways to incorporate visitor voices into the exhibition development process.

The initial challenge considered was to determine whether it was feasible to experiment with 3D virtual installation design in a realistic and meaningful way without having to create physical mockups and, if so, to explore whether it would be possible to invite people from outside the museum to explore the virtual installation to more fully engage them in a co-creative design process.

This initial challenge proved to be the seed that germinated into the creation of the museum's Kristallnacht Installation on the Second Life main grid.

## Why 3D?

The founding director of the Holocaust Museum felt that the museum's narrative exhibition must affect visitors not only intellectually but also emotionally. Similarly, the building architect wanted visitors to experience the museum "viscerally" and be taken in its grip. People who move through the museum must not only learn and understand, but they must also feel.

In many ways, the museum learning experience is as much about the environment as it is about the content. Installation design is not just about reading a passage or looking at a photo or observing an object; it is about contextualizing these artifacts within a space in such a way that they elicit an emotional response. People learn in museums by moving through an installation in a way that allows them to absorb the content in a kinetic and synthetic way.

Museums are also social spaces. Visitors frequently enter exhibitions in pairs or in groups. They share their thoughts about content they encounter. And sometimes they experience vicarious or incidental interactions with strangers responding to the same exhibit content at the same time.

Given that a virtual world can function in much the same way as the physical world, the Holocaust Museum wanted to explore the possibility of building virtual installations to learn more about the ways in which visitor experiences mimicked or differed (both for better and for worse) from those in real-world exhibitions.

## Making the Case

In many ways, since the application of virtual world technologies was being applied to address a known set of issues facing the museum, the main challenge was for those involved in the project to overcome their own skepticism.

Initially, there was some concern that the Second Life environment itself had too high a barrier to entry and that there were not enough residents in Second Life to warrant the kind of investment required to create a captivating virtual installation that yielded a visceral experience for the visitor.

Ironically, the fact that virtual worlds were not yet mainstream helped this effort. The fact that the bulk of the twenty-five million visitors to the Holocaust Museum's website were not likely to also frequent Second Life is one of the reasons the project was approved. If virtual worlds had been as prevalent as the web, the perception of associated risk would likely have slowed the project down significantly. However, since this was not a high-profile project and given that it was aimed at experimenting to address the potential of the technology to improve installation design, visitor engagement, and visceral learning experiences, the project was executed fairly rapidly with few bureaucratic hurdles.

## The Solution

During the summer of 2008 the Holocaust Museum partnered with the youth civic leadership non-profit, Global Kids, in New York City to help them train teenage interns at the museum to design a space on the Second Life teen grid that would allow their peers to learn about Kristallnacht. This turned out to be a wonderful learning experience for all the parties involved, as the teenagers (most of whom had never set virtual foot inside of Second Life) quickly became comfortable within the Second Life environment, and the museum project members were able to help them understand the subtleties of virtual installation design through an iterative process. Ten weeks later, the resulting installation entitled "Witnessing History: Kristallnacht—the November 1938 Pogroms" was launched on the teen grid.

As the ability of virtual worlds to enable kinetic experiences became more obvious as a result of this work, the Holocaust Museum decided to build a more elaborate and nuanced installation on the main Second Life grid based on the design document originally created by the teenage interns at the museum.

The museum partnered with a design firm called Involve to create the main grid installation. Building on the original notion of witnessing history, participants take on the role of a journalist whose charge is to investigate and report on the events of Kristallnacht in November 1938. At the installation entrance, visitors enter a period press room (see Figures 6.18 and 6.19).

As they pore over notes, images, and eyewitness accounts, a wall of the press room dissolves and—as if in a movie dream sequence—the journalist is transported back in time to the events of Kristallnacht. Walking through the dissolved wall, visitors enter a German street scene and witness first-hand the burned synagogues, ransacked homes and schools, propaganda in the town square, and graffiti on walls (see Figures 6.20 and 6.21).

At regular points throughout the installation, the visitor experience is narrated by audio of survivor eyewitnesses explaining what they experienced during the depicted events. All of this is part of an effort to more deeply immerse participants in experiential learning and witnessing history.

**Figure 6.18.** Visitors Adopt the Role of Journalists as They Enter a Period Press Room Scene at the Kristallnacht Installation

**Figure 6.19.** Period Photographs of Holocaust Survivors Whose Testimonies Narrate the Visitors' Experience

**Figure 6.20.** Witnessing a Burning Synagogue

**Figure 6.21.** Street Scene Depicts Nazi Propaganda

The installation visit culminates with a set of video testimonial mini-documentaries from survivors who experienced Kristallnacht, and participants are encouraged to log their thoughts and experiences on a public comment board.

## The Macrostructure Map

The macrostructure map in Figure 6.22 provides a quick visual summary of the archetype coverage in the 3DLE design (see Figure 6.22).

## The Benefits

From an educational outreach perspective, a cursory reading of the public comment board is more than sufficient to convince anyone that the Holocaust Museum succeeded in delivering a kinetic, intellectual, and visceral learning experience for participants.

---

**Figure 6.22.** Macrostructure Map for Kristallnacht Installation

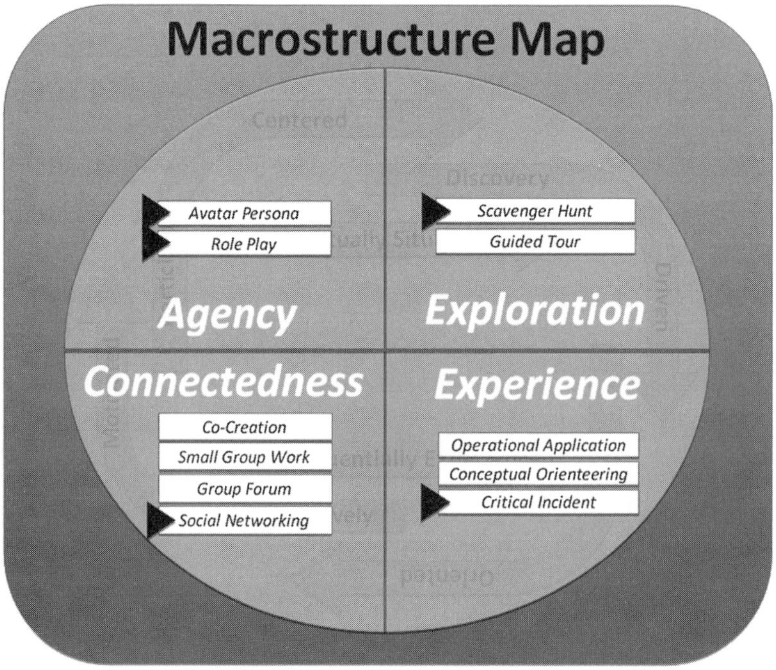

While the same artifacts used in the installation could have been made available on the museum's website (and many are), it is clear that the situated context of the virtual installation allowed these artifacts to be woven into an immersive experience that allowed participants to viscerally feel the connection between history, personal action, and place. And thus, it is hoped that visitors gain a better understanding of what it was like for those who experienced the tragic events of Kristallnacht in reality.

## The Results

From an outreach perspective, to create a more intimate relationship between the institution and a group of constituents is a key goal of the Holocaust Museum. For the museum, moving people to confront anti-Semitism and hatred and working to prevent genocide are central to its mission. It quickly became clear that the Second Life environment is as much a social medium as it is a virtual world. Agency is central to both the museum and to members of Second Life. In Second Life, residents have the ability to take action around endeavors where they see value.

Within a week of its launch, one of the visitors to the Kristallnacht installation sent an instant message to museum staff in-world, "hi my name is [. . . .] want to know who created the museum we want to make a donation. thanks." Others pointed out typos or inactive primitives within the installation itself because they wanted to take agency in ensuring that the environment could render the most authentic and visceral experience possible. Still others asked if the museum had a Second Life group associated with the installation, prompting the Holocaust Museum to create one to better communicate with its Second Life "membership." Just as the CIO had wished, the participants were voluntarily becoming co-curators of the virtual Kristallnacht installation and providing ideas about how the museum might enhance its real-world programming through integration with the museum's outreach in virtual worlds.

Because Second Life is a social medium, visitors use it to communicate with the museum and with each other, sometimes via instant messages (IM) to museum staff, but more often with comments posted to the public board in the installation. Here is a representative sampling of comments that clearly demonstrate the impact that this virtual installation made on those who visited:

- "I haven't wept so much for such a long time; I'd like to think I'm not related to the species who committed such horrors. I can only honor all that suffered by my witness and my vigilance in the future."

- "I don't know if you are a single person or a group, but I just had to thank you. I was at the DC Holocaust Museum last year, and hate to say—the noise and crowds somewhat diminished the powerful effect of it for me. but this, at my own pace, in my own space— wow. perhaps the most emotionally powerful place I've seen on Second Life. THANK YOU for your awesome work."

- "I felt this place to be so important, so moving, I gathered pictures so that I could show my friends who cannot be in Second Life and may never get the chance to go the Museum in Real Life."

- "Never expected a part of a 'game' to be so powerful. What a moving experience."

- "Curiosity brought me here. I entered skeptical, thinking this exhibit couldn't add much to what I had already learned about these horrible times. But after my visit, I had to log off and sit quietly. I came back to leave this message."

## Lessons Learned

The three key pieces of advice for those considering embarking on 3D learning experience project such the one outlined above are these:

**Lesson 1.** While the virtual world context brings a lot of value in being able to integrate 2D artifacts into a situated context that can create a kinetic learning experience, it is important to recognize that the real power of these environments lies in the ability of people to affiliate with an idea or cause, synchronously or asynchronously, and connect and share with one another. The vicarious social interaction that these spaces afford enables rich and meaningful exchanges between the constituents convened in the virtual space.

**Lesson 2.** The affordances of the virtual world can be used to create a stronger sense of authenticity and connectedness. Space and co-presence create a context of shared experience. In the Witnessing History installation, there is a small hiding place where visitors may learn about the experiences of Jewish people forced to hide during the events of Kristallnacht. That space feels a whole lot smaller if there are two or three other visitor/journalists hiding there too. The experience is also a lot more visceral when you know that others are sharing it with you. People process and talk with each other differently about *experiences* than they do about *content*.

**Lesson 3.** Think deeply about how you plan to demonstrate the value of the virtual world solution and build your measurement strategy in parallel with your learning experience design activities. The Holocaust Museum mistakenly assumed that the Second Life browser included a mechanism to measure visitation within a sim. As a result, they are currently not able to log the number of visits to the installation. Thankfully, the comment board has served as a useful proxy and the qualitative comments have provided ample justification for the value that the Witnessing History installation has brought to visitors.

# Case 4: Virtual First-Responder Learning Experience
## Organization Background

The purpose of the Center for Advanced Transportation Technology (CATT) Laboratory at the University of Maryland is to conduct applied research on complex transportation issues. The lab is funded by the Maryland State Highway Administration, federal sources such as Homeland Security, and independent organizations such as the I–95 Coalition, which is focused on ensuring the safe and efficient flow of people and goods up and down the I–95 corridor from Maine to Florida.

This case study chronicles the development of a 3DLE focused on training emergency-responders to more effectively and efficiently respond to traffic accidents on the I–95 corridor.

## The Challenge

An average of 117 people died each day in motor vehicle crashes in 2006. That's one person every twelve minutes. On any interstate highway, for every minute that a lane is closed due to an accident, the chance of a secondary—often more significant—collision occurring goes up 3 percent (see Figure 6.23). Each year, more police and fire personnel are killed as a result of responding to traffic accidents than in any other line of duty.

One of the primary objectives of this 3DLE program was to address the need to improve quick clearance: clearing the scene of an accident as quickly as possible. Achieving quicker clearance of accidents on the I–95 corridor would have a positive impact on first-responder fatalities, but there were also other benefits, such as reduced pollution (since vehicles spent less time on the road) and increased productivity (as goods flowed more efficiently up and down the East Coast).

A core issue in dealing with quick clearance was that police departments in each state had different training programs with varying response protocols. This lack of uniformity caused confusion and clearance delay for accidents near state lines where emergency-responders often came from different states.

A delegation from the I–95 Coalition made a trip to The Netherlands to examine that country's approach to addressing a similar set of issues. They

**Figure 6.23.** National Statistics for Accidents in the United States

15 to 30 percent of crashes on freeways are secondary to other minor incidents, often more serious than the initial one, and incident responder injuries are significant

| 2006 National Statistics | | |
|---|---|---|
| Crash Type | # Crashes | # Victims |
| Fatal | 1,784,000 | 42,642 |
| Injury | | 2,575,000 |
| Property Damage Only | 4,189,000 | – |
| Total | 5,973,000 | 2,617,642 |
| Cost of Crashes, 2000 (last avail.) | $230.6 Billion | |

learned how that country had created a national certification program that aligned the emergency-response protocols and training programs to ensure that all emergency-response personnel had a common understanding of the most effective approach to quick clearance.

As a result, the I–95 Coalition challenged the CATT Lab to develop a certification program that would increase quick clearance and responder safety on the I–95 corridor by providing standardized first-response training to emergency responders up and down the East Coast.

## Why 3D?

There were two primary drivers that led to the application of 3D technology in the development of the certification program: evidence of differentiated value and cost of scale.

While in The Netherlands, the I–95 Coalition had seen how a 3D simulation was applied to ensure that all first-responders were "singing from the same song sheet" upon arrival at the scene of an accident. Although the 3D application used in The Netherlands was not a massively multiplayer solution, it was clear to the I–95 Coalition delegates that the immersive qualities of the 3D environment helped drive alignment and understanding among participants.

The second reason that 3D was explored was cost of scale. Traditional training approaches for first-responders are somewhat akin to running a movie production. They are very costly and often include as many role players as trainees. Typical training activities take a full day and only thirty responders could be trained at a time. The immersive qualities of a multiplayer 3D environment could address the need for responders to be placed in authentic response situations at a much lower cost and with the ability to scale much more rapidly than traditional training approaches could.

Given that the ultimate goal of this certification program is to train police, fire, and EMS, transportation, and towing and recovery personnel up and down the East Coast, the application of 3D technology seemed to be the most logical choice.

Nonetheless, the lab had to address some key challenges in securing sponsorship to develop this program. First, the perception that this learning environment looked too much like a video game and the perception that games have no pedagogical value was a challenge that had to be overcome. Second, the high price tag associated with developing the 3DLA, about $1M at the outset, caused some raised eyebrows among coalition members.

In the end, however, persistence in demonstrating how this immersive approach was superior from a learning alignment perspective and nuanced argument that the solution would be much more cost-effective as it scaled, prevailed. Members of the I–95 coalition who had seen first-hand how alignment around best practice had been achieved in The Netherlands championed the Lab's recommended 3DLE solution and the project was funded.

## The Solution

The solution was designed via a highly iterative process. At the outset, the design team developed a steering committee made up of subject-matter experts from each discipline. Over the past two years, the 3DLE design has been refined and improved upon eight times. In addition to these formal reviews, the design team demonstrates the 3DLE at first-responder conferences every month to solicit first-hand feedback from the front-line responders on how to make the learning experience as authentic as possible.

The 3DLE itself is a part of a larger blended program. Students must first take and pass an online course that teaches the core competency topics such as quick clearance, vehicle positioning, and personnel safety. Once they pass that course, they are required to take and pass a second online course that teaches the mechanics of the virtual world: how to run, how to walk, how to pick things up, and how to communicate. Once both of these prerequisites have been completed, participants are then signed up to participate in the actual 3DLE.

The 3DLE itself is contextually situated around the scene of an accident (see Figures 6.24 and 6.25). Participants play the role of emergency-responders as they work though a series of activities where they discover new issues and challenges associated with the accident along the way.

The application of the knowledge required to understand the core competencies is evaluated by comparing the actions of the first-responders within the 3DLE to a best-practice timeline that outlines the optimal set of actions

**Figure 6.24.** Emergency Responders Arrive on the Scene of an Accident

**Figure 6.25.** Emergency Responders Figuring Out Best Course of Action

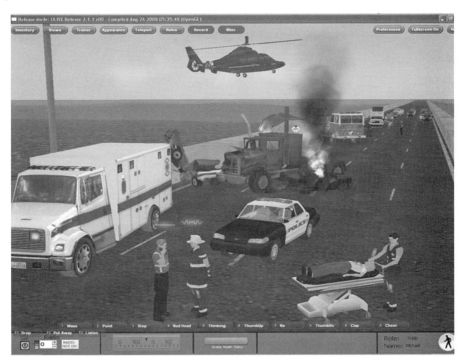

to be taken by the responders. This timeline is built into the moderator's interface. This allows the moderator to evaluate the participants' actions in real time as they move through the 3DLE activities.

Once the exercise is complete, the system generates a recording of each participant's actions relative to the best-practice timeline. The moderator then reviews the tape recording that includes every single action and interaction with the participant, providing contextually specific feedback on where his or her actions deviated from best practice. The moderator also reviews the resulting consequences of the variance from best practice. This after-action review process provides participants with a visceral perspective on who did what when and how well they performed relative to best practice.

There are also some consequential experiences built into the activity itself. If the first-responder fails to put on a reflective vest upon arrival, the likelihood of being struck and killed goes up. If the team is unsuccessful in quickly clearing the accident, the likelihood of a second accident goes up. Surfacing these real-time consequences brings a heightened sense of authenticity to the learning experience.

## The Macrostructure Map

The macrostructure map in Figure 6.26 provides a quick visual summary of the archetype coverage for this 3DLE design.

## The Benefit

The ability to situate first-responders from states up and down the East Coast within an authentic 3DLE that drives alignment around best practices for quick clearance at a cost that is significantly lower than conducting physical training is the primary benefit of this solution.

## Lessons Learned

The four key pieces of advice for those considering embarking on a 3D learning experience project such the one outlined above are the following:

**Lesson 1.** Understand the benefits and limitations of 3D. The virtual environment is actually better-suited for teaching participants how to best act and interact

**Figure 6.26.** Macrostructure Map for Emergency Response Learning Experience

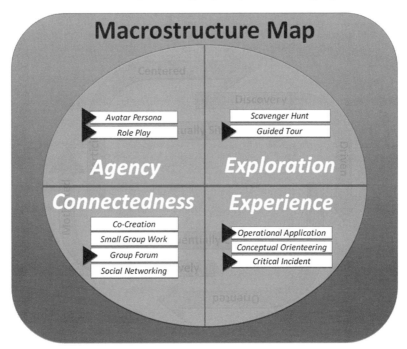

under unsafe situations than it is for teaching physical skills like rigging up a vehicle.

**Lesson 2.** Know the limitations of the software package you will be using to create your 3DLE. Most software in this space is still immature. It will take you longer to do things in the environment than you think. Plan twice as much development time as you think you will need to account for the immaturity of the technology platform and learning curve required to get up-to-speed developing 3DLEs.

**Lesson 3.** Pay attention to the technical issues associated with deploying a 3DLE solution. In this case, the Lab had to deal with multiple agencies in multiple states. All of these agencies had different IT infrastructures and different client machines. This kind of deployment landscape can cause significant technical challenges.

**Lesson 4** Manage expectations up top. It is always better to under-promise and over-deliver rather than the other way around. Being clear on what 3D can deliver and what it cannot and knowing the limitations of the software package you are using and the network issues you will face is a good starting point to ensure you do not over-promise on what you can deliver in the given time-frame. In general, it is best to be overly conservative in planning your first foray into the development of 3DLEs.

# Case 5: Virtual Border Service Officer Training
## Organization Background

Loyalist College, located in Ontario, Canada, has a Justice Studies program that offers a customs and immigrations track for students who wish to pursue a career in customs-related fields. A number of graduates pursue employment as customs officers at the Canadian border working for the Canadian Border Services Agency (CBSA). One of the essential skills for a Border Service Officer (BSO) is the ability to conduct traveler interviews. These interviews are part of the standard screening process when monitoring individuals entering Canada.[3]

Before 9/11, the CBSA (then Canada Customs) participated in a program that allowed seniors at the college enrolled in customs-related studies at Loyalist to experience a three-week field placement opportunity at a customs port, where they could observe BSOs practicing their skills. The arrangement allowed learners to gain first-hand knowledge of the customs function and operations at points of entry into Canada.

Unfortunately, after 9/11, the need to reconsider security-related matters at our points of entry resulted in the termination of placement programs. This gap meant that students did not have any first-hand knowledge of the border patrol process and how travelers were actually interviewed or how they acted or the types of situations they might encounter.

This case study chronicles how Loyalist College developed a 3DLE solution to train BSOs on appropriate interview techniques.

## The Challenge

Because of the inability of the students to experience a field placement opportunity at a customs port, the instructor noticed a decrease in student performance related to conducting interviews with travelers as measured by an end-of-course live role-play exercise. Eventually, the instructor witnessed a drop in student grades because the students did not achieve the same level of standards on the authentic assessment as former students who had been involved in the program of observing actual BSOs. The current students could no longer draw upon their experience of being at the border witnessing a real officer conducting an interview. The chance to observe was no longer available. As a result, the instructor had resorted to in-class role plays and other techniques, but found them ineffective for conveying the right tone, approach, and information that the live border patrol experience afforded.

A BSO has to remember to ask a series of mandatory questions related to citizenship, nature and purpose of visit, and items to declare. Additionally, the officer must be professional, provide a bilingual greeting, and, most importantly, read between the lines and look for unusual and/or inconsistent activities or behaviors.

## Why 3D?

The program instructor was looking for a method to replace the visits to the border sites but had been unsuccessful. Ken Hudson, managing director, Virtual World Design Centre at Loyalist College, thought it was a great opportunity: "We had been experimenting with the virtual world of Second Life and thought that it might be a solution to having the students perform a role play in a realistic environment."

Hudson and the instructor believed that a 3D solution could provide a border patrol station that allowed the students to not only observe (as was the case pre-9/11) but to become involved in every aspect of travel processing. The students would no longer just be observers. Rather, they would become virtual officers expected to handle all of the duties of both primary and secondary officers and to deal with emergent issues that could reasonably be expected at a port of entry.

## Making the Case

From the instructor's point of view, given the fact that actual visits were no longer possible, the virtual experience seemed like a good substitute. In fact, the faculty member was a former employee of the agency who had performed as a BSO and understood the issues involved in preparing someone for a job in this field. She was aware of the high fail rate of BSOs and was interested in finding innovative methods to both train students and current BSOs for the demands of the job. Additionally, since the instructor had been trying various other techniques and not encountering a great deal of success, she was open to trying a virtual world as a method of role playing the crossing process.

From the institution's perspective, it was a little more difficult. Whenever the concept was initially explained to the administration. "They gave the 100-yard gaze. They heard what we were saying but they didn't understand it," lamented Hudson. "We had to demonstrate a tangible need to the college. Once we did that and provided examples of the type of learning experiences the students would have, the administration agreed to allow us to use the technology for the class."

The collaboration between the Virtual World Design Centre and the Customs and Immigration program aimed to create a simulation that would address the challenges of creating realistic role-play experiences set in a true-to-life environment. The case was made that it would be an innovative and effective method of replacing the field trips to the border patrol portals and that the Design Centre would provide the support and instruction needed to make the process as easy on the instructor as possible. It was agreed, and the process of building the border portal in Second Life was undertaken.

## The Solution

The development process began with the creation of a Canadian Border Patrol station that was initiated three months prior to the beginning of class. It involved collaboration among faculty, instructional designers, 3D designers, and in-world builders. The goal was to re-create the Lansdowne, Ontario, border crossing with as much accuracy as possible. This was achieved by going to the site and taking photographs, using Google Earth to view the layout of the crossing site, and working with active members of the Canadian Border Patrol.

Once the crossing station was created (see Figure 6.27), the next step was to create vehicles to cross the border. Different vehicles needed to be created, and each one had to have doors, trunks, and glove boxes that opened for the purpose of searching for contraband. Additionally, different types of contraband had to be created so the students could encounter the contraband while searching some of the vehicles.

It was also coded so that the vehicles generated a random license plate number from a database of images, and that license tag was displayed both on the vehicle and on a virtual computer monitor inside the border officer's booth. The booth monitor provided vehicle flags in the same percentage level as that in an actual crossing area. Warning holds such as stolen vehicle, immigration, and smuggling issues added realistic data for the BSO who must evaluate all factors throughout the interview.

**Figure 6.27.** Canadian Border Patrol Crossing Station in Second Life

Another crucial element of a border crossing is the evaluation of travel documents. The development team created a range of passports and other identification that would be passed to the BSO for inspection. When a BSO looks at a passport, the most important information is determining proof of citizenship. The final bit of authenticity in the preparation of the immersive learning experience was to create accurate BSO uniforms for the students' avatars to wear. The uniforms were created using real examples of the uniforms.

The exercise was conducted in the classroom using a combination of the Second Life software and a large monitor that could be observed by all the students in the classroom. Individuals, playing the role of travelers, would assemble in a room other than the classroom housing the students. The separation ensured that the students role playing the BSOs would not know who was playing the avatars or what they would plan to do as they portrayed the role of someone trying to enter the country. In the classroom, several students would assume the roles of BSOs. Some had primary roles, like asking interview questions, and some had secondary roles, like supporting the primary BSO if a problem arose. The remainder of the students observed the role play and interactions.

After a role play, the class would pause and the instructor would facilitate a discussion about the traveler interview. The discussions raised a lot of questions and engaged dialogue because of the realistic scenario, the complexity of the interview with the traveler, and the items found or not found during the process.

To aid in the realism, the people playing the roles of travelers passing through the border were able to develop their own scenarios from the artifacts provided (which included identification, avatars, clothing, ethnicity, gender, citizenship, and license plates). There was no "standard" script. Travelers were encouraged to express specific emotional states as a part of their characters, such as anger, defensiveness, agitation, overt friendliness, just as occurs at real crossings. The scenarios were intended to be representative of typical border crossings, including shopping trips, vacations, business trips, and other types of travel. For variance, immigration issues and other flag issues such as firearms, smuggling, and vehicular issues were introduced at random (see Figure 6.28).

**Figure 6.28.** Interview at the Border Crossing

The students role playing the BSO used both verbal and visual cues to determine the eligibility of the traveler to enter into the country. If the traveler was acting "cagy" or had no identification, the BSO had to take the appropriate action and ask the right questions.

## The Macrostructure Map

The macrostructure map in Figure 6.29 provides a quick visual summary of the archetype coverage for the 3DLE design.

## The Results

An external researcher interviewed the students, asking them about the results of the simulation experiences. Students were asked to sum up their entire learning experience. They gave the following responses:

- Met or exceeded expectations;
- As close as it could be to being true to life;
- Great alternative to traditional role play;

**Figure 6.29.** Macrostructure Map for Canadian Border Crossing BSO Training

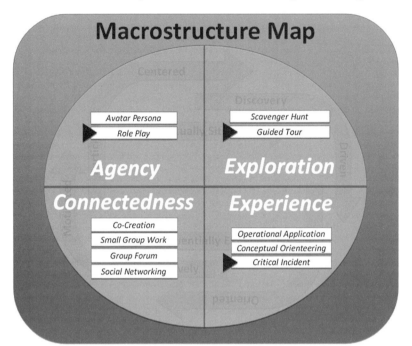

- Advantage over people who have not had an immersive learning experience;

- Made the course more interesting; and

- Seeing, hearing, and doing: we were actually there.

Additionally, in the first year of conducting the in-class 3DLE, the students' grade standing increased 28 percent from previous years without the role play or visit to the border crossing location. In the second year, the grades rose another 9 percent above the first year of using the 3DLE.

The realistic scenarios required the students to draw together all the information they had learned into applicable examples and connect the dots to provide an effective interview of the travelers they encountered. The result was an above-average amount of discussion among the students and the opportunity to address a wider range of topics than were addressed using other approaches.

An unexpected benefit was the speed with which the students were able to commit to memory the interview process. While using notes is normal at first, students quickly began using the full range of their observational skills during the interviews, rather than relying on a script. This gave them a much stronger sense of the process at the real border, where observation is the key to successful job performance.

Students also indicated that their confidence levels increased as they progressed through the experience. The confidence made them perceive themselves at an advantage in a competitive workplace screening process, where most felt they would outperform those without this type of prior training.

## Lessons Learned

The top three pieces of advice for those considering embarking on an immersive learning experience such as what Loyalist College has done with its customs and immigrations track are these:

**Lesson 1.** Make sure the environment you create to conduct the immersive learning experience is contextually relevant to what the participants will be doing on the job. Great pains were taken to accurately re-create the environment—from the proper uniforms, to travelers' cars, to the papers needed for access to the country. The context in which the role play occurs is important to the level of immersion for the learner. The attention to detail meant that the participants felt they were at a real border portal interacting with real travelers. This added to the educational experience of the learners.

**Lesson 2.** Have the resources in place to make sure the development and delivery of the learning can take place as smoothly as possible. Test and retest the environment and programming so the instructor can focus on what she or he does best and not have to worry about technological issues.

**Lesson 3.** Only teach the navigational skills that are absolutely necessary for success within the context of the role play. For this instruction, the participants didn't need to learn to fly or build. We only needed to teach the students how to put on the BSO uniform, how to walk to the booth, how to sit down, how to speak, and how to use the camera controls. That was it. Stick with the core skill set needed to learn within the environment.

# Case 6: Teaching Rhetoric in a Virtual Environment
## Organizational Background

At Ball State University, located in Muncie, Indiana, one of the general education courses is Introduction to Rhetoric and Academic Research, taught through the English Department. A total of ninety sections of the course are offered every year to introduce students to primary research techniques and to help them understand the varying media in which writing takes place and how these affect communication. The course has a significant visual rhetoric element as well as an emphasis on digital writing. According to Sarah "Intellagirl" Robbins, an instructor of the course, "This is one of the first times these students look at themselves as 'knowledge makers' as they participate in a number of activities, including gathering data and observing groups and reporting on the results."

## The Challenge

The ultimate goal of the class is to have the students be able to compose a coherent argument for a specific audience. As Robbins states, "During the class, we look at how arguments are formed, who the students are writing to, and why they should care about their audience." A big part of what a student needs to consider, understand, and be aware of is his or her own bias. This is not always visible to the students.

In an effort to expose bias and teach how preconceptions impact writing, a large part of the class is having students observe behaviors within a group and write about them as objectively as possible. Traditionally, the freshman and sophomore students would go with whatever was easiest. They would conduct the observations in their own dorm or interview fellow classmates. In a few of the sections, the students would conduct their research in a local non-profit organization while aiding the community. Since the students at the school were fairly heterogeneous, interviewing and observing friends didn't give the students enough interface with truly different groups. As a result some students were rather biased because of low exposure to other cultures. While it was important for the students to interact with different cultures to gain an understanding of the realities of conducting observational ethnographic research and their unseen bias, the options were limited.

It was not feasible to send the students to another country and it wasn't safe to send the students into certain local cultures. The options because of geographic and safety constraints were limited.

## Why 3D?

One option for teaching the class was to use chat board and forums, but one of the elements Robbins wanted the students to grapple with was the concept of identity perception. There are ways that students (and all of us) manipulate wardrobe, hairstyle, and shoe choice to impact how we are perceived by others and others, in turn, do the same. It was thought that a virtual world that allowed the customization of avatars would help make perceptions and bias more evident when the students had choices in how to dress in the virtual world. The virtual world made the topic more accessible to discuss.

Additionally, there are niche cultures in Second Life in which students can interact with others in a relatively safe and harm-free environment. Robbins indicated she wanted the students to be "exposed to cultures where they couldn't make sense of what was going on right away. They had to inquire, observe, and ask questions to really gain an understanding of what was valuable and meaningful within that niche culture."

Another reason for a 3D environment was that it contributed to the sense of community among the students. It was thought that the sense of co-presence would help students form a community. This is important because writing is risky, and if students don't bond, then they don't give good reviews to each other. So Robbins decided on implementing a 3D immersive learning environment, hoping that playfulness would encourage the students to bond with each other.

## Making the Case

The first step was to prove to the department that the learning goals could be met using this approach. Robbins recounts that, as a graduate student teaching the class, she was given the syllabus and layout for class with specific goals that had to be met. Since at that time no one else had done this, it was a challenge to get department personnel on board. She stuck with it by showing how the department and class goals could be met using a 3D immersive learning environment. She showed them that the goals could be met within this new technology.

The technical side also proved to be a bit of a challenge. The software labs in the English department could not run the Second Life software, so support was needed from other departments. Robbins had to use another department for access to the labs, had to convince others to allow this to happen, and had to obtain monies to pay for the VIE software. Luckily, the Center for Media Design at Ball State was looking for someone to assist with exploring virtual worlds and the two created a mutually beneficial partnership. Robbins could use the center's island if she reported on her experience and helped them understand the value of 3D immersive learning experiences for students. Making the educational case was the most important element of getting the class in place. Robbins stated, "If I couldn't justify the approach, it wouldn't have mattered if I didn't get funding or lab. The educational element was the most important."

## The Solution

Fortunately, the course was to be taught in the fall semester and permission was granted at the end of the spring, so Robbins had three months in the summer to prepare the learning space for the students' arrival. She indicated that at first she overbuilt the space and created formal spaces that were not used as much by the students. She later allowed students to add to the space and contribute their own structures.

One of the most successful elements created on the island for the class were the dormitories. The dorms worked out well because it gave the students their own space and they had ownership of part of the space. The design for the dorms was based on a panoptical circular structure created by Jeremy Benthem who originally designed an asylum so the guards could see everyone at all times. Robbins and her students turned the asylum concept on its head and made sure the rooms looked out on each other so the students could have informal conversations when accidentally meeting in the common space. They could also decorate their rooms and discuss the decoration choices they made with fellow students. In the end, the students really developed the island. They created the spaces and items they wanted in the environment (see Figure 6.30).

The class was conducted twice a week for seventy-five minutes. The first class of the week was conducted face-to-face and the second class was conducted entirely in Second Life. The face-to-face classes were used to discuss reading from the textbook and to explore writing skills and reflect on the writing process. The in-world meetings became lab time. During that time, the student engaged in exercises to practice the skills they learned in the previous class session. For example, as the topic of participant observation research techniques was reviewed, the group discussed how to become part of a community in which the class could conduct research. During the in-world session, the students dressed as Kool-Aid men and visited a popular Second Life dance club. The Kool-Aid

**Figure 6.30.** Dorms in Second Life

men costumes were cumbersome and awkward and made the students unpop-
ular at the dance club (see Figure 6.31). The owner of the dance club eventually asked the Kool-Aid men students to leave, politely but firmly. When the
students returned to class they reported that they felt too big for the space as
they bumped into other dancers. Generally, they felt unwelcomed and ignored
because of how they were dressed. They didn't fit into the crowd enjoying the
dance club.

The students then changed into attire more appropriate for the club
and returned. The reception at the club was much different, as the students
were accepted into the group. The exercises, not possible in physical space,
allowed the students to feel discrimination in a real and visceral way. The
exercise pointed out that bias can be subtle but still hurtful. Because they
now had first-hand knowledge of being excluded from a group, they gained

**Figure 6.31.** Students Wearing Cumbersome Kool-Aid Man Costumes as They Go Clubbing

valuable insight into what is needed to blend in and become part of a population they wanted to study.

## The Macrostructure Map

The macrostructure map in Figure 6.32 provides a quick visual summary of the archetype coverage for the 3DLE design.

## The Benefits

The primary benefit is that the students had authentic experiences dealing with concepts and issues that are difficult, if not impossible, to re-create in the physical classroom. For example, the students could read articles about gender and identify but didn't really grasp the concepts at a deep level until they switched genders. When they switched genders for an evening, it gave them a new understanding of the feelings and issues involved with gender roles and expectations. They visited places dressed as aliens and as Kool-Aid

**Figure 6.32.** Macrostructure Map for Rhetoric Course at Ball State

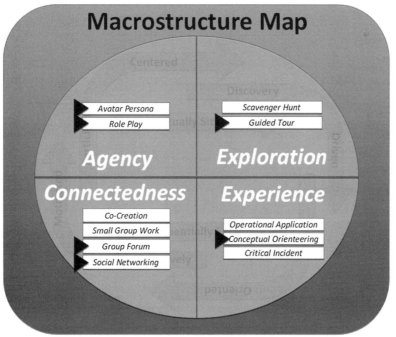

men, they encountered random strangers, and entered into conversations. The students conducted activities that could not have been done in the physical world without significant potential harm to students. The 3D immersive learning experience allowed students to participate in activities that had an impact but were safe.

## The Results

One of the main results was that the students were very engaged in the course. When the class sessions ended, the students stayed in Second Life and continued working on projects for class. An advantage for the instructor was that she was able to stay in the space and observe the behavior and interactions of the students. The resulting level of community in the class was universally high. When asked, most students expressed that they felt closer to one another than they did in other classes, and that their collaborative projects were easier to accomplish because they "know where to find each other," meaning that the online space provided a persistent meeting area. Several students reported logging in to the space when they felt lonely or just wanted to find someone to chat with about an assignment. The students were vested in the course and the space within Second Life. Some indicated that they felt "at home" on the island and that they thought of it as more than a classroom. Student evaluations were high; they talked about applying knowledge learned in the course to other activities; and they expressed that they not only had fun but learned as well.

## Lessons Learned

The three key pieces of advice for those considering embarking on a 3D learning experience such the one outlined above are these:

**Lesson 1.** Start with the learning goals and work backward from there. The most important part is the learning. If the learning goals are not clear and not in place, the technology won't work. The learning goals must come first. If just focused on the technology, the learning experience won't scale.

**Lesson 2.** Make sure learners and decision-makers clearly understand the desired outcomes of using a 3D immersive learning experience for teaching. Be very transparent as to why you are conducting the instruction in 3D. Clearly state the benefits and make sure you establish the benefits up-front.

**Lesson 3** Teaching within a VIE that involves many people means that the classroom can be opened up to a larger community beyond the classroom. Too often faculty teach in isolation, but in a virtual environment, students can interact with people seamlessly from all over the world. Robbins indicated that "frequently, individuals from countries hundreds of thousands of miles away would visit the class and share insights and ideas with students." From the instructor's perspective, other faculty could easily slip into the session and observe the interactions and participate in the classroom.

# Case 7: Environmental Science in a Virtual Green Home

## By Mary Ann Mengel
## Organizational Background

The Berks College of the Pennsylvania State University, located in Reading, Pennsylvania, is one of twenty campuses in the Penn State University system. Penn State Berks has an enrollment of approximately 2,800 undergraduate students. The student-to-faculty ratio is 19:1. Students can complete one of fourteen baccalaureate degrees or eight associate degrees at Penn State Berks; or they may begin the first two years of over 160 baccalaureate degrees that can be completed at Penn State's University Park campus.

## The Challenge

Environmental Science (Bi Sc 003) fulfills a general education natural science requirement at the college. Traditionally, the course consists of lecture, reading assignments, quizzes, projects, and five exams. Professor John M. Meyers teaches two sections of the course. Meyers has difficulty covering all of the material for the course in class and has not previously covered the subject of considerations for green home design, due to lack of class time.

By adding a self-paced, online instructional component to the course, students would learn about considerations for a green home, a timely and relevant topic, without sacrificing valuable class time.

## Why 3D?

Three-dimensional virtual worlds offer unique educational possibilities to teach students about a real-world three-dimensional space, such as a green home. A virtual visit might mimic the experience of visiting a green home, something that would not otherwise be possible within the schedule of this course.

By participating in a virtual field trip to a green home, students might gain a better understanding of the spatial characteristics and design elements as their avatars walk through the structure. By experiencing their avatars' presence in a virtual green home, students can freely explore the 3D space at their own pace, observing and learning about eco-friendly home considerations. During the virtual visit, students might meet other avatars and engage in conversation about the green home. By participating in a virtual field trip to a 3D virtual green home, students could perhaps come away feeling as if they had actually visited the site—a much more memorable experience than reading a textbook that describes green homes.

## Making the Case

Mary Ann Mengel, multimedia specialist in the Penn State Berks Center for Learning and Teaching, suggested the idea of incorporating a 3D learning experience into the environmental science course to Meyers.

Mengel, who was researching the educational usage of Second Life, proposed that a visit to a virtual green home might be an effective way to add an engaging, interactive, online component to the Bi Sc 003 course. An instructional site in Second Life could expose students to additional course content in a self-paced experience outside of the classroom. Mengel demonstrated Second Life to Meyers, who was intrigued by the idea. Because Mengel was already developing a virtual educational site about green homes as part of her research, there were no development costs incurred by Penn State Berks to create the virtual site and little time investment upon the part of Meyers to develop course content.

Consequently, the decision to try presenting the unit in a virtual world was easy. Meyers agreed that incorporating a visit to a virtual green home into his course would be a valuable addition.

## The Solution

Mengel designed and built a virtual green home on a Second Life island owned by Bloomsburg University, where she was doing graduate work (see Figure 6.33).

To engage students in an activity during their visit to the virtual world, a scavenger hunt was incorporated into the site design. Learning stations, represented by blue discs, were placed at twenty-two locations throughout the home's interior space, exterior space, basement, and roof. Visitors are instructed to search for and locate all twenty-two learning stations. Each blue disc offers a note card when touched. The note card describes a particular facet of a green home and explains the associated design considerations.

**Figure 6.33.** The Virtual Green Home on Bloomsburg University's Second Life Island

For instance, visitors can read note cards that describe solar panels on the roof, bamboo flooring in the main living area, a geothermal heat pump in the basement, and a native plant garden in the yard.

Several interactive features are included to further engage students with the content (see Figure 6.34). By clicking on a section of the wall, students can reveal the cotton insulation inside of the wall. Or by clicking on each of two buttons on the toilet, students can hear the differences in sound produced by the two flush options on a dual-flush toilet. Students see and hear rainwater being collected with a rain barrel. An animated compost tumbler demonstrates how to make compost. The television displays a slide show depicting pictures of real-world examples related to the site's content. A mailbox at the end of the home's sidewalk allows visitors to leave note cards to communicate with the site's owner.

**Figure 6.34.** Interactive Features of the Virtual Home Further Engage Students

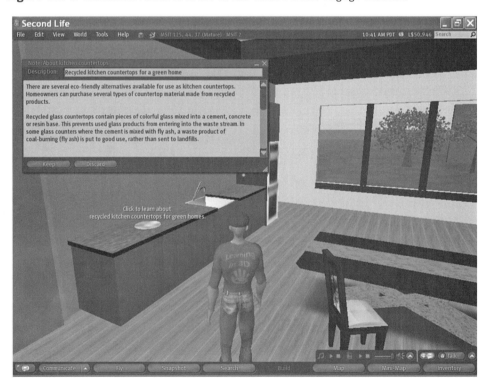

Adjacent to each learning station, students are able to view a 3D representation of the feature described on the corresponding note card. Students can walk around each featured item and view it from multiple angles, thereby visualizing each eco-friendly characteristic within the context of a home. When building the home, photorealistic rendering was not deemed necessary. The home design includes just enough realism to convey a sense of presence in a green home and to suggest an accurate picture of each feature.

Some aspects of the design are modified to better facilitate navigation within a virtual world. For instance, the roof contains a large opening that allows avatars to fly in and out of the home. Teleport pads are strategically placed throughout the grounds to assist with visits to the basement and the roof. An interactive teleport map in the yard displays the locations of the learning stations and enables avatars to teleport to a selected station by clicking on the map.

In the environmental science course, the green home unit was deployed over a period of three weeks. During the first week, the students took a pretest during class to benchmark their prior knowledge. Mengel presented a brief demonstration of Second Life during class after the pre-test. In order to further prepare students for the learning environment, an introductory document was placed in the online course management system. The document provided instructions about how to download Second Life and set up an account. In addition, links to several YouTube videos that illustrate how to use Second Life were included.

During the second week, a document containing a Second Life URL for the virtual green home was placed in the course management system. Students were tasked with visiting the green home over the next week, participating in a scavenger hunt to collect all twenty-two note cards, saving the note cards to their inventory for review, and leaving a record of the visit by placing note cards with their names into the home's mailbox. Students had the option to visit the virtual green home at any time that was convenient. They could visit alone or accompanied by a friend's avatar. They could choose to visit only once, or return for multiple visits. A test about the characteristics of green homes was announced for the following week. It was suggested that students could create their own study guides by pasting the contents of each note card into a Word document.

During the third week, the class took a post-test to access what they had learned during their virtual visits. In addition to questions about the content related to green homes, students were asked questions about the quality of their experience in the virtual world.

## The Macrostructure Map

The macrostructure map outlined in Figure 6.35 provides a quick visual summary of the archetype coverage for the 3DLE design.

## The Benefits

By delivering the course content related to green homes in a virtual world, students were able to experience a field trip to a green home, which would not otherwise have been possible. Through the presence of their avatar, students walked and flew inside and outside of the home, observing the home's green features. During their visit, students attempted to locate and save the note cards. By utilizing the interactive features incorporated into the

**Figure 6.35.** Macrostructure Map for Virtual Green Home

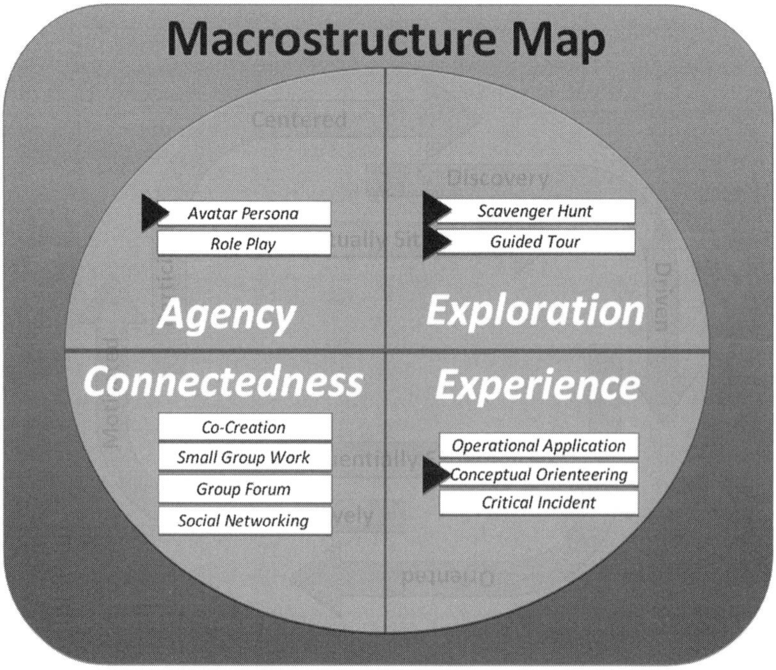

instructional site and wandering in and about the three-dimensional content, the students' virtual presence was physically immersed within the content they were studying.

Students seemed to enjoy this method of content delivery. One student stated, "I liked it because the material I learned was not only informative, but I felt like I got to experience it first-hand, since I could see it in the home." Another stated, "I liked it because it was sort of like experiencing a green home." Another participant said, "Learning in a virtual green home was an effective way to interact and learn because I got a chance to see first-hand what everything was and its functions."

The site visitors indicated that they enjoyed the interactive elements of the virtual green home. When asked which elements helped them to learn, one participant said, "I liked how you could click on things like the toilet, the insulation, television, etc., and they did things." Another participant noted the importance of the interactive map, stating "When I couldn't find one of the notes, I could look on the map and teleport where they were located." Another mentioned the importance of "being able to type freely to people to ask for help." When asked for recommendations to improve the virtual home, one participant said, "Add more methods to interact with the home."

One participant stated that the feature of the virtual home that helped him learn was "being able to fly and teleport. Since I could fly, I could easily move around the site." Similarly, another student cited flying as important, saying, "Being able to fly around . . ., I got to see what all the house had to offer." Similar thoughts were echoed in the comment, "Flying [was important to my learning] because I could move freely and explore where I wanted first."

Clearly, the participants' comments refer to "experiences" and "interactions" that they feel as though they participated in—within a virtual environment. This ability to intermingle students' sense of presence within the content they are studying is difficult, if not impossible, to achieve outside the realm of a virtual world.

## The Results

There was a significant difference between the pre-test and post-test scores of students who visited the virtual green home ($t_{(57)} = -10.545$; $p = .00$), so the instructional site was effective. The amount of time spent in Second

Life ($r_{(57)}$ = .385; $p$ = .003) and whether a participant had used Second Life before ($r_{(57)}$ = .339; $p$ = .009) had a significant correlation with a higher post-test score. Spending a greater amount of time at the virtual home increased the likelihood that participants would receive a higher post-test score by 14.8 percent. Also, having prior experience with Second Life increased the likelihood that participants would receive a higher post-test score by 11.5 percent. Since the students had only one week in which to become familiar with the virtual world environment before visiting the virtual home, the fact that they showed significant increases from pre-test to post-test score is very promising. One student commented, "I had to learn how to navigate around instead of just learning the material." There is no getting around the fact that the learning curve is high, and it takes time to become fully acclimated to the environment.

Over 58 percent of the students indicated that they enjoyed the instructional experience in Second Life. Over 55 percent of students thought they learned more from their visit to a virtual green home than they would have learned from a textbook or lecture. Several students commented that they enjoy using computer-based instruction, and that they liked the self-paced nature of the instruction. In general, students who indicated they did not enjoy the instructional experience gave reasons such as they do not like online games or Second Life, or they prefer a textbook or lecture to online instruction.

## Lessons Learned

The three key pieces of advice for those considering embarking on a 3D learning experience project such the one outlined above are as follows:

**Lesson 1.** Don't let technology get in the way of learning. It is crucial for students who will be learning in a virtual world to first become comfortable with the technology. The skills required to navigate a virtual world are not yet common knowledge, much in the same way that only a few technically savvy people understood how to locate and click on a hyperlink when the Internet was very new. It is essential to provide thorough orientation and training to make sure students are comfortable with the methods to navigate and communicate in the world, so that their ability to concentrate and fully participate in the instruction will not be compromised. Create a plan for how you will ease your students into the virtual world. Expect to spend time preparing the students for participation, perhaps setting up a series of small training milestones to be met before expecting full involvement in instructional activities.

**Lesson 2.** Don't go there unless there is a reason. It's tempting to use a new technology just because it sounds fun. A virtual world is not necessarily a good fit to address each and every learning objective. There are some types of instruction that can be enhanced through delivery in a virtual world; and there are other types of instruction that may be far easier—and perhaps more effective—solutions. If a virtual world is utilized, maximize the world's unique educational potential. Incorporate interactive elements, plan collaborative group activities, leverage the possibilities created by 3D space. Ask your students to do something they can't do in another instructional environment. Otherwise, the resulting instruction may not be worth the time invested in preparing for the visit.

**Lesson 3.** Don't get wrapped up in the details. It's not necessary to build or have a site built that replicates the real world in exact detail. Visitors to a virtual world seem to interpret their surroundings in symbolic terms. A simply rendered object can be understood and mentally translated as the real-world object it represents, even if it is not rendered in photorealistic detail. Invest the majority of your instructional design energy in planning what will happen in the world, rather than in building an extremely detailed environment.

# Case 8: Creating a Virtual Challenge for Global Graduates

## Organization Background

BP (formerly British Petroleum) is one of the largest companies in the world. Given the company's global reach and highly technical work activity, the chief technology officer (CTO) engages in a strategic process called "Game Changer" to identify and apply emerging technologies that can be leveraged to advance BP's vision and mission.

In 2008, the CTO team named 3D Virtual Environments as a Game Changer technology. Since that time, the CTO team had spearheadied a number of BP initiatives for which this technology is being applied. This case study chronicles BP's Global Graduate Challenge (GGC) migration from a physical meeting to a 3D learning experience.

## The Challenge

BP takes training and development very seriously. In the past, graduates embarked on a two-year early development program that culminated in a three-day forum with three key objectives:

1. Ground participants in an understanding of BP's broader business objectives to enable them to become managers of the future;

2. Create global networks to allow BP to quickly identify and share best practices around the world; and

3. Expose BP's future leaders to the company's current senior leadership.

In 2007, the Global Graduate Forum (GGF) brought 300 of the 750 global graduates to London for a series of presentations and activities that included many of BP's senior executives. While the physical meeting was well received by those participants who were able to attend, many graduates were unable to secure support from their business units to come to London due to cost and/or time constraints (in some geographies only 1 in 10 were allowed to attend, selected by a lottery).

In 2008, due to increased economic global pressures and the challenges, BP made the decision to find a different graduate development opportunity that still addressed the objectives of the GGF solution. Having heard of the CTO 3D Virtual Environments Game Changer Initiative, human resources approached the team in search of such a solution.

The development of a solution was not trivial. Two years earlier, the 2006 graduate new-hires were brought into BP with the expectation that their program would culminate with a global graduate forum that afforded them the opportunity to network with senior leadership. Often this networking led to opportunities and placements that launched successful leadership careers within the firm.

It was important to come up with a solution that met the original learning objectives of the global graduate forum, provided the opportunity for access to those who traditionally may not have been able to attend the forum, while at the same time ensuring that the solution maintained the networking aesthetic that the physical forum afforded to allow synergistic and serendipitous interactions between participants and senior leadership. Hence the Global Graduate Challenge (GGC) was born.

## Why 3D?

Given the learning objectives of the global graduate forum, it was clear from the outset that teleconferences, video streaming with discussion boards, and web-conference presentations alone would not be sufficient. While some of the content may have been effectively transferred via these approaches, the ability to build social networks that often happens outside the presentation context itself would have been very difficult to achieve.

The CTO team had been researching virtual world technologies for quite some time as a precursor to naming it a game changer in 2008. In examining the capabilities that differentiated this technology from other enterprise learning and collaboration platforms, it was evident that the 3D environment brought with it a sense of immersion and co-presence that, if leveraged appropriately within the design, could keep participants engaged over a three-day period while simultaneously allowing for serendipitous and spontaneous interactions between participants and senior leadership.

## Making the Case

From a financial perspective, given the economic situation, the company could no longer justify the significant cost associated with supporting a physical global graduate forum. Simply put, another alternative had to be created and it had to be a lot more cost-effective than convening people physically.

From a human resource perspective, an expectation had been set that such a meeting would occur when the graduates where hired in 2006. Not doing anything to recognize the culmination of the graduate program would clearly have upset the graduates, even those who may not have garnered support from their business units to attend. The need to develop an innovative solution that maintained the original objectives of the physical global graduate forum while increasing the ability for participation and networked interaction was paramount.

To address the simultaneous needs to be good stewards of both the company's financial capital and its human capital, the team made the case that hosting a 3D learning experience built around a futuristic challenge called Fordadland 2025 (based on a highly relevant issue) could address both the financial and human resource stewardship needs of the business.

From a human resource perspective, the creation of a 3D Global Graduate Village in which teams worked virtually to complete the Fordadland Challenge and interacted with senior leadership around key strategic decisions related to the challenge would fuse learning and networking in a unique way. From a financial perspective the creation of the Global Graduate Village environment and all other aspects of the design of the Fordadland Challenge was achieved at one-tenth the cost of hosting the physical global graduate forum.

Allowing more people access in an environment that facilitated virtual learning and networking for 10 percent of the cost proved to be the value proposition that brought the CTO and HR teams together to create, execute, and evaluate a pilot project build around the Fordadland 2025 challenge concept.

## The Solution

The GGC 3D learning experience was designed around a critical incident wherein seventeen cross-functional GGC teams took on the role of BP senior leadership in the year 2025. At that time, the world has reached a point at which a decision must be made as to whether or not we should tap our last remaining oil reserves on the pristine continent of Fordadland (a fictitious land mass). And if so, how it should be done in a way that preserves our increasingly fragile environment. This challenge presented a real-world challenge of securing energy demand in an environmentally responsible manner. The Fordadland Challenge culminated with team presentations that recommended a strategy and execution plan. These team presentations were evaluated, and the top three teams were recognized for their efforts at the senior leadership level. The winning team was rewarded with a week-long trip to Egypt, where BP has extensive operations.

All activities associated with the challenge were conducted virtually within BP's 3D Global Graduate Village (see Figure 6.36). Participants were asked to spend four or five hours per week over a four-week period to research and develop their team presentations. The Global Graduate Village was staffed by HR and CTO personnel from 7 a.m. to 7 p.m. to assist with

**Figure 6.36.** The Arrival Platform at BP's Global Graduate Village

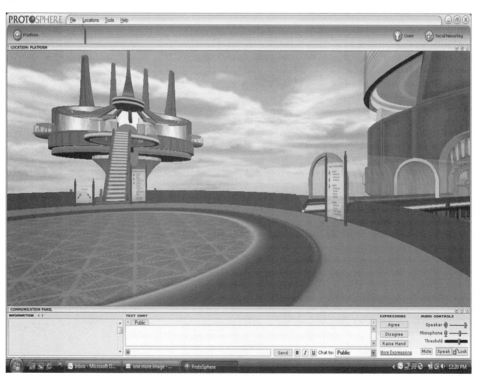

general technical and challenge-related queries and to help deal with procedural decisions and team dynamics.

In the eight weeks prior to the first week of the Fordadland Challenge, the team was dedicated to ensuring that all the teams understood what was required of them by providing a guided tour of the Global Graduate Village to ensure that the GGC participants were familiar with the environment and its capabilities. Additionally, each team had a designated super-user (called a pathfinder), who was provided with additional training on the capabilities of the Global Graduate Village. The team also dedicated themselves heavily in the first week to ensure that the teams knew what was required of them in terms of developing a strategy and set of recommendations related to the challenge.

In the central presentation area of the Global Graduate Village, senior leadership and subject-matter experts provided briefings related to the challenge (see Figure 6.37). Over the four-week period, sixteen briefings were

**Figure 6.37.** GGC Participants Attend a Senior Leader Briefing

delivered to the GGC teams covering topics such as alternative energy, compliance and ethics, competitive intelligence, and environmental policy and operations, to name a few. This group forum also provided the opportunity for the graduates to meet informally with the senior executives and experts following the briefings to seek guidance from them as they iteratively refined their presentations.

Each team was also provided with a 3D virtual team room. This team room served as a virtual hub for all synchronous and asynchronous small group work activity for the team. Each team room was pre-populated with key documentation and reports that enabled the teams to establish a fact base upon which to build their strategies and recommendations as well as an embedded video presentation of the challenge itself. The challenge culminated with submissions from each team that were reviewed according to a pre-established set of criteria.

## The Macrostructure Map

The macrostructure map in Figure 6.38 provides a quick visual summary of the archetype coverage for the 3DLE design.

## The Benefits

The business case for the creation of the Fordadland Challenge was driven by needs to reduce the significant cost ($5M) associated with conducting a physical global graduate forum and the ability to provide better access for graduate participants.

From a financial perspective, the Fordadland Challenge was successful in that this pilot effort, which included 178 GGC participants, was completed at 10 percent of the cost of the physical GGC forum.

Furthermore, now that the Global Graduate Village has been constructed, subsequent Global Graduate Challenges can achieve further cost reduction while simultaneously increasing access. The incremental cost will go to additional user licenses for participants to access the environment. It

**Figure 6.38.** Macrostructure Map for BP's Global Graduate Challenge

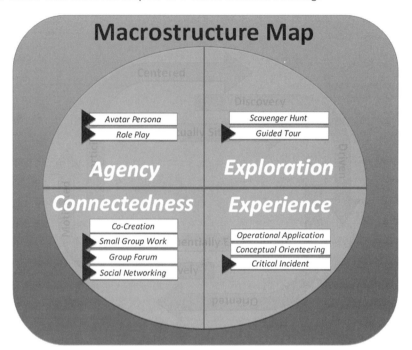

was also successful in that it attracted participants from regions further away, such as China, Australia, New Zealand, and Trinidad and Tobago.

Finally, an additional benefit of hosting the challenge in the Global Graduate Village is that senior leaders, subject-matter experts, and GGC members are finding new ways to leverage the environment to run virtual meetings or create virtual communities of practice for a given set of disciplines.

Significant cost savings, increased access and reach, and additional usage of the environment outside the global graduate program are all solid benefits that have been derived from this pilot activity.

## The Results

All pilot participants were surveyed following the Global Graduate Challenge. Participants were asked to rank their perceptions on a number of questions on a 7-point agreement scale (Strongly Disagree = 1, Strongly Agree = 7). Tabulated below are some aggregate results of the data related to the original program objectives:

**Objective 1:** Ground participants in an understanding of BP's broader business objectives to enable them to become managers of the future, as shown in Table 6.1.

**Objective 2:** Create global networks to allow BP to quickly identify and share best practices, as shown in Table 6.2.

**Objective 3:** Expose BP's future leaders to the company's current senior leadership, as shown in Table 6.3.

## Lessons Learned

The three key pieces of advice for those considering embarking on a 3D learning experience projects such the one outlined in this case are on the next page.

**Table 6.1.** Results of Survey Concerning BP's Broader Business Objectives

| Survey Questions | Rating Average |
| --- | --- |
| The Fordadland context was relevant to BP's business. | 5.7/7.0 |
| The program has expanded my understanding of BP's business. | 5.1/7.0 |

**Table 6.2.** Results of Survey Concerning Questions About Networking with Others

| Survey Questions | Rating Average |
| --- | --- |
| The program allowed me to build new global networks. | 4.3/7.0 |
| I was able to acquire important "know-how" through the project. | 4.6/7.0 |

**Table 6.3.** Survey Results Concerning Interaction with Senior Leadership

| Survey Questions | Rating Average |
| --- | --- |
| The SME/senior leaders who presented were relevant and insightful. | 5.6/7.0 |
| The SME/senior leader sessions were enjoyable and engaging. | 5.4/7.0 |
| The program provided the opportunity to present business opinions and solutions to BP senior Leaders. | 4.5/7.0 |

**Lesson 1**  Don't underestimate how long it takes to ensure that all the technical aspects associated with launching a new environment are identified and addressed. BP did extensive stress-testing of the Global Graduate Village, including testing access from seventy offices world-wide before making it available for the Global Graduate Challenge. The GGC project team also built contingency plans to address the possibility of the GGC failing during a briefing and had set up alternate access mechanisms for those who were unable to connect to the Internet due to their locations.

**Lesson 2**  Don't underestimate how long it takes people to become familiar with a new learning and collaboration platform. Great care was taken to embed expertise within each team via the super-user (known as a pathfinder) prior to the start of the challenge.

Also, for the first week, primary emphasis was placed on getting the participants comfortable in navigating the environment and understanding how the features and functionality of the environment could best serve the team as they worked on their strategy and recommendations. Separating the learning curve associated with becoming familiar with the environment from the learning curve associated with the activity itself is key.

**Lesson 3**  While the first two pieces of advice focused on technology, the final piece of advice is to bring all of this back to the business need. In this case, the needs of the business intersected with the capabilities of the technology in such a way that value could be derived from a 3D solution. Careful articulation of what the specific business need is and how a 3D solution can provide a more effective and efficient solution is central to securing sponsorship and demonstrating value once the solution is implemented.

# Case 9: Hosting Virtual Academy of Technology Events

## Organization Background

As the world's leading information technology company, IBM has a long tradition of leading the charge in developing and implementing new technologies that drive significant business benefit. IBM's Academy of Technology (AoT) has long been at the forefront of emerging technology research and exploration. This select group of 330 thought leaders and technology innovators are responsible for providing technical leadership to IBM—identifying and pursuing technical developments and opportunities, improving IBM's technology base, and developing IBM's technical community.

This case study chronicles how VIE technology was leveraged to host two virtual events for the AoT members. Following their experience in these two events, the AoT has concluded that virtual worlds will have a big impact on business, on IBM, and on IBM's clients.

## The Challenge

By late 2007, based on an external scan and the activities of IBM's Virtual Universe Community (VUC), it became clear to several AoT members that virtual environments had the potential to change the way business was done globally.

As a result, it was proposed that an AoT conference dedicated to virtual worlds be convened in October of 2008. Two key requirements for this conference were that it be hosted in a virtual environment and—due to the confidentiality of the information being shared—that it be held in a secure environment behind the company's firewall.

Given that the best way to understand the potential that virtual worlds provide is to experience them, the primary cultural challenge with hosting a successful event was to ensure that AoT members who had not previously been exposed to virtual world technologies felt comfortable with their avatars and with navigating the virtual conference space. The primary technical challenge revolved around working with Linden Labs to create a stand-alone behind-the-firewall environment for the AoT Virtual Worlds Conference. In many ways, the due date for the conference catalyzed the efforts on both sides to solve the technical issues associated with delivering a behind-the-firewall solution.

The AoT's annual general meeting was scheduled to be held in Florida the month following the Virtual Worlds Conference. Each year at the annual general meeting, AoT members get together to compare stories and give presentations on their accomplishments over the previous year. They hear from key IBM executives on the business strategy for the firm. They plot the agenda for the upcoming year and, most importantly, they network and reconnect with each other as members of this strategically significant group within the company.

Following the Virtual World Conference, Joanne Martin, president of the AoT, and her leadership team decided that it would not be appropriate to hold a large physical meeting given the economic situation at the time. At the same time, Martin's mission of transforming the Academy to become more active and regularly engaged could not be put on hold. She needed to find an acceptable alternative to physically hosting the annual general meeting—and she needed it fast.

As she explored the agenda for the physical meeting, she made mental notes on what different technologies might be best leveraged to virtually convene the meeting. Webcasts, video-conferences, and online brainstorming sessions were all factored into the mix, but Martin still felt that there was something missing. The need to network, share, and reconnect and reenergize members of the community, so much a part of the physical AoT annual general meeting, simply could not be re-created with these technologies.

Having had a positive experience at the AoT Virtual Worlds Conference, Martin decided to leverage the virtual environment created for that meeting to host 120 poster sessions for the annual general meeting.

## Why 3D?

For the Virtual Worlds Conference it was clear to the organizers that abstractly talking about the benefits of virtual worlds would be far less compelling than viscerally experiencing them.

For the annual general meeting, the primary motivation for the use of a VIE was to enable serendipitous networking and to enable the community to really feel a virtual sense of community in attending the conference. The connectedness and presence that Martin had experienced at the Virtual Worlds Conference was something she felt strongly could be leveraged to build the sense of community that was as strong in the physical annual general meeting.

The 3D space, she hoped, would become the home base for the virtual annual general meeting, where the persistence of the space and the sense of presence and connectedness allowed AoT members to interact with each other with the same level of serendipity and spontaneity as in the physical world.

## Making the Case

For the Virtual World Conference, the design of the event itself required that it be held in a virtual world context. The AoT had agreed that, if they were to really learn about the benefits of virtual worlds, they would have to experience them first-hand. That being said, it is estimated that IBM saved over $250,000 in travel and venue costs and more than $150,000 in productivity gains due to travel time savings by hosting the conference virtually. Given that IBM invested roughly $80,000 to create the virtual environment and run the virtual world conference, this amounts to a net real savings of $250,000 for hosting the event virtually.

For the annual general meeting, the economic climate at the time necessitated that Martin take on the challenge of replacing the physical meeting with a virtual one. With the wide array of collaborative technologies at her disposal, it was clearly possible to host a virtual event. The bigger challenge for Martin was to re-create the sense of community that was the glue that transcended the events themselves.

Had she not attended the Virtual World Conference and experienced first-hand how the sense of community could be cultivated virtually, she might have considered this approach a bridge too far. But based on her positive experience and the lack of other alternatives, she decided that it was an acceptable risk.

In the end, the risk did indeed prove to be acceptable. The annual general meeting was very successfully executed at one-fifth the cost of a real-world event.

## The Solutions

**Solution 1.** On October 21, 2008, the three-day AoT Virtual World Conference was launched. It attracted over two hundred members globally who attended three keynote presentations and thirty-seven breakout sessions chosen from over sixty-five submissions. IBM's Virtual Universe Community members served as volunteer conference concierges, and kiosks in the reception plaza allowed participants to automatically teleport to the sessions that most interested them.

Many breakout sessions were delivered by experienced VUC members who took full advantage of virtual world affordances to make their presentations more engaging. One presenter used a 3D model of a server to show participants how to service a machine (see Figure 6.39).

**Figure 6.39.** Instructor Shows Participants How to Service a Machine

Another used a "walk around" presentation format whereby each slide was displayed on a set of viewers mounted within a wonderful garden landscape. There were no boring page-turning pitches at this conference!

Most importantly, the space itself was used as a venue to socialize. One thing the team realized after the first few sessions was that, just because you can instantly teleport from one session to the next, does not mean you should only schedule five minutes between sessions. As AoT and VUC members lingered in rooms following sessions or as they moved out to a commons area to continue their discussions, the conference organizers had to update the conference wiki schedule to accommodate these self-organized informal gatherings. Furthermore, at the end of the day, it was not uncommon to run into several AoT distinguished engineers gathered in the commons area, reflecting openly on the conference and where they thought this technology might go in the future.

**Solution 2.** The annual general meeting was larger, with over three hundred registered attendees. The busy three-day agenda included many different activities such as:

- IBM technical agenda brainstorming sessions;

- Executive sessions;

- "Read out" presentations from AoT research projects;

- Birds-of-a-feather sessions; and

- "Poster sessions" where new academy members present their credentials and seek to find opportunities for research collaboration with other AoT members.

Although other technologies were used extensively to host different parts of the annual general meeting, Second Life quickly became the persistent meeting place for the over three hundred conference participants to hang out. The conference planning team decided to reuse the behind-the-firewall Second Life solution to host the 120 poster sessions (see Figure 6.40).

Recognizing a similar pattern of spontaneous self-organized informal gatherings in the virtual space, the organizers decided to officially schedule networking breaks and cocktail hours, just as they would have for a

**Figure 6.40.** One of the 120 Poster Session Sky-Pods

physical conference. They also scheduled a two-hour picnic social at the end of the conference. AoT members gathered around, drinking virtual beers, while others took virtual hang-gliding or jet-ski lessons (see Figure 6.41).

The VIE had provided Martin with the opportunity to virtually re-create the positive social and technical exchange that AoT members needed when faced with the challenge of not being able to meet physically. Furthermore, this outcome was achieved at one-fifth the cost and without a single case of jet lag.

## The Macrostructure Map

The macrostructure map outlined in Figure 6.42 provides a quick visual summary of the archetype coverage for in the 3DLE design. Both the Virtual World Conference and AoT annual general meeting are represented on the same map, as they leveraged the same set of 3DLE archetypes.

**Figure 6.41.** Academy of Technology Social Picnic at the End of the Conference

**Figure 6.42.** A Macrostructure Map for the Academy of Technology Virtual Events

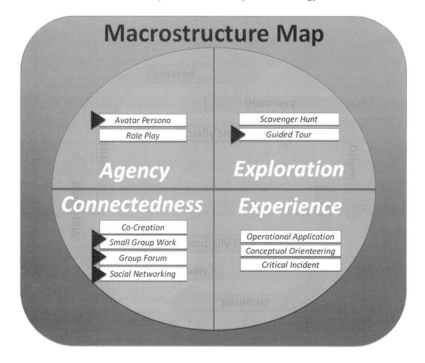

## The Results

IBM surveyed participants from the AoT Virtual World Conference to determine how the virtual experience compared to face to face in four categories.

1. Content: 96 percent said the same, or better.

2. Presentation Style: 85 percent said the same or better.

3. Learning: 78 percent said the same or better.

4. Networking: 62 percent said the same or better.

Clearly, not all of these results can be solely attributed to the use of a VIE. However, when it comes to networking, it is clear that the persistence of the virtual world platform created an environment that encouraged an organic pattern of social networking and connectedness that was positively regarded by the participants.

Another result worth noting is that, immediately following the annual general meeting, twenty different organizations within IBM have asked the VUC for help in hosting meetings on the behind-the-firewall environment. There are now over fifty requests for meetings pending, with many successful events already completed.

## Lessons Learned

The four key pieces of advice for those considering embarking on a 3D learning experience projects such the ones outlined above follow:

**Lesson 1.** Make sure you deal with all cultural and technology issues before the event. There must be a structured communications strategy that parses out the work to be done to have participants download, troubleshoot, and acclimate to the technology in such a way that it is perceived to be neither too obnoxious nor too onerous. Striking the right balance on communication and acculturation is a key success factor.

**Lesson 2.** If participants are not comfortable with the technology before coming to the event, they will not see the benefits of attending the event virtually. Establish orientation sessions and make them available often. Establish buddy systems and schedule weekly goals to help novices move through the steps necessary to achieve a level of comfort with the platform before attending their first event. It pays to over-invest in getting people up the learning curve, because once you do they will reap significant benefits in the future.

**Lesson 3.** Ensure that the experience itself takes advantage of all that virtual worlds have to offer. The in-world activity needs to prove to the novice that it was worth his or her effort to build an avatar and become familiar with the environment. If all they are shown is virtual slides in a virtual classroom, the non-believers will leave as critics. Virtual-world learning experiences cannot just be presentations. Presenters must be pushed to do something creative, memorable, and meaningful.

**Lesson 4.** Necessity is a wonderful motivator. The economic challenge left Martin with little alternative but to take a risk on a technology that might previously have been considered a bridge too far. Take advantage of a crisis to push people all at once to realize the benefits that these technologies can provide.

# Part Three

**Breaking New Ground**

# Overcoming Being Addled by Addie

## Avoiding the Virtual Ghost Town

Deciding where to start in designing and developing a 3DLE can be overwhelming. There are many considerations and elements to juggle. Fortunately, many of the same processes used to develop more traditional instruction can be used when developing virtual learning worlds. With specific modifications and changes, more methods of developing instruction can be utilized to create an engaging, focused, and productive learning experience. This chapter explores using the process of Analysis, Design, Development, Implementation, and Evaluation—the ADDIE model—to create effective virtual world learning. It also describes some general guidelines needed for success and some considerations for working with vendors to create a 3DLE.

One common mistake organizations make in designing 3DLEs is failing to have specific learning objectives, either formal or informal, for the intended interactions. Some organizations create a virtual space with only vague learning outcomes and no formal assessment plan. Then, after a few months of inactivity, no visible learning outcomes, and frustration, the organization drops the VIE because it doesn't seem productive.

The lack of learning in these instances is not a result of the VIE; rather it is a result of poor instructional design. VIEs, like other types of planned learning events, require attention to instructional design to meet their desired goals. Even if the goal is to foster informal learning, the VIE must be structured appropriately to encourage and enable interaction between and among learners. If not, the result is a virtual ghost town. No one comes to visit, and the place is empty.

When creating a VIE and 3DLEs, the basic tenants of instructional design still apply, as they do with any new technology that enables learning. Organizations do not need to completely throw away the concepts of aligning objectives, tasks, and measurement just because a new technology is available. A systematic process is required to ensure that optimal learning can occur.

Having said that, the development of a 3DLE is far more complicated than the creation of a few slides and a couple of multiple-choice questions. Ultimately, the design process for creating a 3DLE requires a modification of the traditional skill set of an instructional designer—a modification, not a totally new approach. As a result of the modification, the design and development efforts for 3DLEs require a higher level of effort both in time and resources. The process demands both a careful crafting of the learning environment (the context) as well as the mapping of the content to the appropriate learning archetype, the creation of learning spaces, activities, and planned interactions.

To highlight the development differences, let's compare and contrast the development efforts needed to create the 2D learning environment versus the efforts required to create the 3DLE behind Jane and Jack's experience with the Model Z drill discussed in Chapter 3.

## Juan's 2D Synchronous Design Story

This too originally appeared in an eLearning Guild publication called "360 Synchronous Learning Report," and we'd like to acknowledge the eLearning Guild for granting permission to republish the stories in this chapter.[1]

Juan has done this before. His job in the learning and development department is to help subject-matter experts create and deliver effective synchronous learning. This includes instructing the sales trainers on the proper method to deliver synchronous online learning, as well as reviewing their training courses the first few times they are given.

Today he is reviewing the slide deck for the Model Z created by Derrick Pablo, the newest guy in sales. Juan mutters to himself, "This needs some work." He mentally creates a list: add an objectives slide so the learners know what they will be learning, reduce the number of words on each screen, add a couple of interactive exercises, add a few instructional design elements, group all like information together, and get some photographs of the Model Z from marketing. He sends an e-mail to marketing asking for images and material explaining the features and functionalities of the Model Z.

First he creates an "objectives" slide and then turns his attention to the rest of the deck. He spends about two hours re arranging the text; he diligently copies half the text on each screen and pastes it onto a new slide. He then adds titles, stock photographs, or clip art to each slide. He re-sequences a few of the slides to present simpler information before more complex topics.

The process is time-consuming but necessary. It helps with the readability of the slides (which they've heard complaints about in the past) and helps learners to better comprehend the material on each slide. At last the deck is to the point at which text-heavy slides will not overwhelm the learner. It doubled in size from twenty-one to forty slides.

Next Juan opens up an older product launch slideshow and grabs the standard "Welcome" slide. It encourages interactivity by inviting students to use their whiteboard tools to mark their locations on a world map.

After Juan adds the "Welcome" slide, he closes the older deck and navigates to the "Features" slide for the Model Z. The slide, as originally provided by the SME, contains a list of features on a blank screen. Being a good instructional designer, Juan knows that linking visual and verbal cues is an important element in learning, so he spends some time fixing this slide. He takes the image of the Model Z that he just received in his e-mail from marketing and adds it to the slide. He then draws arrows from each new feature to its location on the drill based on a marketing brochure attached to the e-mail. He creates a few additional slides with images of different Model Z displays so the instructor can show product placement.

In about six hours, the deck is ready for the lesson. It is properly sequenced, includes two interactive polling questions, and has at least one image on each slide.

Juan contacts Derrick, the course instructor, who has never taught using the 2D synchronous tool. They get together the next afternoon and discuss how to progress from slide to slide, how to go back to a slide if necessary, how to see whether a learner has a question, how to record the session, and how to operate the chat function of the software. In the training Juan emphasizes the use of interactive techniques like the whiteboard and conducting ad hoc polls to gauge the understanding level of participants. In about an hour Derrick feels comfortable and is ready to practice on his own and then teach the lesson early in the next week.

## Sylvia's 3D Synchronous Design Story

Sylvia, the 3D project manager, looks around the room at the assembled team. In attendance are Fred, the VP of sales; Larry, who heads up new product development; Kaylee, the instructional designer; Mark, a context developer; and Horatio, who will be conducting the lesson in the VIE in less than three weeks. Sylvia is feeling the time crunch. She has developed two of these 3DLEs in the past and knows it takes time, commitment, and resources.

Today Sylvia wants to review with the team the space in which the instruction will take place and the information still needed to create the instruction. She has distributed a drawing and storyboards to each attendee showing the various educational areas within the VIE and what activities will take place in each area. It took her and her team about two weeks to review the content, create objectives, and develop learning activities to support the course objectives. They have decided on two scavenger hunt–type activities, providing examples of store and tradeshow displays, as well as an exercise to allow the learners to practice setting up displays; and a last-minute addition was a role play at a construction site. Now she and her team need to start building the environment, but she can't move forward without help from the subject-matter experts on the sales team.

She opens the meeting by carefully listing the remaining needs for the Model Z training session: creation of large and small store displays as well as a trade-show floor display, creation of a giant Model Z drill, development of "feature cards" to place on both the giant drill and the smaller drills to provide information about the new features, providing sales representatives with a "selling experience" role play, and, finally, the creation of interactive displays for the learners to create as a final exercise.

Larry interrupts Sylvia and wants to know why they can't just create a virtual classroom and deliver slides to the learners via the virtual classroom. He wants to know why the company has to spend all this time and money on these crazy activities. He insists that a virtual classroom would be just as effective.

Sylvia takes a deep breath; she has explained this at least one hundred times to both Larry and Fred. She looks at Larry and slowly begins the explanation yet again. She reminds him that, to achieve its fullest potential, 3DLEs must avoid the routinization trap of re-creating old, inefficient processes with new technology. For the learning to be effective, it cannot simply mirror the classroom, but must go beyond the classroom. It must allow learners to explore and learn in ways that are not possible in current learning formats. She points out that VIEs provide for a higher rate of retention in many cases than 2D synchronous events during which everyone is checking e-mail or surfing the web.

Suddenly, Fred remembers the previous discussions and reminds Larry that they have already made the decision about using a VIE. He tells him this meeting is to find out what Sylvia's team needs to make this work, not to debate the already chosen approach.

Everyone agrees and Sylvia begins to run down her list of items necessary to complete the project. She first tells Larry she needs schematics of the drill and not just photographs. In fact, she wants one of the physical prototypes so she can reference the real thing when creating the virtual 3D drill. She knows it needs to look as realistic as possible if the learners are going to be able to properly identify the new features.

Larry tells her there are only three prototype versions available and that the marketing team needs them for photographs and sizing displays. Sylvia insists on having a prototype of the Model Z and tells Larry and Mark that she only needs it for two days. Larry finally acquiesces, when Fred speaks up and reminds the team that, while marketing is important, a properly trained sales force is more important to the overall success of the product launch.

Next, Sylvia tells Fred she needs him to provide photographs of large and small store displays and the planograms or diagrams used to set up the displays. She needs to know the placement of the hangers, location of the signs, and how everything fastens together so they can realistically re-create the displays in 3D. She knows the reproductions need to be as accurate as possible. She also needs the same information for the trade show display. Fred tells her she will have the information by the close of business that day.

Fred wants to know how long all this will take. Sylvia asks Mark how long it will take to create the giant drill. He estimates about three or four days once he has the physical prototype in his hand and then another day or two to accurately re-create all the displays and then a couple of days to set up the virtual product display exercise. Sylvia also explains that her team will need to create "teleporters" to place at each location so the class can move quickly from environment to environment, and she reminds them of the creation of the construction site for the role play.

Sylvia suddenly asks Kaylee to make a note. They need to create a scoreboard for keeping track of all the features to award the learning bucks properly. Kaylee reminds Sylvia that they have a scoreboard from the Model Q launch and should be able to modify the scripting to accommodate scoring for the Model Z exercise.

When the room quiets for a moment, Horatio speaks up for the first time. He wants to know about his training as a 3D facilitator. While he is a great stand-up instructor and has conducted dozens of 2D synchronous learning sessions and studied the Model Z, he knows nothing of facilitating a training session in a 3D environment. He has an avatar and has been to the company's help station in the VIE, but is uncomfortable with conducting a 3D session.

Sylvia tells him they can meet tomorrow to go over the controls and interface, and then he will need to practice for a few days until he gets the hang of it. She then asks for any other questions, reminds the team of how important it is to get the information as soon as possible, and adjourns the meeting.

The next day Sylvia and Horatio meet in the virtual space and she explains to him what he needs to do to teleport learners from place to place, how to monitor the activities of the learners, and how to look for the gestures of the learners to gain input on their level of activity and whether or not they have any questions. She laughs to herself when he keeps flying into walls and he always seems to have his back toward her. Eventually, he gets better. She tells him they can have another session in a few days but that he needs to practice on his own in the meantime. Horatio is still nervous and eagerly schedules another training session with Sylvia. What he really wants to do is to practice in the actual 3D space in which he will be teaching, but from the sounds of the meeting, that may be a little while.

# Development Team

The contrast between the design process of Sylvia and that of Juan is striking. The efforts required by Sylvia and her team are much more complex than the required efforts of Juan for a number of reasons. First, the process that Juan is following is not unlike the process required to put together a slide deck for a physical environment. Juan doesn't create the environment in which the learning occurs. It is already determined; it's the desktop of the learners attending the session. On the other hand, Sylvia needs to create the context of the learning, the scavenger hunt with large drills, the construction site, and the content that must be learned by the participants in the virtual world. She has a much more involved task.

To successfully accomplish the task of creating a VIE for the Model Z, Sylvia must work with a team. She cannot possibly create the entire learning experience herself. A typical team required for building a VIE consists of:

- Project Manager
- Instructional Designer

- Subject-Matter Expert

- Context Developer/Builder

- Scripter/Programmer

- Information Technology Representative

- Representative of Learner Population

**Project Manager.** The project manager is responsible for coordinating the activities of the other members of the group. This is a critical role in the development of a virtual learning space. The reason is because of all the interconnected and dependent activities. The project manager must ensure that the different individuals on the team are speaking the same language and working toward the same instructional goals.

**Instructional Designer.** This team member is responsible for developing the instructional framework and the pedagogy to make the learning effective within the 3D space. The instructional designer chooses the correct learning archetype and determines the methods by which learners will interact both formally and informally within the space. This is the person who is responsible for thinking through the entire learning experience of the participant and determining how the space and environment will foster learning. The instructional designer often creates the storyboards and design document that will be used as the foundation for the others to build the 3D spaces required for the learning.

**Subject-Matter Expert.** This is the person who knows the subject matter to be learned within the VIE. Sometimes the environment is carefully developed and scripted, like the creation of a burning building that is being used to provide first-responders with an opportunity for repeatedly practicing how to coordinate activities, or it can be an environment that is less formal, allowing for interaction like a series of diagrams placed on virtual billboards that avatars can review and discuss as they meet together in-world.

**Context Developer/Builder.** This is the person responsible for building the 3D environment in which the instruction will take place. This often requires knowledge of third-party 3D development software such as Autodesk's Maya or 3ds Max or knowledge of how to use in-world modeling tools. A context developer/builder needs to have the knowledge and skill necessary to align surfaces and primitive elements (cubes, pyramids, cones, spheres, and torus) to create an object that looks realistic in the VIE. Additionally, this person needs to understand how to use textures, light, scale, and spacing to create the appropriate environment in which the learning is to occur.

**Scripter/Programmer.** This person is responsible for writing code that makes the 3D world function as desired. Often within the VIE certain actions will be desired, such as the opening of a door or the specific operation of a gage on an instrument panel. For the elements within a 3D world to function, they need to be scripted to perform as desired. This is the job of the scripter/ programmer, who writes scripts so objects and avatars interact as required.

**Information Technology Representative.** When implementing a VIE, a representative from the information technology department must be a team member. This is because of the technical requirements necessary to run a robust and effective VIE. If the world is being hosted internally, there are server and bandwidth requirements, not to mention requirements related to video and sound cards. If the world is hosted externally, there are requirements related to opening portals and firewall issues. Regardless of the actual physical location of the server housing the virtual world, a representative of the information technology department is required to minimize the technical issues that will be encountered.

**Representative of Learner Population.** One often overlooked team member is someone who represents the typical learner. This is someone from the target population who can help to inform the team of the mindset of the learners. This person can help make suggestions and contribute ideas that will help to shape the virtual learning experience and hopefully make it more comfortable for the learners who will be entering the VIE.

# Design Points for Virtual Learning Worlds

When designing instruction in a VIE, it is critical to remember that you are designing a learning "environment" and not an e-learning module or course.

The primary objective of a VIE is to design engaging experiences that logically lead the learner along an optimal flow state to rapidly assimilate new learning. The learning that occurs with a virtual learning world surfaces at the moment when the lack of knowledge or capability of the learner intersects with the need to have that knowledge or capability to overcome a given challenge. The learning is engineered so that teachable moments surface at every turn. Those teachable moments are not the same for everyone, but areas covered in the 3DLE are encountered, consumed, and applied based on the experience of the learner, not the mandate of the instructor. No two people can be expected to come out with the same experience in having gone through a virtual learning world experience. That is precisely the design point for these environments.

Experience is much more about context than content. In VIE, as stated before, content is king, but context is the kingdom. Context renders explicit topics and principles and makes them actionable. The true value of virtual learning worlds is not how well they can mimic the classroom but how purposeful they can be in allowing learners to act and interact toward a common goal, fail, try again in a different way, and eventually (but *much faster* than in real life) achieve the learning outcome desired.

Given this backdrop, there are a number of general design points to keep in mind when creating virtual learning experiences:

- Create the right context;
- Create specific objectives;
- Provide minimal guidelines;
- Encourage collaboration;
- Allow opportunities for demonstrating learning; and
- Build in incentives.

## Create the Right Context

In a traditional classroom or in a 2D synchronous learning space such as WebEx or Centra, the context is pre-established. The learners are faced with a slide of content, a shared application, or a whiteboard on which they can collaborate. There is little variation from session to session in terms of context. The content may change, but the environment is static—a digital interpretation of the physical classroom.

In a VIE, the entire context of the learning can change many times within one session. For example, in Chapter 3 when the learners first arrived to learn about the Model Z, they found themselves in a room looking for features on virtual drills; within a few moments, they were flying around a giant drill; and then they whisked from store display to store display; and in the next instant were at a trade show, then a role play and, finally, were placed into a workspace to create their own displays. The responsibility for creating those environments and anticipating the needs of the facilitator within a virtual learning environment is the job of the designers of the 3D learning environment. It is not possible for a facilitator to "whip up" a VIE with the same speed she could whip up an ad hoc slide to clarify a point in a 2D synchronous learning situation.

The learning context is critical to the learning process in VIEs. How you create the context impacts the learners and influences how much they will learn from the facilitator, each other, and the environment. The designer must establish a context that: (1) encourages collaboration, (2) helps learners achieve specific learning goals, (3) fosters peer-to-peer interactions, and (4) provides the right context for the instruction to occur. In 3D learning, context is as important as content.

## Create Specific Objectives, But Don't Tell the Learner

In a 2D synchronous learning space; the instructor typically presents the learners with an introductory slide labeled "objectives" or "agenda" that tells him or her what he or she is going to learn in the session. The objectives are specifically spelled out for the learner. In a similar fashion, the 3DLE designer needs to have specific objectives and goals in mind for the learners to achieve. However, the objectives do not need to be explicitly spelled out for the learners on a virtual slide. You should not provide a myopic step-by-step sequence of events or step-by-step objectives. Instead, take advantage of the openness of a VIE and let the learners explore the area in a sequence and flow directed by them. Create the environment to achieve the objectives of the learning. Rather than provide objectives such as "You will be able to identify seven safety violations," pose questions of the learner. "What safety violations do you see on this virtual shop floor?" Or provide tasks that lead to an understanding of the objective such as "Examine this machine and place the required safety guard in the proper position" or "Correct seven safety violations within this production line."

## Provide Minimal Guidelines

While the learning objectives should be specific in the design of the 3DLE, the methods for achieving those objectives should be open. VIEs allow for real-time collaboration and interactions among learners. However, the learners typically need some level of guidance to achieve a learning goal. Establish a set of minimal guidelines and then allow the learners to engage with the environment. This can happen when you transport learners from one example to another, such as with the displays for the Model Z. At the end, the learners did not receive specific instructions; instead, they were shown several examples and then asked to create their own based on what they had seen.

Minimal guidelines will direct learners toward the "Aha!" learning moment you are trying to encourage. If you provide the right context and the right guidelines, people will learn from each other, from the environment, and from the immersive experience. They will learn in a manner that increases retention and recall of information.

## Encourage Collaboration

A huge advantage of a VIE is that it naturally enables peer-to-peer collaboration. The collaboration afforded within the VIE includes the co-creation of items, pointing out features of a specific environment, and participating in the same activity at the same time in the same virtual space. When designing these types of learning events, create a context in which collaboration is necessary and required for success, such as working on team exercises to create a display as indicated in the example. Sylvia's team created many different collaborative activities, which started with the group looking for features on small drills and continuing to the final exercise. Other examples include avatars working together to solve puzzles or to play a game together in a virtual

**Figure 7.1.** Two Avatars Working Together to Win a Virtual Game Against a Team of Co-Workers in Another Part of the Physical World

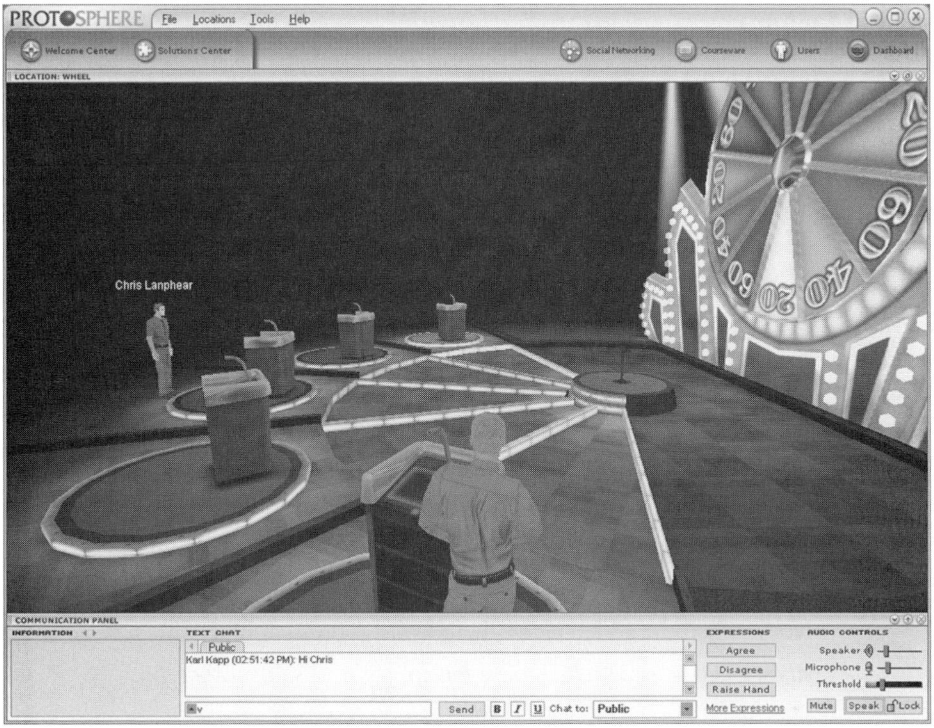

space—the facilitator could even serve as the host in these situations to monitor the game and the associated learning, as shown in Figure 7.1.

## Allow Opportunities to Demonstrate Learning

One of the most critical aspects of training is the transfer of skills learned in the classroom into the actual work environment. VIEs provide learners with the opportunity to practice skills under the guidance of the facilitator in an environment that mirrors the actual workplace in digital form.

When designing a context for these types of sessions, provide time for both instructor review of the application of the skills taught and peer-to-peer review of actions and results. Having an avatar go through the exact same motions as the person will need to on-the-job, in an environment similar to the workplace, is an excellent assessment of the ability of the person to transfer the skills learned in the VIE session to their job.

## Build in Incentives

In designing a VIE, context that leverages immersion and interactivity to increase engagement, incentivization, or "tokening" becomes a key lever. Sylvia's team created exercises for Jack and his colleagues to win "learning bucks." The promise of winning those tokens drove much of the engagement in the specific challenge activities. Game developers have long leveraged tokening to drive a perpetual flow state in gamers. Managing the fine line between challenge and boredom by introducing leveling and tokens is central to the huge adoption and usage numbers that successful games such as *World of Warcraft* have achieved. As we move into delivering instruction in a virtual learning environment, it makes sense to learn from our colleagues in the gaming industry to help leverage incentives and tokening to make learning both instructional and engaging. However, there are risks with this approach, such as making it seem like a game to upper management; incentives needs to be added carefully to avoid too much of a game feel. A careful balance needs to be struck between tokens and self-motivation.

# Leveraging the ADDIE Model

How does Sylvia know how to design learning for a VIE? First, she follows the general design points described above. Second, she relies on a proven method of designing instruction known as the ADDIE model. She follows the basic process of Analysis, Design, Development, Implementation, and Evaluation. Creating valid instruction within a VIE requires following a systematic process of the five-step ADDIE model. While designing a virtual learning experience requires some different considerations, affordances, and concepts, the basic underlying process of the ADDIE model cannot be ignored.

Perhaps the biggest difference is that a team creating a VIE needs to take into account not only the design of the content but also the design of the environment in which the learning is going to take place. This is much different from traditional instructional design, where you simply design the sequence and content of the instruction. With VIEs, you also need to design the context in which the instruction occurs. The instructional designer must become a context designer and consider things like building architecture, peer-to-peer interactions, informal learning spaces, and learner-to-object interactions. Other considerations include whether or not the environment "talks" to the learner through voice, text, or note cards. Can the learner experience "death" within the VIE? What degree of realism is required for successful learning? Is a surreal environment meaningful to learning?

Let's examine how these questions can be addressed within the ADDIE framework to create an optimal virtual learning experience.

## Analysis

Without a careful analysis of content, learners, and technology, problems will occur and the virtual learning environment will become a large software investment that failed to pay off. Without analysis, problems such as developing instruction that doesn't match the needs of the learners, designing instruction that is not really needed, reconfiguring poor stand-up materials as poor virtual-world learning, or developing spaces that don't attract learners are bound to occur. Problems can even occur when the virtual world doesn't run on the current network. None of these situations is favorable.

To help ensure success, an analysis must be performed prior to launching into a virtual world learning experience. Typically, the analysis step of the ADDIE process consists of examining four main areas. The first is the *task, concept,* or *skill* to be taught. The second is the *environment* in which the learning should occur. The third is the *technical considerations* required to have learners interact within the VIE, and the fourth area is an analysis of *the learners* who will be interacting within the VIE.

**Task, Concept, or Skill.** When deciding whether a task, concept, or skill can be appropriately taught in a virtual learning world, consider several variables. The first is determining the type of content being taught. Is it facts and jargon or concepts and procedures, or is it problem solving? Identifying the type of knowledge, as shown in Table 5.1, will help with the rest of the process of creating the instruction. The analysis of the content provides direction in terms of selecting the right learning archetype.

Another variable to examine is whether or not the instruction requires group coordination. If the task is related to multiple groups interacting and working together in real time to accomplish a goal or solve a problem, a virtual world makes sense.

A VIE will allow learners who are spread out in different geographical locations to practice coordinating activities and working together. For example, creating a real-life full-scale exercise in the area of a mock disease outbreak or natural disaster takes a lot of advanced preparation, requires day-long drills, and often involves the coordination of dozens of mock patients, which is expensive and time-consuming. But a VIE allows for the run-through of a mass casualty event numerous times, with the ability to easily change the parameters. First-responders can practice working together in a variety of virtual situations.

VIEs can also be effective in teaching people how to react in group settings when individuals have to work together under pressure. Because of the realism of a VIE, it is possible to place learners into situations in which emotions may run high and the pressure is on for them to perform. When people are put into these types of situations in which they must work together, they react as they would in the actual situation. For example, some people will make bad decisions or they will do or say inappropriate things. These tendencies can be examined in the relative safety of a training event.

**Environment.** The next area to consider is the environment in which the learning should occur. Should the learning be in a realistic environment? Should it be in a more stylized or surreal setting—or even a setting not possible in real life? The immersion can be realistic, such as putting a person in a sales situation and asking her to perform, or it can be more surreal, like having a doctor walk through a giant heart to gain another perspective on human anatomy.

When the learning environment requires realism, virtual worlds are an effective solution. They can mimic the physical world by realistically depicting cityscapes, vehicles, and machinery. If the fidelity required to ensure optimal performance is high, virtual worlds can provide the necessary realism. The graphical and auditory realism of many virtual worlds allow for highly realistic depictions of realistic objects. This can be critical when teaching the operation of gages, dials, and switches. It also provides an authentic environment in which the learner can practice. Virtual worlds can also allow for the inclusion of realistic settings, clothing, and weather conditions. All of these visual cues become encoded in the learner's mind and make it easier for him or her to recall the learning in the exact setting in which it is required.

The realistic virtual environment also makes it ideal for teaching learners a dangerous process or a procedure in a safe environment. Simulations have been used for years to teach how to conduct dangerous procedures such as fighting a battle or troubleshooting a nuclear reactor in a safe manner. VIEs offer the same protection. VIEs have the ability to immerse the learners in a realistically depicted replica of the dangerous environment in which they need to perform.

Conversely, another advantage of VIEs is that they can provide the learner with an immersive experience in which he or she could not otherwise venture. For example, a person can be dropped into the center of a volcano or shrunk to the size of a molecule and explore the blood stream or even experience life as a member of the opposite gender. VIEs can provide a context for teaching difficult-to-grasp concepts through immersion of the learners into a completely foreign environment.

Another element of the environment is the level of stress. Virtual worlds can create a great deal of stress on the leaner through moving objects, sounds, surprise elements appearing on screen, and other techniques to induce an uneasiness within the learner. This can be highly useful if the actual environment in which the learner will be performing will be stressful, such as a military action or dealing with an evolving natural disaster. In these types of situations, a VIE can provide a fertile training ground for the affective or emotional domain of learning. VIEs can be used to instruct a learner on how to handle stress and work within a difficult environment while keeping his or her emotions in check.

Examples of such environments include:

- Emergency room team;
- Team selling;
- Combat;

- First-responder activities;

- Compliance activities;

- Event planning/coordination;

- Multiple scenarios; and

- Security (building, ports).

**Technical Considerations.** One area that can quickly derail a virtual learning effort is technical obstacles. Many organizations do not have the graphical cards or processing power to run VIEs with any level of proficiency. This can be a problem when the VIE lags or operates slowly. Ineffective operation can greatly detract from the learner experience. Additionally, many organizations have problems with bandwidth requirements. VIEs can utilize a great deal of bandwidth, which can slow an operations system to a crawl. If an external host is available to work with your VIE, you still may encounter IT department problems such as ports that are not open, inability to download client software to run the virtual world, and other problems. Conduct an analysis of the types of servers available, firewall issues, client computer capabilities, and other technical specifications to ensure that the virtual learning world will function properly when launched.

**Learners.** One of the most important elements is the readiness of the learners to engage in a VIE. It is important to understand that the best developed VIE will not be successful if the learners don't understand how to gain access to the world, how to navigate through the world, or how to set up their avatars. All of these items can be trained, but first the organization needs to understand the level virtual world acumen of the learners. If they are not familiar with virtual worlds, plans will need to be made for some basic education and instruction before a full-scale learning event can be planned in a virtual world.

To determine knowledge and familiarity with VIEs, consider conducting surveys to determine whether learners use similar worlds at home or if they are completely unfamiliar with the concept. If they have not participated in virtual worlds, this will inform the process of creating the instructional experience for the learners.

# Design

This element of the ADDIE model involves the application of appropriate instructional strategies to the design of a 3DLE. An instructional strategy is a method of influencing a learner's ability to understand and acquire knowledge, skills, and information. Strategies are the techniques used to ensure the learner is actually learning from the VIE. They involve sequencing, interaction, and methods of instruction. The design process is informed by the analysis. The information gathered in the first step feeds into the design considerations of the learning.

**Synchronous or Asynchronous.** One of the first decisions to make in designing a 3DLE is to determine whether the learning will occur in a synchronous environment led by an instructor or in an asynchronous environment in which the learner proceeds at his or her own pace. VIEs can accommodate both types of learning, but each must be planned and coordinated to ensure the optimal learning occurs. As indicated in Chapter 5, certain types of learning archetypes such as tours and scavenger hunts can be done effectively in a self-paced environment, while problem solving works well in an instructor-led format.

Some questions to consider are

- Will an instructor or facilitator be present to guide the activity and set the parameters for interaction?

- Is interaction with other learners required for the activity?

- Is the activity supported by the 3DLE (meaning the environment matches the activity, like teaching security checks in an environment in which the security guard will be working)?

- Can the learners self-navigate through the environment and learn simultaneously?

- Can educational elements be placed within the environment and learners interact with those elements independently? Does the environment "talk" to the learner through text or voice?

**Sequence and Instructional Elements.**  Designing the 3DLE requires careful consideration of the entire educational experience of the learner. Consider the following questions when designing a 3DLE:

- What happens first?

- How do learners interact (voice/text)?

- Where do you want the learners to go?

- What are the desired learning outcomes?

- Do you add pressure elements (time, score)?

- How realistic do you want actions?

The design of the learning should also consider learning activities that will occur during the instruction.

- What do learners do?

- How do they receive instructions?

- How do they know what to do?

- How are the learners going to be observed?

- Do actions in the environment adversely impact the health of the avatar?

- How will you score success?

- How explicit are the instructions?

**Environment and Structures.**  Another consideration for the design of a 3D learning event is the creation of the environment in which the learning takes place. This involves determining the level of realism but, even more than that large decision, it requires consideration of the type of structures and spaces that are created to facilitate the learning.

One mistake many people make in designing spaces for 3D learning is to attempt to mimic as closely as possible actual structures or spaces. This can be limiting and makes it difficult to navigate with the avatar. In a VIE, an avatar needs more room to walk down hallways and to move around objects than a real person in the physical world does.

For example, make the ceilings a little higher than normal because avatars may jump or teleport to an area and land on top of each other and may become confused. Additionally, an avatar may attempt to fly within a room, and a low ceiling is a flying hazard. When designing a 3D learning space, consider the movement of the avatar and do not make the buildings 100 percent to scale. When creating a meeting space for a large group of people, there is no need to add a roof or walls; it is possible to control the weather in a virtual environment so there is no need to have a roof. Also, in many VIEs it is possible to create transparent or phantom walls or roofs. If one of these types of structures exists, an avatar can pass right through the seemingly solid object like ghosts. This is convenient when you want the space to look as realistic as possible but want to simplify the navigation for the learners. See Bart Pursel's advice on building 3D spaces for learning in the sidebar.

When considering the creation of gathering spaces, a method that IBM has found to be effective is to create a large meeting space in the middle of an area and then create smaller breakout spaces surrounding the main meeting space. They design such spaces in an X pattern with the large meeting space in the middle and the small breakout rooms at each end of the X.

---

## Designing Learning Spaces in VIE

### Barton Pursel

Designing 3D spaces in virtual worlds can be tricky business. Depending on the goal of your design, several domains exist that can help shape a good 3D environment in a VIE. One domain that jumps to mind is architecture, but be careful. Architects are normally trained in the design of 3D spaces in the physical world, which is *much* different from the various 3D virtual worlds available today. Using a blend of instructional design, game design, and web design, you

*(Continued)*

can begin to prototype environments in VIE that offer a wide breadth of experiences for end-users. Some tips on designing for VIEs:

1.  Always begin with a clear goal before thinking about design. If you are working on an instructional project, identify the need that your 3D environment will address or the overall objective you are attempting to address. If it is more of a game-like environment, be sure you can succinctly and clearly state the experience(s) you want your users to have within the environment. Once you do this, it helps to identify what specific 3D environment you might want to use for your design, as well as what type of affordances exist in these 3D environments that will reinforce your objective or intended experience.

2.  Align the affordances of the virtual world with your objective or experience. Affordances in virtual worlds refer to the qualities the virtual world exhibits that allows a user to perform specific actions. For example, Second Life provides a user with several modes of transportation, including teleporting and flying (*Note:* these can be disabled on individual areas in Second Life). These affordances alone make Second Life a *very* different place compared to the physical world, where we cannot fly or teleport to specific locations. If we were designing a museum in order to educate students on various types of dinosaurs in the physical world, we would need to include things like walking directions from exhibit to exhibit. If we did something similar in Second Life, due to the affordances the environment provides, we can simply create teleporters that will take the students' avatars to each exhibit with a single click.

3.  Design for avatars. Controlling avatars in VIEs can be difficult, much more difficult than controlling our own physical bodies in the real world. Things like navigating a hallway or a flight of stairs in a virtual world can be very difficult at times. One reason for this is the camera controls for the virtual world. To borrow terminology from video games, most virtual worlds use what is called a third-person view. We see the world from a third=person perspective, often looking at the backside of our avatar as we navigate 3D space. In the real world, we see through our eyes, what is called first-person view in games. This difference in perspectives makes navigating in virtual worlds much more difficult at times. This can also cause what is called "camera clipping." As your

avatar makes a 90-degree turn in a narrow hallway, the camera may actually swing outside of the hallway, cutting off your view of your avatar and essentially forcing you to navigate blindly. Another consideration is latency. Some virtual worlds require a great deal of graphics and CPU horsepower to render hundreds of textures and animations on the computer screen at a time. This occasionally causes some objects or textures to load slowly, taking several seconds to fully come into view. This can cause confusion at times, as an avatar may not see a wall blocking the path to an exhibit he is trying to navigate.

One rule of thumb is to design everything in virtual worlds 30 percent larger than the real world. This rule of thumb is used by several VIE designers because it helps to compensate for the sometimes awkward or complex controls for moving an avatar in 3D space as well as camera clipping.

4. When prototyping, make sure the specific things you prototype have a purpose. Returning to the museum design, focus on prototyping specific exhibits featuring content that is critical to the objective or experience you're creating for the end-user. Many designers become bogged down in designing everything at once, including things like doors, walkways, staircases, and so on. These are elements of the virtual world that serve very little purpose but will take someone time and effort to design and develop. You want to spend the majority of time and energy working on specific elements that are directly applicable to your goal and can also be tested. Once you have created a single exhibit, ask other designers to interact with it. Better yet, try and gain access to a sample that represents your intended audience.

You may even find that you do not need certain elements in a virtual world that exist in the real world. Doors are a great example of this. Why does my avatar need to open and step through a door to move between rooms? In the real world, doors have a variety of purposes, such as safety or temperature control. In the virtual world, often these purposes are irrelevant. Make sure the parts of your design all serve some sort of specific purpose. After you brainstorm the design, it can be helpful to list all the different elements that need to be modeled and go through them one by one, making sure these elements serve some sort of functional purpose.

*(Continued)*

5. Familiarity versus usability. This is a very delicate balance to strike and something many designers struggle with. When working on your design, ask yourself: How realistic should this be? If I'm building a virtual museum as part of an architectural course to demonstrate my knowledge of museum layout and structure, the final museum should be realistic and will likely be familiar to end-users; they will arrive and enter a structure in the virtual world that looks and feels like a museum does in the real world, as shown in Figure 7.2.

If I'm building a museum to house a collection of paintings, I am no longer bound to create something realistic or familiar. I can now turn my attention to creating something that is usable based on the affordances of the virtual world. Does my museum require rooms? Multiple floors? Does it even need to reside in a virtual building?

If I'm building this in a VIE where learners can fly, why not take advantage of the fact that users can fly (as shown in Figure 7.3)? This allows you to build upward (which can also save space). What about the problem of latency and camera clipping? Typical museums are comprised of various rooms with

---

**Figure 7.2.** Designing a Virtual Museum Using a Paradigm Bound by the Physical World

hallways and doorways. If these elements are not critical to the design, why not create the museum outdoors? Now avatars can maneuver in 3D space without worrying about camera clipping or navigating from room to room without any idea of the exhibits being displayed around a corner.

The great thing about VIEs is that they allow us to create powerful experiences for end-users. Not understanding how to design for these spaces will have an immediate adverse effect on the end-user's experience. Think of a bad website experience you've had. Was it a site that had specific information, but you could not find it due to poor information architecture or search? Was it a website that was difficult to navigate? These types of usability concepts should be considered when designing VIEs because they all impact the experience of the end-user. If you create a fantastic virtual museum with phenomenal exhibits, but the end-user struggles to navigate the 3D space or becomes lost in the vast corridors of the structure, you are adversely impacting the user's experience. Be sure you are continually testing and iterating your design so when the final build is complete, you can be confident the end-user will have a great experience.

**Figure 7.3.** Designing a Virtual Museum Using the Affordances of a VIE

**Design Outside of Reality.** One strong advantage of virtual learning worlds is that they can be used to create extraordinary places and have the ability to transport learners back in time. One can create ancient Egypt or an ancient battlefield and let learners explore. It is possible to design an underwater scavenger hunt and allow learners to walk on the bottom of the ocean or explore a constellation. Create environments that excite the senses, that are fun, and that are educationally challenging.

**Consider the Debriefing.** One important element of learning in an interactive environment is to provide a proper level of debriefing so the learners can understand the experiences they had and reflect upon their learning. In fact, reflection is one of the seven principles discussed in Chapter 4. The debriefing process can be important for both a synchronous learning experience as well as an asynchronous experience. Some questions to consider for a debriefing are

- Who conducts debriefing?
- What will be the focus?
- How does the instructor observe?
- Is it provided in a written format?
- Where does it take place?

**Storyboard.** Because the development of a 3DLE is complex and multi-layered, many developers first design the 3DLE with a storyboard and actually build the environment only after the storyboards have been created and the learning event "walked through." The step of creating a storyboard helps to ensure that the environment that is created encourages the desired learning. Storyboards also enable the expensive development process to run more effectively because it is easier to alter a storyboard than a completed virtual environment. This is similar to the storyboard process used to create movies. The learning experience is planned and then it is made a reality in the next step of the process. An example of a storyboard is shown in Figure 7.4.

## Develop

Develop is the part of the ADDIE model wherein the virtual learning environment is created. This is where the combination of 3D structures, spaces,

**Figure 7.4.** Storyboard for the Creation of a 3DLE Within a VIE to Teach the Concepts of Volume and Surface Area

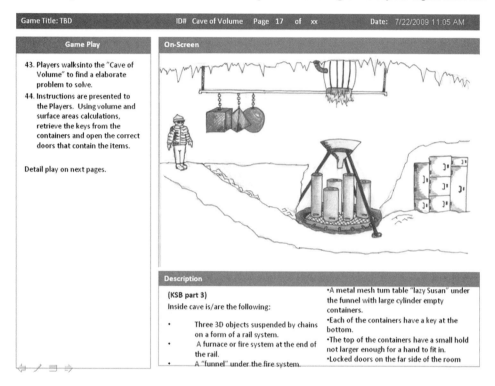

and design combine with other elements to create the instruction. The develop step of the model involves translating the instructional strategies into the 3DLE that will be used to deliver the instruction and provide the learner experience. While this is an important part of the ADDIE model, it can only be successful if the analysis and design are done properly.

To develop a VIE, the instructional designer, context developer, and programmer must work closely together to make the vision outlined in the design step a reality. This team takes the storyboards and makes them a reality within the VIE. This process occurs when the context developer creates the spaces, buildings, vehicles, and/or machinery that needs to be created and the programmer scripts the proper functionality.

While many times a 3DLE is built from scratch, with the increasing popularity of virtual worlds, it is possible to purchase many items that might be needed to create a learning experience.

For example, if you were training first-responders in Second Life, it is possible to purchase virtual helicopters, police cars, fire trucks, and other items to complete the learning environment. Organizations can take advantage of the growing popularity of virtual worlds and can purchase many items that, only a few years ago, they would have had to build from scratch. Organizations can even take advantage of the fact that many items already exist, even if they are not creating the virtual learning worlds themselves. Readily available digital assets mean that the overall development cost charged by vendors can be lower because they can use pre-existing items in the virtual learning experience.

## Implement

The next step in the ADDIE model is the implementation of the 3DLE. This is the process of rolling out the virtual learning instruction to the learners or organization. To help with the smooth implementation of the VIEs, consider the following items prior to starting the learning event:

- Make sure everyone can access the VIE prior to the actual event. Consider having a "dry run" exercise.

- Ensure that all technical specifications, potential firewall issues, and other requirements are addressed prior to the learning event for learners who will be engaged during the event.

- Send advance notices about when and where to meet.

- Set up a site outside of the VIE for correspondences and messages using a wiki or an online community.

- Make sure learners have an avatar prior to the learning experience.

- Encourage learners to explore the VIE prior to class so they are somewhat oriented when the learning event begins.

During the implementation of the learning event, consider the following:

- Make sure everyone can do basic navigation. Start with an orientation exercise.

- Make sure learners know where to go before starting the instruction.

- Regardless of the instructional archetype, create a gathering place for learners for pre- or post-briefings.

- Establish methods of communication with the entire group.

- Make sure instructions are clear. Vague instructions are hard to follow, so provide instructions in written format if possible.

- Provide a time limit for the instructional exercise.

- As the instructor, go group to group to see how the learners are doing and to answer any questions specific to a particular group (if a group exercise).

- If the setting is more classroom-oriented, provide a mechanism for hand-raising and for developing an orderly method of calling on learners.

- Establish rules of behavior in terms of gestures, sounds, building, and other activities that might interfere with instruction.

After the 3DLE event is over:

- Conduct a debriefing.

- Make sure future assignments are clear so everyone understands.

- Assign in-world activities outside of formal meeting time to keep learners involved with the VIE when not officially meeting. This fosters informal learning.

- Provide opportunities for after-class, informal, peer-to-peer learning and exchange of information.

Marketing of the VIE, creating a roll-out plan, and convincing the organization to adopt the created 3DLE are also important factors in the implementation step and are addressed in Chapter 8.

## Evaluation

This is the quality control process that ensures an instructionally sound, bug-free 3DLE. The evaluation process needs to occur at all stages of the process. The goal is to create a high-quality experience for the learners. Plans should be made to evaluate both the learners' acquisition of knowledge, skills, and information, as well as the quality of the VIE.

In some instances, evaluating the learners should consist of assessing their ability to perform the desired task. This can be a cognitive task such as problem solving or a procedural task such as inspecting a container for possible damage. In these cases, the assessment should be as authentic as possible. The goal is to provide practice in an environment as realistic as possible, as shown in the EY example in Chapter 6. When teaching concepts such as having someone fly around a molecule or witness a virtual tsunami, the goal is to assess the knowledge gained from the experience.

The second type of evaluation is to determine whether the instruction is sound. This is done by aggregating results across multiple learners to determine whether the instruction was effective. Tracking results and keeping measurements on successful learning is important to ensure the design and approach are effective for the desired learning.

# Step-by-Step Designing Process

Here is a step-by-step process for designing and launching a VIE within an organization.

*Step One:* Identify the learning objective and outcomes required of learners.

*Step Two:* Determine the content that must be learned to enable participants to achieve the desired outcomes. Analyze the learners, environment, technology, and organizational readiness for VIEs.

*Step Three:* Determine that content is appropriate for learning within a VIE. Choose the dominate macrostructure and ensure the other macrostructures are addressed at some level.

*Step Four:* Decide the learning archetype most appropriate for the content. Consider whether instruction should be synchronous, asynchronous, or a combination.

*Step Five:* Create storyboards outlining the environment and flow of the instructional sequence, and map content to the environment in a manner appropriate with the chosen learning archetype.

*Step Six:* Build or purchase the necessary digital assets for the virtual learning environment.

*Step Seven:* Determine a method for evaluating the learning, and map learning outcomes to business outcomes.

*Step Eight:* Ensure that technical obstacles such as downloads, open ports, firewalls, and graphic cards have been addressed.

*Step Nine:* Create guidelines to inform the facilitator and learners of what they will be doing in the virtual learning environment. Create debriefing exercises to ensure learning.

*Step Ten:* Conduct a pilot test of the environment with a small group of learners to work out any issues or obstacles.

*Step Eleven:* Provide sessions to teach learners how to navigate in a virtual world if they are novices to ensure that navigation issues don't interfere with learning.

*Step Twelve:* Launch and conduct the 3DLE.

*Step Thirteen:* Debrief the learning experience.

*Step Fourteen:* Gather feedback on the experience and modify the virtual learning environment as required.

*Step Fifteen:* Measure learning outcomes against on-the-job performance to measure impact of learning.

# Working with a Third-Party Virtual World Vendor

For most organizations, even with full knowledge of ADDIE and a team of instructional designers, the cost, expense, and effort involved in creating a

3DLE will not be borne internally. Most likely an organization will contract with a vendor. Ideally, it will be an experienced vendor that has created successful virtual learning experiences before. This can be difficult given the myriad of different virtual learning world products. Some vendors offer perpetual worlds that are always available, others offer one-time events like virtual conferences, while still others offer a specific virtual scene or scenario.

There are a number of preliminary things to consider when beginning to look for vendors to assist you in developing a virtual learning world and the upcoming essay by Eilif Trondsen provides a list of questions you should ask any VIE vendor before working with him or her. Tying the following considerations with the top ten list by Trondsen will put your organization in a good position to purchase the services of VIE vendors.

## Tie Your Request to a Business Need

Successful projects start by aligning virtual world needs with your organization's goals. Whether the goal is to reach out to alumni through a shared virtual space or to create a virtual machine shop to teach safety to mechanics, the underlying purpose, academic goal, or business objective must be articulated to the vendor. When the vendor understands the business requirements or academic need, he or she can better craft the solution.

## Know What to Expect

The virtual learning marketplace is relatively young and is just now beginning an accelerated growth path. This means that companies will appear and disappear; mergers and acquisitions will occur at a high rate; and companies will suddenly arrive out of nowhere with new and improved virtual world technologies. The virtual world marketplace is growing fast, and there are many different players. It is still too young for any major shakeouts to have occurred. So it is important for you to understand the vendor landscape, the technologies, the learning potential, and the affordances of VIE. You need to understand what is happening within the field before you can make informed decisions. Attend tradeshows focused on 3DLEs, read blogs by virtual learning thought leaders, read publications and vendor brochures, look at websites, and educate yourself on the vast number of virtual world options. Immediately limiting yourself to one or two well-known virtual world vendors will limit your choices and options. Speaking only with vendors provides a limited view of the field. You need to explore. Take the time to read industry literature and become educated on the direction of the field before you rush into choosing a vendor to build a learning space.

## Be Specific About Your Requirements

Vendors cannot read your mind. They need a direction and a concept of what you want to achieve with the virtual learning world. It is acceptable to speak with vendors to help clarify what you want at trade shows and venues created for such interactions, but when you finally craft a request for proposal, make sure you have a clear understanding of the requirements you need. The clearer you are about what you need from a vendor, the better able he or she will be to provide you with a solution that meets your needs. Even if you want the vendor to help craft your solution, be clear that you are looking for advice and counsel, versus implementing a fully developed idea.

## Do Your Homework

You need to research the vendor to gage his or her level of experience and knowledge before undergoing a project. It is okay to take a chance on a smaller or less experienced vendor (or even students) if you are launching a small-scale proof of concept virtual learning experience. However, if you are launching an enterprise-wide initiative, you need to ask some serious and difficult questions to potential vendors (see the sidebar by Eilif Trondsen).

## Visit the Virtual Space Yourself

It is one thing to hear or read about a virtual learning space; it is something altogether different to immerse yourself in a 3D world. You need to become immersed in any potential virtual world you plan on purchasing. Ask the vendor whether you can log in to a demo site or into an example of a virtual world and explore that world for a while. Watching a machinima or example is not enough. You need to test drive the virtual learning environment yourself to determine how it functions, ease of navigation, and comfort level with speaking to other avatars. Take time to log in and see it first-hand. You want to have some time by yourself to explore the product and understand how it works before you commit to a large scale implementation of that particular vendor's virtual learning environment.

---

# The Top Ten Questions You Should Ask Any VIE Vendor Before Hiring Him or Her
## Eilif Trondsen

1. What are the five most successful VIE projects you have done for clients and what data/metrics did your client collect that prove the success of the project?

2. How do you work with your clients to make their projects successful? And please give specific examples.

3. What is the current status of the VIE projects you have worked on last year? What kinds of challenges did you and your clients run into, and how did you overcome them?

4. What are the most difficult use/adoption issues you have faced with your clients, and what lessons learned will be of value to our current project?

5. What is your future vision for VIEs' use and adoption, and what are some of the key elements in your roadmap that will support us in building long-term, sustained success of our VIE project?

6. What have you learned from your past projects when it comes to how to get target users involved, excited, and engaged?

7. What do you see as your most important competitive differentiator, and what do you expect to do in the next few years to stay ahead of your competitors?

8. Who can you connect us with in your clients' companies so we can hear their perspectives of what some of their key VIE deployment issues were?

9. How can we integrate some of our Web 2.0 tools and technologies and enterprise systems with your VIE platform to achieve the greatest benefit?

10. How can you support us globally as we deploy your VIE platform, and what is your previous experience in operating globally?

# Implications for Trainers and Educators

Developing a VIE requires the crafting of a learning environment, as opposed to a focus solely on content. The implication is that teams are going to be required to build effective virtual-world learning experiences. In addition, the time frame for building these worlds will be greater than putting together a slide deck to teach within a virtual classroom. It will also take more effort to mold the environment into a state where it can be used effectively in the teaching process. The traditional methodology of using analysis, design, development, implementation, and evaluation is still valid; it just needs to be modified slightly to accommodate the richness of virtual learning worlds. Trainers and educators will need to work closely with designers and others to create the right learning. The process will most likely involve the use of an external vendor, and plans have to be made to ensure the vendor will meet the needs of your VIE. While the process of designing your own or hiring a vendor to create a VIE may seem long and cumbersome, the results can be dramatic as learners gain knowledge and experience by participating in these environments.

# Steps to Successful Enterprise Adoption

## Introduction

Convincing an organization to adopt the use of a VIE for learning and collaboration is a difficult task. While immersive learning environments provide tremendous value, the effective adoption and implementation of a VIE does not occur without focused effort. Some opponents see the use of 3D technology as childish; others see it as a waste of resources; and others view it as yet another learning fad. Successfully overcoming objections and implementing a VIE requires identifying potential adopters of the technology, overcoming obstacles, choosing the right implementation strategy and pilot group, selling the attractive attributes of VIEs, and properly building a business case. If these steps are carefully navigated, the implementation process achieves success. Without a careful plan, the results will be another technology on the scrap heap.

The planning process starts with an understanding of the answers to the questions: What makes technology attractive to people? And why are some technologies adopted rapidly while others like the doomed Betamax or the 3Com Audrey are not adopted and eventually disappear? Research has shown that the adoption of new technologies and ideas follows a specific trajectory through social groups. Knowledge of that trajectory and what makes technology attractive to potential adopters is an important element in helping an organization adopt VIEs for learning.

After the technology trajectory is understood, the next step is to identify how certain individuals react to the implementation of new technological innovations. Again, research provides insights into positioning the "technology sale" according to a potential adopter's location on a technology adoption continuum. One size does not fit all when positioning innovative technologies with potential adopters. The study of the convergence of technology attractiveness, the adopter's location on the technology adoption continuum and the rate of acceptance of new technology is called the *diffusion of innovations*.[1]

Understanding the diffusion of innovations process within an organization serves as a required foundation for creating a meaningful business case to bring VIE technology into the organization. A formal business case makes the adoption of VIE technology more palatable to executives and others who must approve the purchase.

Although gaining approval with the backing of a well-conceived business plan is critical, the real struggle occurs during the implementation phase. Even if upper management approves the new technology, getting others to adopt it can be a challenge. To combat this reluctance, a combination of an effective implementation plan and an understanding of the diffusion of innovations come into play. Leveraging those concepts makes the implementation less painful. Starting with a pilot group keeps the initial implementation manageable, helps to work out any potential organizational issues, and can be instrumental in avoiding obstacles to ultimate success and adoption within the enterprise.

# Diffusion of Innovations

The pioneer of the Diffusion of Innovations Theory is Everett Rogers, who researched, experimented, and wrote extensively on the subject. Rogers defined the term *diffusion* as "the process in which an innovation is communicated through certain channels over time among the members of a social system."[2] Rogers contends that *diffusion* as a type of communication has special characteristics because of the newness of the idea in the message content and the degree of uncertainty and perceived risk to the potential adopter. Rogers' ideas have been echoed in such works as *The Tipping Point* by Malcolm Gladwell and *Crossing the Chasm* by Geoffrey Moore. The difficulty with diffusing an innovation is that no one wants to adopt a new technology and have it fail, especially within conservative organizations like corporations and universities.

## Attractiveness Criteria[3]

In his research, Rogers uncovered a list of "attractiveness" criteria that influence the adoption of technology into an organization. Rogers indicates that, when positioning a technology for adoption, it is advantageous to the rate of adoption to focus the message on these attractiveness criteria. This is especially important when the innovation carries with it a stigma of being childish or gimmicky, as is sometimes the case with VIEs that tend to get lumped together with commercial games like *World of Warcraft*, *City of Heroes*, *EverQuest,* and others.

The attractiveness criteria must be leveraged when trying to influence executives, college deans, managers, and even peers on the value of VIEs; focusing on these criteria make the job of selling the concept of VIEs easier.

**Relative Advantage.** The first criterion is *relative advantage*, which is the degree to which an innovation is perceived as being better than the idea it supersedes. Executives, managers, students, faculty, or employees must see the use of VIEs within the organization as having an advantage over existing training methodologies such as classroom instruction, traditional e-learning, or even 2D virtual classrooms. The concept of relative advantage is an important predictor of an innovation's rate of adoption. The more VIEs are seen as an advantage over other methods, the faster they will be adopted. If they are seen as equal or inferior to other types of learning environments or techniques, their adoption will be slowed.

To help others see the relative advantage of VIEs, emphasize the seven sensibilities, the collaborative aspects of the environment, and the ability for learners to travel to different locations, times, and environments—all from the safety of their favorite keyboards. It is important to show the advantage because many people don't see it themselves. In one example a faculty member who was already using 2D virtual classroom software didn't see how 3D software was any different, "It is just the same, only with avatars, and why would I want to be an avatar?" This person needed to be shown the relative advantage because he was not seeing the relative advantage on his own.

An effective method of showing a relative advantage is to benchmark against other organizations. A good place to start is to provide examples and case studies of how similar or rival organizations benefited from a VIE implementation. Let the executives, presidents, provosts, and managers know that they are not the first organization to try VIEs. This is where it becomes important to let individuals within the organization know that the use of VIEs is being rapidly adopted and some early pioneers have already had success. A good place to start is the case studies in Chapter 6. Also let them know that, if they fail to adopt, they may be at a disadvantage. The adoption of VIEs has begun to occur and within a few years will reach what Malcolm Gladwell calls the "tipping point," the point at which widespread adoption will occur on a massive level. The same process occurred with the Internet, cell phones, and with the social networking software such as Facebook and the messaging program Twitter. Helping others to see the widespread adoption of VIEs will help them see the advantage for their own organization.

Not only do executives, managers, deans, and provosts have to be convinced, but often rank-and-file employees and faculty shy away from VIEs for fear of the unknown or the perception that experimentation in these environments would be seen by colleagues as a waste of time. Employees may feel guilty or apprehensive about using VIEs.

To help overcome this resistance, teams must implement some type of "marketing" campaign to articulate the advantages of the technology.

The marketing campaign must show real business or educational reasons for the use of VIEs as indicated in many of the Lessons Learned sections of the case studies. While many of the advantages will be geared toward the entire organization, an effort must be made to "personalize" the advantages so each individual realizes the potential for personal gain by using VIEs.

**Compatibility.** Compatibility is the degree by which an innovation is perceived by the adopters as being consistent with the current mission of the organization, past experiences of the workforce or students, current technology, and needs of the learners. Positioning VIEs as a natural extension and convergence of existing technologies such as synchronous learning tools, video games, Web 2.0, and social networking—and not as a science-fiction-dream-come-to-life will go a long way toward the concept of compatibility.

The objective with showing compatibility is to let people see how the VIE fits with the overall learning strategy, goals, and culture of the organization. To help convince others to adopt the innovation you are selling, the use of the new technology or technique must not be perceived as an "overthrow" of all the methods that have come before—a complete overthrow is too radical for most executives, managers, faculty, students, and employees to accept. For example, the abandoning of all other types of training, e-learning, classroom instruction, and so on in favor of nothing but virtual learning worlds is an overthrow mentality—that may be your eventual goal, but it cannot be the battle cry.

Compatibility can be achieved by illustrating how the use of a VIE fits with the current practices of the company. For instance, if employees are now using classroom role plays to learn how to sell products in a traditional stand-up training class, explain how placing those same role plays into a virtual environment is an advantage in terms of time and opportunities for practice, as well as the ability to allow a company expert to virtually train dozens of employees without having to travel. Or show in an academic setting how the instructional objectives achieved within the virtual world are congruent with the objects accomplished using classroom techniques.

A critical aspect of compatibility is how well the innovation meets the needs of the current workforce or students. To create initial acceptance and leverage compatibility, build a strong case to show how virtual learning worlds augment and enhance existing training or educational curriculum.

**Complexity.** One justifiable fear many potential adopters have is a lack of knowledge of how to navigate in a VIE. They don't know how to interact or function within these 3D software platforms. People know what to expect in a 2D virtual class session or in a face-to-face classroom; they've attended dozens of similar sessions. Not so with a VIE. The interface, functionality, and experience level with VIEs are not universally high, and the lack of familiarity causes resistance and/or fear among potential users and decision-makers.

As Rogers points out, the complexity of an innovation, as perceived by members of a social system, is negatively related to its rate of adoption. The higher the perception of complexity, the slower the rate of adoption. Efforts must be made to train members of the organization on how to navigate and function within the VIE to reduce the perceived complexity.

One method to overcome the complexity issue is to conduct face-to-face classroom instructor-led sessions to teach learners the technology, etiquette, and navigation within VIEs. This technique was used by Sarah "Intellagirl" Robbins when she conducted her class in a VIE. One day a week the class was face-to-face, and the other weekly session was virtual.

An advantage to this approach is that, in a classroom, inexperienced learners can receive help from an instructor or more experienced peers if they are stuck or have a problem. This immediate, in-person assistance reduces frustration and the overall perception of complexity. The classroom environment can also be used to provide the mental message that it is "okay" to visit and interact in VIEs. This method was used often in the early days of e-learning when learners still were not familiar with web browsers or the conventions of the Internet. Nowadays, little time is spent explaining how to close windows or click on navigation buttons, but in the early days, training was needed on the interface. In the future, training will not be required on 3D interfaces either. The conventions will be universally known, as they are for Internet browsers.

Another method to minimize frustration and to keep the complexity issue in perspective is to help the learners understand that not all 3D learning experiences will be fun. Some will be difficult and frustrating, as is learning in many instances. Learners need to understand that frustration during the learning process is not necessarily a bad thing as long as it is centered on the learning process and not on some technological or navigational issue. Points of educational frustration often lead to memorable learning. Tying emotions to learning is a powerful combination, but the emotion shouldn't be tied to bumping into virtual walls with one's avatar. It should be tied to the desired learning outcome.

Another method to help reduce the perception of complexity is to team someone experienced or comfortable with VIEs with someone who is not. This provides the person who is not as knowledgeable with a tutor or mentor who can help him or her learn the ropes of a VIE in a one-on-one setting. Often the questions asked by the novice will encourage the experienced person to learn even more about the environment because he or she will be forced to seek answers for questions asked by the novice that he or she doesn't readily know.

Providing a basic tutorial on how to navigate and function in the VIE is also a good method for making the virtual learning world more accessible. Many learners skip right past the "tutorial" or "how-to-play" button, but a surprising number will take the time to learn how to operate within the VIE if the instructions are available. With many VIEs, orientation activities and instructions are available in-world. When the avatars enter the space, they are immediately placed into an orientation area and given specific tasks, which provide them with opportunities to learn how to navigate and interact within the environment.

Other organizations have a virtual greeter in-world at all times. The virtual greeter welcomes newcomers to the space, answers questions, and guides learners toward appropriate activities. The presence of a virtual greeter goes a long way toward reducing the perception of complexity and reduces learner frustration over navigation and functionality.

Finally, to keep the complexity to a minimum, design the VIE with avatar movement in mind and do not try to make it 100 percent accurate or to scale. As mentioned in Chapter 7, designing VIEs with the avatar's world in mind instead of the physical world will help remove confusion. Remember to make hallways larger, create outdoor venues, and think carefully before adding doors or windows to a virtual room.

**Trialability.** Trialability is the idea of "kicking the tires." People want to check out the VIE technology before they totally commit. According to Rogers, "New ideas that can be tried out on the installment plan will generally be adopted more quickly than innovations that are not divisible."[4] An innovation that is trialable represents less uncertainty to the individual who is considering it for adoption. The trialability of an innovation, as perceived by members of a social system, is positively related to its rate of adoption.

Set up a space with the VIE that people can check out without a specific goal or objective. This can be a large office, a dorm room, conference room, or even a garden or a campus—an open space with no objectives or specified activities that is easy to navigate. These types of environments can provide people with a chance to try out the VIE without feeling that they have to commit to using it right away.

Hold informal "tryout" events like a virtual cocktail party where people can go and just meet each other and explore the environment. It is important to note that early adopters of VIEs will perceive trialability as more important than later adopters will. The more innovative individuals will have no precedent to follow when they decide to adopt. Therefore, they need to try it out themselves. The later adopters will typically be surrounded by peers who have already accepted the innovation. The peers act as a vicarious trial, so later adopters don't have as much need to conduct their own trials.

**Observability.** Observability is the ability of one person to observe another person working within the technology. Establish the ability for someone to observe a 3DLE without being asked to participate. Arrange it so that colleagues can observe a role play in a VIE before being asked to participate.

An important aspect of observability is that the person being observed is of a similar status as the person doing the observation. The closer in status the observed person or organization is to the potential adopters, the more likely the adoption. Have executives and managers greet other executives and managers in the VIE. Have students greet other students and faculty greet faculty members. Provide examples of people at every level of the organization participating in the VIE. On an organizational level, find companies or educational institutions similar to your organization that are using VIEs for learning and education. Share those examples liberally.

Observability can also be provided via machinima. Machinima is a video created in the VIE using the avatars as actors and the environment as a set. The machinima should illustrate how 3DLEs are conducted and how people interact and navigate within the environment. Additionally, consider providing tip sheets and job aids that clearly define what happens in the VIE and what learners can expect to encounter within the environment. The more students and employees understand what happens within the VIE, the more likely they are to actively participate.

## Technology Adoption Continuum

While highlighting attractiveness criteria increases the speed of adoption of VIEs, different people are drawn to different criteria, depending on where they are on the technology adoption continuum. Certain employees or students will accept the use of VIEs more quickly than others. In any organizational system, there are five types of individuals on the adoption continuum. On one end of the continuum are the technology enthusiasts who embrace, almost blindly, any new technology just because it is new. On the opposite end are skeptics, who reject any use of new technology in a corporate, academic, or government setting.

In between there are technology visionaries, pragmatists, and conservatives. Each one is more hesitant to adopt technology than the last. The challenge is to present VIEs to the individuals within these different groups appropriately. The difficulty is that the "sales pitch" used for the technology enthusiasts and visionaries is exactly the opposite of the pitch used for the pragmatists, conservatives, and skeptics.

Another piece in the VIE adoption puzzle is a person known as a "knowledge broker," "gatekeeper," "opinion leader," or, as Malcolm Gladwell called them, "connectors."[5] These are the people within an organization or group who are connected to everyone and who exert a large amount of influence over technology adoption. The connector is a person who is able to influence other peoples' attitudes and behavior informally but doesn't tend to lead the charge.

The person leading the charge is called a change agent or, sometimes, the "champion." Champions typically leverage opinion leaders in a social system to help in diffusion activities. The champion is the person who sees the potential and possibility of VIEs and serves as an evangelist.

For the evangelist's message about VIEs to gain traction within an organization, the final person needed is a "sponsor." The sponsor is typically at the management or executive level of an organization and has money and resources to put behind the implementation. Sponsors are needed to ensure sustainable change. Champions can quickly run out of steam if they aren't backed by a sponsor.

To understand how to diffuse the innovation of VIEs into an organization, one must understand the motivation, triggers, and characteristics of each type of person on the technology adoption continuum. Once the unique characteristics are understood, the message can be tailored appropriately.

**Technology Enthusiasts.** These are the hard-core techies of the organization. These folks love technology because it is technology. Technology enthusiasts will be the first to embrace a new technology. They enjoy and are fundamentally committed to any new technology. They like to fiddle with various types of technology and want to be the first ones to explore new software tools. In fact, many of the true techies within the organization are already involved in some type of virtual world such as Second Life or World of Warcraft or Whyville or City of Heros or one of the other hundreds of virtual worlds already on the consumer market. These individuals are heavily vested in virtual world technologies at home and would enjoy using them at work.

The technology enthusiasts want to know all of the specifications, the system requirements, and any other technical aspect of the VIE that can be known. These are the people in the organization who are able to pick out the next big thing; they always have their eyes out for new technology. They subscribe to RSS feeds from dozens of technology blogs and websites and delight in being the first to know about some new technological advance. Techies are not interested in the business or educational advantages of virtual learning worlds; they are into the "newness" or "wow" factor of these worlds.

They ask the questions, "Is it cool?" and "Does it do neat stuff?" and "What are the specs of this software?" "How does it compare to other 3D virtual worlds?"

**Visionaries.** While the techies might not be interested in the business or educational advantages of VIEs, the visionaries are only interested in the business or educational advantage. They are not interested in technology for technology's sake. They want to know how this new technology is going to position the organization ahead of competitors or how it will help students learn more effectively and be more engaged. How are VIEs going to give them a strategic or tactical advantage? How are students going to become more educated by interacting in a 3DLE? How are employees going to benefit from participating in a 3DLE?

The visionaries typically look to the techies for advice and information about new technologies. They are able to effectively communicate with the techies. Visionaries will "quiz" the techies about the potential business and educational uses and whether or not other organizations are using these technologies. These individuals are important during the adoption of new technologies because they are able to translate the technological advantages of the VIE into business and educational advantages.

Visionaries are highly interested in VIEs because they are new to the business and educational environment and can be used as an advantage over competitors precisely because they are new.

Visionaries ask the question, "How can I use this new technology to my advantage before the competition gets hold of it?"

**Selling to Techies and Visionaries.** Together, the techies and the visionaries will be the early adopters of VIEs within an organization. Both the techies and the visionaries like the idea of a brand new technology, even if their reasons are slightly different—techies want to explore it, while visionaries want to exploit it.

VIEs appeal to both groups precisely because they are new and few other organizations are deploying them on a widespread basis. When selling the use of VIEs to these two groups, stress the newness of using them for business and distance education applications.

Specifically when selling to techies, let them know the software specifications, the hardware capabilities, and the technology behind them. Stress the newness of the technology and the innovative uses of VIEs. When selling to visionaries, let them know that it provides an advantage to themselves and their organization. Show them how the VIEs will provide a competitive advantage over others. Sell the "advantage" of the idea and the newness of the technology.

Unfortunately, the newness of VIEs is exactly what the pragmatists, conservatives, and skeptics dislike. These individuals, many of them organizational decision-makers, are not interested in pushing the envelope in either business or educational practices—and especially not with technological features. They want a solution that is more in line with the status quo. They want the "tried-and-true" approach and wonder what's wrong with classroom instruction.

**Pragmatists.** This group typically deliberates for some time before backing an innovation like the use of VIEs. This group wants the "proof" that VIEs are better educational tools than traditional methods. They want the white papers, the peer-reviewed research, and all the facts before proceeding. They want to know VIEs are being used by hundreds of other organizations before they will adopt them themselves.

While deliberate and demanding of proof, the pragmatists do not want to be the last group to adopt a new technology. If they see something is working and it seems to make sense, they will move to adopt. Not as quickly as the techies or the visionaries, but they will adopt VIEs after they see a few positive case studies and learn how other organizations are benefiting from the innovation. These are not the pioneers, but they follow close behind.

The pragmatists ask the questions, "Does this really work?" and "We aren't the pioneers, right?" Once they learn that it does work and that they are not the absolute first adopters, they will embrace VIEs.

**Conservatives.** Even less eager to embrace innovation are the conservatives. These individuals are extremely slow to adopt VIEs as business and educational tools and are extremely cautious about new technologies in general. Whereas the pragmatists want to know that VIEs are being used by hundreds of others, the conservatives want to know that they are being used by millions of others. This group is hard to please and a little cynical about new technologies.

Members of this group will not adopt the use of VIEs until the techies, visionaries, and pragmatists have all done so. They are unconvinced about the ability of VIEs to add any value to the organization. Conservatives want assurances that the use of new technologies is more or less like the use of older technologies—just better.

One mistake that is often made when trying to sell the concept of VIEs is spending a great deal of time concentrating efforts on trying to "convert" the conservatives to becoming enthusiastic about using VIEs. The effort is not worth the payoff. It is better to concentrate on the first three groups, and then the conservatives will eventually adopt VIEs because they will no longer be "new."

Conservatives ask the question, "What's the matter with doing this the traditional way? It has worked for years, and I don't understand why we need to change methods."

**Skeptics.** Skeptics will never think that VIEs are appropriate for learning. They delight in challenging the hype and claims of the advantages of VIEs. "This is childish." "Yes, it might be entertaining, but it doesn't teach." "Where is the evidence that 3DLE are better than instructor-led classroom teaching?" "It takes me three times as much effort to set up a lesson in a VIE; plus we need so many people in place to make it work." "The advantages don't outweigh the work." "Doesn't virtual classroom software do the same thing as VIEs for a lot less money?"

Skeptics will continually ask "innocent" questions in an attempt to undermine the implementation of VIEs. "What if people goof off in these virtual worlds?" "What if I get lost in the virtual world?" "What if my computer doesn't support the graphics?" They will even try to locate stories of failure to support their case.

Skeptics are quick to point out problems and exploit any mistakes or weaknesses in the implementation of VIEs. They are the ever-present critics of the new methodologies. Fortunately, there are usually only a few skeptics within any particular organization. Unfortunately, they tend to be highly vocal and attempt to persuade the pragmatists and the conservatives to become skeptics. The point of reference for skeptics is the past.

While you will want to educate the conservatives and pragmatists to avoid having them influenced by the skeptics, it is impossible to convert a true skeptic. Spending energy and resources attempting to convert skeptics is a waste of time. Let the skeptics vent, but focus energies on the other groups to achieve success.

Skeptics will tell you, "This will never work; it's a fad and a gimmick."

**Connectors.** Connectors know people throughout the organization. They easily move in and out of the social circles and are well respected by everyone for their knowledge and insights in a variety of areas. The connector influences the attitudes and even the overt behavior of others informally in a desired way with relative frequency. This informal leadership is not a function of the individual's formal position or status within the system. Opinion leadership is earned and maintained by the individual's technical competence, social accessibility, and conformity to the systems norms.

Connectors have a social network that allows them to serve as a social model whose innovative behavior is imitated by other members of the system. Connectors talk with the techies, find out what is cool, new, and provides a competitive advantage, describe those attributes to the visionaries, and influence the pragmatists and conservatives with their knowledge, confidence, and enthusiasm about VIEs.

Because of their influence, connectors are extremely important in the adoption continuum. If they are enthusiastic and pro-VIEs, then others in the organization will follow. If they are opposed, others will be as well.

Early in the adoption or sales process, identify the connectors of the organization and get them on board. This can be done by surveying or interviewing people in the organization to see whose opinion they value and respect. Once you have identified the connectors, provide them with information, resources, and evidence that the innovative use of VIEs will be valuable to themselves and to the organization. Send them to conferences, buy them books on the subject, and send them to benchmark against other organizations. Money invested in bringing a connector on board is well spent.

**Champions.** These folks tend to identify themselves as champions by their enthusiasm and energy surrounding the topic of VIEs and are usually visionaries. Champions are the ones who see the potential of the technology and want to let everyone know. For the champion to be effective, she needs to work with the connectors. Organizations need to have champions to spread the word and generate enthusiasm for the use of VIEs. Champions are willing to work through adversity and obstacles, even when it seems the organization is not ready or willing to adopt VIEs. The champion is usually a visionary on the technology adoption scale, but sometimes is a technology enthusiast.

**Sponsors.** The sponsor is the person who supports adoption of VIEs for learning but is typically not as loud or as enthusiastic as the champion. A sponsor is usually someone in a high position within an organization and can provide support via personnel or budget to help get a VIE project started. Sometimes the sponsor is the same as the champion, but that is usually not the case. The ideal traits of a sponsor is that he or she has money to put behind the project, a certain degree of autonomy from the rest of the organization, can assign personnel to the project, and is open to the use of new technologies. A manager of sales is typically a good prospect because he or she tends to have a group of employees who act relatively independently of the rest of the organization, tend to be geographically dispersed, and, in many cases, has what John Coné, former vice president of learning and development for Dell and Motorola, calls "lots of feet," meaning enough employees to have an impact with the technology and on the organization. Having a large number of employees who will benefit from the implementation of a VIE can help in the implementation and give the sponsor a good deal of leverage.

# Crafting the Business or Education Case for VIEs

The steps to building a business case for the introduction of VIEs into an organization is similar to building a business case for other tools, software acquisitions, or large-scale purchases. For an educational case, the steps are similar to requesting any new pedagogy or resources. A key element in the process is to analyze where the potential sponsor is in terms of the technology adoption continuum and use that knowledge to craft your argument. Additionally, use the attractiveness criteria to position the VIE relative to the needs of the organization. The specific steps in the process are

1. Create a problem statement.

2. Provide a problem description related specifically to the business or educational need you are trying to meet. Describe the current situation and indicate the cost of maintaining the status quo both in dollars and in lost productivity or opportunity.

3. Provide a proposed solution—the rationale for choosing a VIE and what you hope to accomplish via the implementation.

4. State the key objectives and success indicators of the VIE.

5. Describe how current systems like the learning management system (LMS) and legacy content will be addressed and/or integrated into the process.

6. Compare solutions by making a financial, business, and/or educational comparison and analysis of the value of the VIE versus other solutions.

7. Make the final recommendation for action.

When creating a business or educational case for implementation of an enterprise-wide VIE, the focus must be on the needs driving the adoption of the VIE and not on the technology. The VIE must solve a specific business need in corporations, and in educational institutions it must fill a specific educational or learning need. Identifying the need and presenting it to others starts by writing an effective problem statement.

## Problem Statement

Clearly state the problem you are trying to address by proposing the use of a VIE. The problem statement must be framed to address an actual need. You cannot write:

> The purpose of this business case is to propose the creation of a VIE to introduce a new technology to teach our sales force how to learn about new product launches without bringing them to headquarters for a training session.

> or

> The purpose of adopting a VIE is to provide students with a new technology environment in which they can study other cultures.

The focus of the above statements is on the technology and not on specific learning or business needs. It would be better to write:

> The purpose of this business case is to increase sales of our new products while simultaneously reducing training costs by providing

the sales force with a method to quickly and accurately sell our new products and overcome objections more quickly to increase overall corporate profits.

or

The purpose of adopting a VIE is to provide students with an immersive learning experience in a realistic environment where they can safely intermix with other cultures without incurring the costs of travel.

Notice that the technology is not the focus of the problem statement. Instead, the goal is to provide a compelling business or educational need and to focus on that need. VIEs are just enablers and should not be viewed as the end goal. The end goal must be the accomplishment of a business goal such as increasing profits or an academic goal such as better-prepared graduates.

## Problem Description

The "problem description" explains the current situation and provides clear evidence of why it is not working or how it could become more productive. This section should answer the question, "What elements are driving the need for the implementation of the VIE?" or "Why is the current state not acceptable?" Again, keep the focus on organizational needs.

One of the best places to begin the discussion of the current state is to look at whether or not the organization is accomplishing its goals as effectively as possible from both a cost and productivity perspective. For example, one pharmaceutical firm decided that its sales representatives were not applying the proper sales model on calls with doctors, and the result was missed opportunities to have their products adopted. To counter the lack of application of the sales model, they created a "sales village" that includes six virtual doctors' offices and, within each office, a different type of doctor with different concerns and needs. The sales representatives could practice in a virtual role play with the different types of doctors to perfect their application of the model.

In another example, a manufacturing plant wanted to teach workers how to work within a newly constructed work cell. The company graphically constructed work cells for applications such as welding, painting, material removal, and machine tending. These virtual work cells are then used to determine positioning, peripheral tool placement, reachability, and other important productivity factors as well as to instruct the employees on proper location and placement during the production process. Loyalist College could no longer take students to actual border crossing stations, and student performance was suffering. They built a virtual border crossing and dramatically improved student grades as a result, as described in Chapter 6.

Describing these types of activities can serve as a foundation for a case to present to the organization to deploy a VIE for use across the enterprise.

## Propose Solution

This section of your case describes your proposed solution and its major features. Here describe the reasons for the investment and the expected tangible and intangible benefits. Describe the VIE and its potential impact. Contrast the benefits of the solution with the shortcomings of the current situation.

It is a good idea, at this point, to provide evidence of the effectiveness of the proposed solution. Most senior executives or university officials will ask "Do 3DLE really teach?" or "Is the investment equal to the payoff?" The burden of proof clearly lies with the person recommending the VIE. Interestingly, the burden of proof tends to be higher for VIES than for traditional classroom instruction or even e-learning.

While the use of VIEs is relatively new, there are some sample data points that can be used to help you build the case:

- In the manufacturing arena, the level of complexity of today's assembly lines cannot be accomplished with two-dimensional visualization. A virtual 3D world is needed to make sure all of the manufacturing equipment and human employees work together flawlessly. The use of a 3D world can lead to significant savings. A small manufacturing plant can realize an annual savings of $1M and a 5-to-1 annual return on investment. A medium-sized plant can realize an $8M savings with an 8-to-1 return on annual investment, and a large manufacturing plant can see a $50M to $100M annual savings with an annual return on investment of as high as 10-to-1.[6]

- At Mercedes-Benz, the use of a virtual world simulating the manufacture of an aluminum component for an S-class coupe saved the company time and money. Initially, after the assembly line was conceived and developed, a compression-modeling die did not manufacture components correctly in the virtual world, so changes were made until the virtual world produced the correct part. If the problem had not been discovered and changed in the virtual stage, it would have meant a three- to six-month delay and several thousand dollars to repair the process on the actual production floor. Overall, use of the virtual world has resulted in cost reductions of up to 30 percent in several areas of vehicle planning for the luxury car company.[7]

- IBM's Academy of Technology held a virtual conference and annual meeting and estimated a savings of hundreds of thousands of dollars. With an initial investment of roughly $80,000, IBM estimates that they saved over $250,000 in travel and venue costs and more than $150,000 in additional productivity gains (since participants were already at their computers and could dive back into work immediately), for a total of $320,000, as described in Chapter 6.

- Grades in a program at Loyalist College to prepare students for service as Canadian Border Patrol officers increased 37 percent over a two-year period after the introduction of a virtual role play within a VIE, as described in Chapter 6.

Use these data points and the other case studies from Chapter 6 to build the argument that the use of VIEs are not just fun and games but improve knowledge transfer, reduce costs, increase performance, and provide a competitive advantage.

## Key Objectives and Success Indicators

In this section, state outcomes you are trying to achieve as well as key indicators of success. Clearly describe measurable objectives and anticipated outcomes from the solution you are suggesting. Indicate anticipated learning outcomes in this section, but only as they relate to identified needs. The success measures should be easy to obtain and agreed upon by others to ensure that the anticipated results are relevant and meaningful.

This is also the place to list intangible benefits such as higher morale, ability to attract and retain the younger generation of students, and other benefits of the solution that are hard to quantify but important to the organization.

## Current Systems and Legacy Content[8]

Existing learning management systems (LMS) do not always have the capabilities to interface with VIEs, and sometimes the VIE technology is not able to easily update or integrate with the LMS. Decisions need to be made regarding how much information from the VIE needs to be shared with the LMS. Once the VIE is in full-scale use, the need to have good communication with the LMS will become critical if there is a desire within the organization to track the action and performance of the learners within the 3DLE. Describe how you plan to address the interface with an existing LMS and what type of measures within the VIE are important for recording in the LMS.

Describe in the business case how you will address legacy content. Organizations have a wealth of content, and deciding how to integrate that content into a VIE is a critical step. This section needs to describe how existing content, classroom processes, and user-generated items will be incorporated into the VIE. It is possible to repurpose some content and display it within a 3DLE for the learners. Other times, it will be necessary to scratch existing content and redevelop the learning materials within the VIE. At this step in the case for VIE, consider the uses and re-uses of existing content. Also consider that the 3D technology for learning will be a portion of the overall learning content of an organization and not the entire offering. It can be helpful at this point to describe how the use of VIEs fits into the overall learning strategy of the organization. As Koreen Olbrish, CEO of Tandem Learning, a company that specializes in immersive learning environments, states, "E-mail did not get rid of the phone, and Twitter did not get rid of instant messaging. VIEs are another methodology we have to interact with people. This needs to be understood by the stakeholders."

## Financial Comparison and Analysis

The last element is to compare the cost of the VIE solution with the cost of other solutions—or even with inaction. Show that your proposed solution is cost-effective. Add up all the development and purchase costs as well as the costs of the human resources. This is the cost side of the equation. (See the sidebar by Erica and Sam Driver later in this chapter for more detailed information concerning the cost aspects of implementing a VIE.)

Once all costs are determined, list all the benefits. Assign a dollar value to as many benefits as possible, and then add together the dollar value of the benefits. It is important to be conservative and gain buy-in on the numbers from the accounting department. Be sure they are in agreement with how you determined the dollar value of the benefits. Now compare the costs of the development with the anticipated benefits. The benefits should outweigh the costs. For VIEs, costs can be impacted greatly by reduced travel costs, but be sure to look at the value of improved performance or the cost of making errors in an actual situation.

## Final Recommendation

The last step is to make a recommendation based on the facts of the case. This usually involves presenting the case to a group of executives or managers or upper-level educators who will need to view the data and make the final decision. If presented well with acceptable numbers, the project is usually funded (but not always). One particularly powerful method of presenting the case to this group is to provide a demonstration of the activities that can be accomplished in the VIE by having the decision-makers partake in activities within the VIE. To really understand the impact of VIEs, it is important to experience being immersed within a 3DLE.

# Implementation Considerations

Once the business/educational case is approved and it is time to implement the VIE into the organization, there are a number of elements to consider. First, an effective implementation strategy must be put into place. Second, the right pilot group needs to be chosen. Third, a governance process must be created to ensure the proper communication and oversight for the project; and, finally, methods must be developed to overcome those obstacles that will inevitably arise.

## Implementation Strategy

A well-written business or education case can serve as a solid foundation for the implementation of a VIE. The information regarding the legacy systems, communicating with the LMS, purpose of the VIE implementation, key objectives and success indicators, and other information provide a road map for implementation. The next step is to determine the group and process for the implementation.

Olbrish advocates starting internally. She believes that a VIE implementation needs to consider three separate groups: the internal team (people who work within the organization); direct customers (people to whom the organization sells its products); and the ultimate customers (people who benefit from the product sold to the direct customer).

In an academic setting, the first group would be faculty and staff. The second group would be the students, and the third group would be the employers who hire the students. In a corporate setting, for example, the pharmaceutical industry, the first group would be the employees of the company, the second group would be the physicians who purchase the products, and the third group would be the patients who benefit from the products.

Olbrish recommends starting internally so that the company can build know-how, acumen, and experience with VIEs and then more easily roll them out to the other two groups. She states that starting internally provides a more controlled and organic adoption of VIEs and the company will better understand the process and policies that will make the VIE work. "Getting internal people to embrace 3DLE experience and establish processes that are easily adopted helps build a base of knowledge. This base becomes important when the organization wants to then extend the VIE to customers. It makes the organization smarter." Olbrish goes on to say that "internal success helps with external VIE activities like recruiting, customer collaboration, and virtual sales calls."

John Royer, former director of sales training strategy at AstraZenca, thinks a different strategy might be more effective for bypassing some of the inertia that might be encountered within organizations. Royer contends that in some cases it might be better to bypass the internal organization and try to position the VIE with direct customers—or even the ultimate customers. Royer sees a huge upside to the community aspect of VIEs and thinks that focusing on creating a VIE for customers is a sure way to get the organization excited about using the technology. Position it with visionary customers and then leverage the knowledge you collect to leap over your competitors. "I think the immersive interaction is something that you don't ordinarily have, and the ability for you and a potential customer to go into a shared space and exchange information and tools is huge in terms of joint problem solving and solution-based selling."

## Choose the Right Pilot Group

Regardless of the implementation strategy chosen, inside out or outside in, many experts recommend starting with a pilot group. Running a pilot means choosing a small group of users to experiment and explore the VIE and asking them for feedback. The advantage is that you can catch problems on a small scale and then adjust, correct, and modify based on the feedback and experience of the pilot group. Skipping the pilot phase is a dangerous gamble. An important element in the pilot process is choosing the right group for the pilot. Here are some suggestions for crafting your pilot group:

- *High-Technology Comfort Level*—You don't want to provide initial access to a VIE to a group that is not comfortable with technology. Choose people who have historically used and embraced technology and are comfortable using technology as a productivity enhancer. This is especially true because navigation can be difficult at first within virtual worlds.

- *Mix in Some Not So Comfortable Folks as Well*—If everyone in the group loves and has a high comfort level with technology, an accurate view of how the technology will roll out to the entire organization will not be created. While it is good to have a lot of people with a high comfort level, make sure you recruit some people who are not so comfortable.

- *Choose a Relatively Small Group*—With employees geographically dispersed, it is important to start with a manageable size group so that any initial unexpected complications can be worked out efficiently. The group should understand that the technology adoption cycle will have a few "rough edges" before it is perfected.

- *Legal and Regulatory Personnel Involved from the Beginning*—Form a committee that includes individuals from the legal and regulatory department. Many questions concerning the use of VIEs will be encountered by legal and regulatory personnel, and the earlier the department is involved, the better. Even if the organization is not operating in a highly regulated environment, involving representatives from these departments can be helpful. The only caution is that the individuals from these organizations tend to be highly conservative. Leverage the sponsor to avoid having this department shut down the VIE before it starts, but knowing their objections early will prevent surprises.

- *Involve IT Personnel from the Beginning*—Just as legal and regulatory need to be involved early, so does the information technology department. Inevitably with new technologies, complications will arise; the IT staff needs to be on board to help quickly overcome technical obstacles. This is especially true with VIEs.

- *Choose a Group Interested in the Potential of Virtual Worlds*—Choose a group interested in the business advantages of VIEs. These people will spend more time and effort working through the technology to get it working correctly, and they will tend to be more comfortable with technology issues they encounter because they will see the business potential. The pilot group needs to have both technology savvy individuals as well as people focused on business outcomes.

- *Choose a Group That Is Easy to Track*—Choose a group that will provide you with access and data when requested. Develop methods of keeping in touch with the group to foster an exchange of ideas and input into the issues and advantages of the virtual world interactions.

## Overcoming Obstacles

Even with the formation of an ideal pilot group, implementers are bound to encounter objections and obstacles to using VIEs for learning. Some of the obstacles can be avoided by laying the proper groundwork prior to an organization-wide rollout of immersive learning. These are listed below:

- *Clearly Articulate the Intended Outcome of the Learning*— Stakeholders need to understand the goal of the learning to focus on the process. This needs to be articulated throughout the organization so everyone understands the goals and does not think the VIE is for playing games.

- *Establish Rules and Guidelines to Prevent VIEs from Becoming a Distraction*—Because of their unfamiliarity and the sense that VIEs could be too "game like," put guidelines in place to prevent these misconceptions from gaining traction. Clear policies and procedures remove ambiguity and force the organization to focus on the learning aspects of the technology.

- *Create a Marketing Campaign*—A marketing campaign can help to publicize the benefits and attract the techies and visionaries (at least for the first round). Anticipate that the technology enthusiasts and visionaries will be interested first, but don't forget the others. Carefully craft an effective message and make sure that the connectors are given special attention.

- *Understand That the Investment Is for the Long Haul*—The use of VIEs to achieve real and sustainable strategic advantage typically takes a while. The pilot group has to be able to go completely through the early phases of the process, realize success, and then spread the story of success throughout the organization. This process always seems to take longer than the champions and visionaries would like. The trick is to work through obstacles with a focus on leveraging the technology for the future. Employ the "Lessons Learned" from Chapter 6 and the process will be successful—and soon the entire organization will embrace VIEs.

## Lessons from the Front Line:
## How Early Adopters Achieve and Measure Success
By Erica Driver and Sam Driver, Co-Founders and Principals, ThinkBalm

### "What's in It for ME?"

Boiled down to the simplest level, "What's in it for me?" is the first question anyone has to answer when challenging others to make a change. It doesn't matter what kind of change, how small, or how sensible. We tend not to change our behavior or thinking unless we are convinced of a compelling-enough reason to do so. When it comes to adopting new technology in the enterprise, that compelling reason is evidence of business value. In the spring of 2009, ThinkBalm analysts set out to answer the "What's in it for me?" question about work-related use of immersive technologies. For the ThinkBalm Immersive Internet Business Value Study, Q2 2009, we surveyed sixty-six highly qualified practitioners and conducted fifteen in-depth interviews. Here are some highlights from that study.

### Early Investments Are in Fact Yielding Business Value

Not everyone who's been implementing immersive technology in the workplace can—or even expects to—quantify the business value of the investments they've made so far. Few Immersive Internet projects done in 2008 and the first quarter of 2009 had rigorous ROI numbers attached. We discovered that many of the practitioners involved in these projects never intended to build an ROI model. Still, various data points we collected via survey and interviews indicate that investments in immersive technologies in the workplace are yielding value:

- *Most of the people who know whether they got business value report positive numbers.* More than 40 percent of the practitioners we surveyed (twenty-six of sixty-six) said their organizations saw a positive total economic benefit from investments made in immersive technologies in 2008 and early 2009, and more than 50 percent of respondents (thirty-four of sixty-five) expect to obtain a positive total economic benefit in 2009.

- *Quantification of business value is all over the map.* In our research we found that measured business value ranged from less than $10,000 USD to more than $1 million. Likely reasons for this are that business value depends heavily on use case and on the maturity and breadth of the rollout.

- *Some practitioners recouped their investment in less than nine months.* Most respondents (forty-four of sixty-six) said either that their organizations had not recouped their investment or that they didn't know. Nearly 30 percent of respondents (nineteen of sixty-six), however, said their organization recouped their investment in immersive technologies in less than nine months once their project(s) launched.

## Money Is Not the Only Direct Measure of Success

The sentiment many practitioners have toward the projects they undertook in 2008 and early 2009 is overwhelmingly positive. We asked how successful people felt their immersive technology projects were. One-third of respondents (twenty-two of sixty-six) said their project data showed success. Another 61 percent of respondents (forty of sixty-six) said the project "felt like" a success, for a total of 94 percent of respondents.

Wait a minute. *Feels* like a success? That could be worrisome. So we did some digging and found that many projects were still underway, so no hard data existed yet. Other projects were not actually driven by direct financial success. Some were R&D efforts, while others were measured in ways that had little to do with revenue or profits. Educators, non-profits, and government agencies take note: strict financial ROI is not the only measure of success. A closer look at some of these success stories shows immersive technology can result in:

- *Improved employee productivity.* One characteristic of immersive work environments is they keep people focused on the task at hand. These environments simplify collaboration and provide a simulated face-to-face interaction. About 72 percent of survey respondents (forty-six of sixty-four) said employee productivity improvement was a very important or somewhat important benefit of their 2008/1Q 2009 immersive technology projects.
- *Increased innovation.* Not originally a part of our survey, we added innovation just prior to launch. Survey results delivered a clear message: innovation isn't just the means to an end, it is often an end in itself. Give people an immersive tool and they'll use it to innovate. Nearly 90 percent of survey

respondents (fifty-nine of sixty-six) said that increased innovation was a very important or somewhat important benefit of their 2008/1Q 2009 immersive technology projects.

- *Revenue from new and existing products and services.* Some early adopters dream of revenue generation or enhancement as a real end goal for their immersive technology projects. One-third of survey respondents (twenty-one of sixty-four) reported that increased revenue from new sources was a very important or somewhat important benefit of their 2008/1Q 2009 immersive technology projects.

- *Cost savings or avoidance.* We asked an obvious question: How important was cost savings or avoidance for your immersive technology project(s)? Nearly 90 percent of those surveyed (fifty-six of sixty-four) said it was at least somewhat important. This is right in keeping with many anecdotes of success: you can do it cheaper or skip some expenses altogether if you swap in immersive technology and swap out the old way of doing things, whether that be getting on a plane or racking up transcontinental telephone bills.

## How to Get Funding and Buy-In for Immersive Internet Initiatives

So you've bought into the value of immersive technology in the workplace. You have a great idea for how this technology could help your organization solve a problem. How do you get funding? The theoretical ideal is you go to an executive, make your case, and the budget-holder approves the idea based on your impeccable logic. But in the real world—certainly with immersive technology—it usually doesn't work quite so smoothly. So you have to:

- *Experiment and conduct a pilot to prove the concept.* Pilots (small projects designed to prove a concept) help you demonstrate the value. It's nearly impossible to convince people of the value of immersive technology without allowing them to experience the technology first-hand or second-hand. One of the best ways to allow them to experience it second-hand is through machinima—videos filmed in immersive environments. Another way is to stream an immersive event to the web so people can watch it without participating fully themselves.

- *Leverage the success of others.* This emerging market is young enough that there is a bit of a "wild west" feel to it. Often, there is only a single advocate per organization, so going outside for support and learning is mandatory. Early adopters band together with common interests that override traditional barriers, like, say, spending time with competitors. In a couple of years, as adoption moves into the early majority phase, competition will heat up and this collaborative attitude won't last. So take advantage of it now.

- *Pick one business problem and focus on a solution before making the pitch.* Immersive technology can be applied in many ways, but don't overwhelm your audience. Keep it simple and keep it about the business—always about the business. Pick a single problem for which immersive environments are a good solution, and work with that. Focus like a laser on this solution before making your pitch. The low-hanging fruit are learning and training, meetings, and conferences.

- *Hand-hold.* Ease people in. Let them watch a productive session before making them dive in. Create machinima. Show what your experiment was able to accomplish. Bring budget-holders into the pilot immersive environment to *show* them what you are setting out to do. Offer potential project sponsors one-on-one sessions during which you teach them the basics—like how to walk and talk in a virtual world. Ease them into it gradually.

- *Watch your language.* One of the most powerful ways to enhance a pitch for immersive technology is to use the right words. One great way to think about it is the real/virtual and real/fake dynamic. People who are not "virtual world geeks" often misunderstand what old-timers mean by "real life" versus "second life" and assume that work done in an immersive environment is somehow less valuable, or fake, compared to work done in the physical world or via traditional means.

## You Can Get Your Feet Wet at Very Little Cost

One of the most important aspects of immersive technology is that it can be very inexpensive to get an experiment or pilot up and running. Many early pilots are performed in public virtual worlds or using free or inexpensive software. Assets are hand-made, donated, or bought for pennies on the dollar. Often, the most expensive purchase for a new user is a headset.

- *You can get going for less than $25,000 USD.* More than half of our survey respondents (thirty-seven of sixty-six) said their organization spent less than $25,000, and the majority of those (thirty respondents) spent less than $10,000. Nine percent of respondents (six respondents) reported they actually had zero budget; this means they got by on efforts by volunteers who used either free software or software they paid for on their own. This is a viable approach for a proof of concept.

- *A solid experiment or pilot may require less than 160 person hours to get up and running.* If we are looking at an officially unfunded project, another way to look at cost is in terms of the hours team members spend. About 45 percent of respondents (twenty-two of forty-nine) indicated their organization spent 160 person hours or less on 2008/1Q 2009 projects. When you do the math, this works out to about $16,000 for a professional employee who carries a fully burdened cost of $100 USD/hour.

- *You'll likely find that immersive technology is less expensive than alternatives.* Almost 60 percent of respondents (thirty-eight of sixty-six) said that immersive technology was less expensive than alternatives. Only 11 percent (seven of sixty-six) said it was more expensive. When we looked at why people chose immersive technology over alternatives, 27 percent of respondents (eighteen of sixty-six) wanted to reduce costs.

- *But don't be misled by low cost of entry.* Okay, reality check: you can do a pilot very inexpensively. That is, if you don't count donated time, working after hours, donated 3D assets, space . . . the list goes on. But the cost of immersive technology projects is heavily dependent on use case. Some projects (such as meetings and some learning and training applications) can leverage inexpensive technology and have fairly simple requirements. Other use cases, like collaborative design and prototyping or remote system and facility management, bear additional required costs like system integration, 3D model translation and import, and sensors and tracking devices. Cost also depends on the maturity of the project; pilots that utilize a public virtual world are often relatively inexpensive. Also, reported costs are deceptively low due to prevalence of a volunteer culture. Early project cost reports often don't count development time or time spent learning how to use or customize immersive technology.

## The Roadblocks Are Many

You've got a vision; you've convinced some people to give it a try. What are the pitfalls you'll run into along the way? Some barriers to adoption are technology-related and others have more to do with people. The most common barriers are

- *Overcoming technology hurdles.* The lack of adequate hardware for end-users is a big issue: particularly video cards, computer RAM, and headsets. Sixty percent of survey respondents (thirty-nine of sixty-five) reported users having inadequate hardware as a barrier to adoption. Nearly half (thirty-two of sixty-five) also reported problems with corporate security restrictions.

- *A problematic learning curve.* Forty-five percent of respondents (twenty-nine of sixty-five) said it took more effort than they expected to train their target user population. Ease of use is an important factor to look at as the vendor market evolves. The one-on-one hand-holding so common today is not scalable or sustainable.

- *Getting buy-in from management and the IT organization.* You may clear the executive sponsorship hurdle just to get bogged down in IT rules and regulations. Never mind the fact that the IT organization is engaged in a constant juggling act, balancing competing priorities. Understanding all of the players in a successful immersive technology project will give you a lead on converting enough of the right people to give it a try.

- *Getting buy-in from target end-users.* Nearly half of our survey respondents (46 percent, or thirty of sixty-five) said that getting target users interested in the technology was more difficult than they expected. Some prospective users resist because the technology appears too fanciful or too complex, or they simply don't feel they have the time to learn to use it. An effective communications and marketing campaign as you roll out a project, even if only viral, will go a long way toward helping you succeed.

- *Driving organizational and end-user awareness.* You've got a project started, people are using the immersive technology as you intended, and you want to expand the breadth of the rollout. How do you get the word out and craft the message to draw more people in? Think back to the section above: hand-holding is critical. One vocal, dissatisfied user—especially if he or she is in a position of power—can sabotage many new users. Language will help condition expectations, and the best chance you have to capture a new user is if he or she is aware something new and exciting is coming down the pike.

### Lessons Learned from Early Adopters: How to Get Past the Roadblocks

The best characterization of the result of the Immersive Internet market for work is probably:

> "Immersive technology is delivering solid business benefit, both financial and non-financial, to a wide range of organizations, for a wide range of use cases. Well, at least to those organizations that are aware of immersive technology, anyway."

Humor aside, the data we have collected about the business value of work-related use of immersive technologies leads to the following recommendations:

- *Start early, gain skills using immersive technology, and grow with the sector.* Hurdles are bountiful, but early experimentation will lead to invaluable experience and fewer mistakes in the future. Business value is to be had if you focus on the right business problem; look first to the low-hanging fruit of meetings, learning, and training.

- *Be prepared to jump a whole host of technology hurdles.* Work with people in your IT organization as early in the process as you can. Make sure they know your target users need powerful-enough graphics cards. Seek funding to order a collection of USB headsets if your target user population doesn't already have them.

- *Be clear about and declare your mission.* The best early projects are small, focused, and set up so that they practically can't fail. Focus first on solving a single business problem. Pick a problem you can communicate about easily—such as the need for salespeople to spend time together and share best practices even though their travel budget has been cut in half.

- *Use hands-on experience to help you get management buy-in.* As with any emerging technology initiative, executive support goes a long way to clearing technical hurdles and changing corporate attitudes. Bring the results of your experiments—as well as something decision-makers can experience, such as a video or a demo—to a planning meeting and watch attention grow. Don't just talk about it. Show it.

- *Know your target user population.* Make sure you understand their motivation for using the technology. If you have people in your sights who like to have a good time, loosen up and have a little fun with the immersive technology. Add a virtual ski trip or hot air balloon ride to the roster of team activities. If the target audience is a more staid bunch, leave out all the extras; show them how to get into the environment, get what they need, and get out.

- *Carefully consider your user base when assessing immersive platforms.* When selecting an enterprise-immersive platform, look for features and functionality that make the user experience easy and fun. Carefully consider the tradeoffs between simple environments, which typically have thinner clients with less functionality yet are easier to operate, and more complex, robust environments that offer more powerful capabilities but have higher technology requirements and a steeper learning curve.

If we acknowledge that the Immersive Internet trend is still in the early adopter phase on Everett Rogers' and Geoffrey Moore's technology adoption curve, it is a difficult climb ahead to reach the early majority phase. Between here and there is the proverbial chasm: lack of awareness, perception problems ("it's just a game"), and technical hurdles. It is a daunting path to follow, but the promise of solid business value is an irresistible lure.

# Implications for Learning Professionals

There was a time when computers themselves were thought of as toys or novelties; now these devices are indispensable business and education tools. There was a time when the Internet was not a part of our daily lives. It's hard to reach back and remember the time before these technologies became ubiquitous—when the same type of implementation and adoption concerns existed for those technologies. For learning, business, and education professionals to leverage and take advantage of VIE technologies, they need to find a way to introduce their organizations to VIEs and to position the technology to provide a competitive advantage. The first step is to understand how to diffuse VIEs into the organization. The next step is to create an effective business or education case for the technology. Then choose the right strategy, the right pilot group, and the right processes for avoiding (or at least minimizing) obstacles that are bound to be encountered. This is a nascent technology and issues and problems will be encountered; however, the point is that VIE technology is arriving and the organizations that are positioned to leverage it will receive the greatest advantage in learning and business success.

# Rules from Revolutionaries

## Meet the Revolutionaries

All revolutions have revolutionaries—those people who see the future before the rest of us and who toil tirelessly to have that vision become a reality despite the greatest of odds. This chapter is dedicated to distilling the rules from four such revolutionaries:

Steve Mahaley is the director of learning technology at Duke Corporate Education (Duke CE). At Duke CE, Steve focuses on creative and effective design of educational programs and experiences for corporate and non-profit clients globally. Recent work has been focused in the area of virtual worlds and serious gaming.

Karen Keeter is a marketing executive in IBM Research and is working to help define the emerging market IBM calls the "3-D Internet," defined as the application of virtual worlds, visualization, and social networking tools and platforms to address real business issues.

Brian Bauer is the founder and managing partner at Étape Partners LLC, responsible for business development and overall company strategy. Looking forward to virtual worlds and an Immersive Internet, Brian is keenly aware that innovation must be revolutionary, but also practical to real business customers.

John Hengeveld has twenty years of experience leading the development of technology and business strategy. John is currently the senior business strategist for Intel's Digital Enterprise group. John is a graduate of the Massachusetts Institute of Technology and holds an MBA from the University of Oregon.

All of these revolutionaries selflessly gave of their time to share their insights on what it feels like on the inside of the 3D revolution. In their essays, they share their candid views and opinions on a number of questions related to driving change and making a difference.

# Essay Format and Questions

The following outline shows the essay format and questions asked of the revolutionaries. The remaining sections of this chapter present each essay in detail. The final section of this chapter attempts to synthesize the wisdom of these change-leaders into ten key rules for revolutionaries.

**Revolutionary Essay Format**

Overcoming Objections

- What are the three most common objections you can expect to immediately encounter and how do you address them?

Establishing a Beachhead

- Where is the low-hanging fruit within the enterprise to quickly demonstrate the value of 3D learning?

Securing Sponsorship

- Who is the most logical person to approach within the enterprise when it comes to securing sponsorship?

- How do you sell the value of 3D to them?

Making the Case

- What are the mot compelling ways you have found to demonstrate the value of 3D learning to sponsorship?
- What are the most compelling ways to make the case for 3D learning within the enterprise?

Crossing the Chasm

- What are the keys to success in moving from concept to execution to avoid falling in the chasm?

Going Mainstream

- What are the most important issues to consider when you move from successful pilot to executing at scale?

Demonstrating Value

- How do you demonstrate value to your stakeholders?

Double-Loop Reflection

- What top three pieces of advice would you have for those about to embark on a journey of implementing 3D within their enterprise?

# Essay 1

### Steve Mahaley, Duke Corporation Education
## Overcoming Objections

Probably the first objection we find is that most of us (myself included) did not have these kinds of learning experiences when we were younger, and our only association with 3D environments is through the media and perhaps our kids. We read of hours of time spent by the "gamer generation" in fantasy games, and we see our own kids captivated by the desire to uncover the clues and patterns in a game and "level up." The whole idea of a "game" as a productive use of time runs contrary to our mental models; games were for recess. Real learning happened in the classroom.

To address this with our clientele, I usually refer to some of the research and writing on games for learning, including works by Gee, Squire, Johnson, Beck, and Wade. I find that if I can help the decision-makers make the positive connection between good game design—the reason people become so hooked on the experience—and memory creation and retention, I can then move on to making a connection to serious gaming. First step: use good game design for serious learning outcomes.

Second, I often draw the analogy that an immersive 3D experience for serious learning is not really different than creating in-class role plays or doing other immersive experiences (such as outdoor team-building events). This helps make the connection that it is not about the game or the technology, it is really about designing an experience to get to relevant learning outcomes.

Finally, there is sometimes an objection related to perceptions of expense—that the 3D solution will be cost-prohibitive. The good news here is that the cost of technologies is coming down as the capabilities of standard hardware and networks in corporate environments have come up, lowering the technical and financial barriers to entry.

## Establishing a Beachhead

3D environments are really useful for learning when the environment itself is part of the training. For example, if you have a need to orient your workforce to the physical environment where some aspect of the work is taking place, 3D worlds can provide a simulated version of the real thing, accelerating spatial understanding of physical environments, how to navigate those, and coordinate efforts with teams in them. Those could be environments that are structured for single-player learning or for scheduled multi-player simulations.

These environments are also best used when you need to create any situation that is difficult, dangerous, or expensive to simulate at scale, giving learners an opportunity to practice and obtain feedback on core skills and behaviors in context before it really matters for the organization for example, when things have gone awry with a customer and challenging conversations need to be held or for hard skills, or for coordinating efforts of a team under time pressure to assess data and present a solution.

## Securing Sponsorship

When we think about developing learning experiences employing 3D environments, it is always important to secure the sponsorship of senior leaders in the organization, not just the learning and development function. Without that connection, forays into what can be perceived as "technology for technology's sake" will be met with questions about levels of support for the initiative at hand.

In addition to C-suite sponsorship, I have found that it really helps to have the learning and development leader, along with HR and IT, present. You may begin with 3D education in the learning and development function, but it is a really good idea to go ahead and talk with HR leadership to gain buy-in and involvement, especially when it comes to specific competency models and integrating those. Also, IT should be involved up-front so they can share ownership and provide the necessary resources for successful integration from a technology perspective.

Selling the value of 3D education to each of them will require slightly different angles; for the C-suite it will be about business performance. I highlight the research around simulation and gaming as approaches that speed time-to-performance, thereby positively affecting business performance. For HR professionals, they will respond well to the notion that key competencies will be brought to life by immersive experiences, providing opportunities for coaching, assessment, and feedback. For the IT professionals, my experience has been that it is less about the pedagogy and business impact, and more about standards and security. Involving them early is always a good idea.

## Making the Case

One of the most compelling ways to make the case to the sponsors is to demonstrate something that their competitors are doing. Provide hard data if you can (scope and scale of the initiative and any business-level impact), and if not, show similar cases from other industries (medical, military, manufacturing, energy, etc.) where 3D worlds are being used.

If you can manage it, I recommend giving the sponsors a direct experience. Arrange for a demonstration of one of these environments, and give the sponsors a guided tour. Words fail to capture the richness of these environments, so seeing them and being "there" is a much more powerful approach. It is helpful to involve one or more of the sponsors in the presentation and to (if the approach in question merits a live environment) actually have live presenters in the environment as part of the demonstration.

I also recommend having a vendor-neutral approach. One of the benefits of my position at Duke CE is that we can select the best platform for the specific learning design at hand. This allows us to demonstrate focus on the learning outcomes and target population, and less on a specific technology.

Making the case also entails outlining a pilot project. Don't just go in with a vague notion that 3D environments are going to improve learning and business performance. Identify a real gap for which you have real data (for example, time-to-proficiency for new hires) and then propose a pilot project. Pilot projects indicate that you are optimistic about the potential and are smart about taking a first, limited step.

## Crossing the Chasm

First, involve the right people. As mentioned above, having a sponsor for the project from business leadership is key. Follow that with the appropriate learning and development individuals, human resources, and IT representation. Have a kickoff meeting to describe the project and to coalesce around time, scope, budget, and evaluation. Be clear with the senior sponsorship about deliverables—what they should expect to see and when they will see it.

Second, select the right project. It would be a bad idea to select a noncritical area for your project, as this will exacerbate feelings about 3D virtual worlds or gaming as superfluous and expensive endeavors. Choose a project that represents a performance gap that, when improved, will positively impact business metrics, and for which the use of 3D spaces is optimal (as described above).

Next, have a design methodology. Our approach at Duke CE is to use a design methodology that describes clear line-of-sight from business strategy, to performance gaps, to target populations, and all the way through appropriate methods, technologies, and measurement to provide effective learning experiences. The risk of not doing this is a failure to provide the rationale for the project from a business performance perspective, and possibly a very negative (and expensive) experience for everyone involved.

Finally, start small and design big. As mentioned, move ahead with a pilot experience. Don't try to roll something out to an entire population as a first experience. Don't kitchen sink the design, either. By this I mean don't try to address every possible learning and behavioral objective. Focus your efforts on the two or three that really matter. And design the environment to be flexible, so that additional uses of the environment can be illustrated and maximum value for the investment made can be realized.

## Going Mainstream

Once you have succeeded with the pilot, you should also have scheduled a time to report out on the delivery to the project sponsors (senior leadership). During that meeting, it will be important to have a draft implementation plan that illustrates the steps and resources required to roll out the new 3D environment and method at scale. Important here will be an understanding of the natural cycles of the business (to connect the learning experience optimally to the seasonality of the business), HR process schedules (for example, annual appraisal schedules), internal and external subject-matter experts needed, any IT implications for roll-out (for example, additional integration with learning management systems, load testing), an idea about internal marketing and communications, and any further investment required.

## Demonstrating Value

If you have done your work to include the right people, identify the right learning need and target populations, developed the right 3D environment, and executed a successful pilot, the good news is that you will have several people reporting on the value of the experience. And you should have some comparative data from performance measures before and after in-world learning events. For procedural learning outcomes using a 3D simulated environment, you should have some key performance indicators from the business to look at. For soft skills (for example, team building in a 3D environment), you should be able to get some subjective reporting and perhaps 360-degree data on individual performance improvements.

## Double-Loop Reflection

Our advice to those beginning to consider 3D environments for learning is to spend some time in a range of them. For example, play a live multiplayer console game. Install Second Life, create an avatar, and attend one of the free educational events there. Read some of the literature and blogs out there (such as Terra Nova).

If you are in the learning part of your business and have an instructional design team, challenge your team to identify five different commercial off-the-shelf 3D environments that they believe represent features and functionality that could be beneficial when designing a similar learning environment for your people. Run a game night, have them all demonstrated in a hands-on fashion, and expose some of your business leaders to the process.

Finally, do your best to identify the business critical performance gap that would best be addressed through the use of a simulated (or metaphoric) 3D world, and gather the sponsorship and resources necessary to design and run a pilot.

# Essay 2

### Karen Keeter, IBM
## Overcoming Objections

The three most common objections we hear are

- It is too hard for new users.

- It looks like a game.

- What about integration (with other business apps), security, or scalability?

Let's take these objections one at a time.

**Objection 1: It Is Too Hard for New Users to Get Up-to-Speed.** This is a very common concern, and my first response is "You are right—sort of." In order to be a successful participant in a virtual environment, you must often download some software, learn how to log into the virtual environment, and then learn how to walk, communicate, examine, and interact with your surroundings. For first-time users, especially in that first hour, this can be quite a daunting experience that may cause some people not to want to try at all.

However, most of us don't remember what it was like the first time we tried to use a word processor, develop a presentation, or create and perform calculations in a spreadsheet. So while the objection is valid, it is true of most new technologies and is not a reason to decide not to try it out in the first place. I have to laugh sometimes, because the people who raise this objection are probably the same ones who are still using numeric keyboards on their cell phones to send text messages!

At the same time, I believe that the onus is on developers to design for new users, while still enabling advanced users. What are some of the things we do here? We put our orientation areas in a circle, so people don't have to know how to walk to go through the orientation when they first arrive. We remind our trainers what it is like to be a new user and ask them to "think like a noob" (new user). We place big signs throughout the space to help people remember what they can do. We have developed seats with built-in camera controls, so they can cycle through multiple relevant viewpoints with just the page up or page down keys. We also try to communicate with soon-to-be new users in small bites, instead of making them drink from the proverbial fire hose. For some of our large events, we may send four e-mails over four weeks, to get people ready and (hopefully) excited.

One might ask them just to install the virtual world client, then the next invites them to go in-world so they can test their audio (sessions hosted by "greeters"). After that, they would be invited to an orientation session. And in some cases, we might also run a pre-event tour to let them practice their newly learned skills. We run on-boarding sessions before any real meeting takes place, and we try to make those sessions informal—with no pressure to perform immediately on a real task—and fun.

We also try to do one-on-one sessions with sponsors, executives, or other key influencers, to allow them to learn in private, so they can look like experts in front of their teams. Ironically, we have found that some of the most senior technical people—whom we would have expected to be the earliest adopters—tend to be more reluctant than less senior people to participate in large meetings or events. Although we can't prove it, we think that the reason for this is that these high-skilled experts are rarely in a situation in which they appear "dumb," and they are not about to start putting themselves in that situation now!

**Objection 2: It Looks Like a Game.** For many business users, their experience with virtual worlds has been as consumers. They, or their children, have used game platforms, either online or on machines in their homes. Many of these games have capabilities similar to what we saw in the early days of virtual worlds for business—as business users attempted to use existing consumer environments to do real business—people represented as animated characters (avatars), often wearing funny clothes, shapes, or weirdly colored hair. My mother used to tell me about first impressions being very important—and she was right! Virtual environments for business should take advantage of the expansiveness and creativity inherent in a virtual world development environment, but at the same time, we must keep in mind that the person responsible for the purchase decision needs to believe that real work can be done in these virtual environments.

So what does this mean? Well, if you are building applications for real businesses, you need to dress for business and build for business. Our approach has been to start building applications in the virtual environment that are familiar to business users. It is hard enough to learn how to interact with a virtual world, without making the interface look like a prop from Star Trek! We use familiar objects such as sticky notes (everyone knows how to write on a sticky note and put it on a wall), flip charts, and presentation screens. These familiar objects take away the initial trepidation and allow new users to become acclimated more rapidly. But—you say—we can do so much more! And you would be right. Start with familiar objects and then show them how much more can be done because these objects are virtual, not physical. For example, in a virtual world, notes on a virtual flip chart don't need to be transcribed, since they can be exported electronically.

As we look at the current market (spring 2009), many of the virtual environments being demonstrated have the same basic functions. An avatar can be created, dressed, and can come in-world. Once there, they can text

chat and voice chat with each other. They can show each other presentations—where the process for getting presentations in-world varies from dirt-
simple "drag and drop" to multi-step processes. In some environments, they
can perform application viewing/desktop viewing—where participants can
watch from in-world as another participant modifies a file. Some applications show true application sharing, where control can be passed from one
in-world user to another for file editing. These are all interesting demonstrations, but for the virtual world "un-initiated"—the majority of potential
clients—none of these are compelling reasons to invest in going "in-world."
Why? Because all of these functions can be performed using a variety of
less complex web-based tools broadly available in the market. These types
of demonstrations add to the belief that virtual worlds are a "just a game,"
because they do not clearly demonstrate the additional value added that a
virtual environment can bring to business users. If we are going to move
beyond this objection, we need to start demonstrating truly collaborative
activities—in-world activities—that cannot be done with web meeting, tele-
conferencing, webcast, or video conferencing tools.

**Objection 3: What About Integration (with Other Business Apps), Security, and Scalability?**  Once
potential clients get past the first two objections, the questions tend to start
shifting from the functionality of the in-world application to more mundane,
but equally important issues. Many clients have existing collaboration tools
and other software that are used by their employees, and they are often looking for ways to integrate these existing applications with any new applications
they acquire—including virtual worlds. Yet most VW business applications
are built as stand-alone, proprietary systems, so integration in an enterprise
environment is not that easy. Many are enabled for the obvious applications,
per discussion above—showing or manipulating common file types.

However, deeper integration is often lacking, such as ability to access
virtual-world applications from other business applications, for example,
import and export capabilities to allow content in one form (a spreadsheet,
for example) to be brought in Word and manipulated in a form that is more
useful in a virtual environment (as sticky notes on a wall), and then be
exported back into the original form.

Security and authentication is another concern, where lack of integration with enterprise authentication tools (LDAP, for example) to allow single sign-on between enterprise applications and virtual world applications means multiple systems for managing access and identity of users. The good news is that VW developers are beginning to realize the need for further integration within the enterprise, and the capability is beginning to appear in newer applications.

Scalability (to hundreds or thousands of users) is still the exception more than the rule. We encourage clients to start small, begin with pilots—perhaps with multiple different applications and platforms—and continue to watch for further improvements in this particular area. We are also of the mind that there is not necessarily one single platform that will meet all of a client's needs. The solution for small collaborative meetings may be very different than the solution for large-scale meetings with thousands of participants, and support for deep simulation capabilities may require a completely different platform or tool.

## Establishing a Beachhead

As I look at the experience at my own company (IBM), there are a surprisingly wide range of pockets within our company that turned out to be low-hanging fruit. And, as I work with external clients, there appears to be a similarly wide range of early adopters out there. Of course, unlike within my own organization, most companies may only have a few pockets of possible early adopters!

**Affinity Groups Within an Organization.**  "Birds of a feather" groups, communities of interest, and other groups are likely a geographically diverse group brought together by a common set of interests. Most likely, these are informal groups, so they don't have a travel budget for meetings. The interest in virtual worlds at IBM was the result of a small, dedicated, and vocal group of "virtual world evangelists" (as they liked to call themselves) who introduced a wide range of IBM'ers—both at an executive level and in the ranks—to the possibilities for virtual worlds. My first experience was as part of an affinity group. It started in November 2006 with a one-sentence e-mail from a global innovation community I was a member of: "Does anyone want to help try to run one of our global innovation meetings in Second Life?" We planned and executed an event for 140 or so people in late January of 2007—most of whom were new to Second Life—and I was hooked.

**Early Adopter Communities.** This is a special form of affinity group. Their affinity is that they like being on the bleeding edge, and will try pretty much anything! In IBM, we have taken advantage of our Technology Adoption Program (TAP), a formal program for getting new technologies out to the IBM community, in particular early adopters. In the spring of 2009, there were more than twelve hundred applications available on TAP. Within a week of when our "Sametime 3D" initiative was announced in a TAP newsletter, over fifteen hundred people had pressed the "Try it now" button to install the application. Even we were shocked by the high level of interest!

**Remote Teams.** Virtual worlds are a very attractive approach for bringing remote teams together for meetings. One place to start is with teams that are more technical in nature (IT, for example). They are more likely to be comfortable with embracing new technology. We run daily development "scrum calls" in-world in one of our collaboration spaces, using a presentation viewer and brainstorming board and other tools as needed. In our case, the team consists of people from multiple U.S. locations, Germany, and Australia.

**Human Resources, Training, and Learning.** HR in particular has a strong employee collaboration focus, so they tend to be looking for ways to improve collaboration across the employee population. Early initiatives included "universities" (training), mentoring, meet the experts sessions, poster sessions, social networking meetings, and the like. In addition, for certain industries (military and healthcare, for example), there are a wide range of training exercises that can be performed using virtual simulation tools and delivered to a wider audience in a safer and more cost-effective manner than real-world simulations. The simulation training market is probably the most mature part of this segment, with a wide range of companies offering different simulation development platforms and pre-defined simulations. Many simulation tools are already integrated with learning management systems to record results of individual students (a sign of more market maturity).

**The "Newly Grounded."** Look for groups who (in the past) may have held in-person meetings but are no longer able to do so. These groups are often desperate for a way to bring their teams together, and virtual meetings provide a cost-effective approach for doing this. After the first major series of in-world events sponsored by the IBM Academy of Technology (see Chapter 6), where a wide swath of people from across IBM started to understand the potential, I joked with my colleagues that every time a travel budget was reduced, we got a telephone call about running a virtual meeting.

## Securing Sponsorship

As with the beachhead, there are different opportunities within different organizations, so there is not just one logical person to approach. Much of this will depend on the organization structure and the "personality" of the organization. Some people to consider:

**The "Chief Innovation Officer."** Look for someone in the company tasked with looking at the leading-edge technologies, envisioning the future for the company. He or she may be called the "innovation executive" or "e-business executive," or it could be the strategy executive in the organization.

**CIO Office.** Especially where there is a visionary leader who has shown inclination to experiment in the past, the office of the Chief Information Officer is often tasked with determining ways to improve productivity for the employees. Use of virtual-world applications for meetings between remote project teams is a great place to accomplish this. Just make sure, as we discussed earlier, that the application can do more than their existing tools.

**Line of Business Executives.** Focus on executives who are responsible for specific functional areas within the company and are high enough in the organization to be able to influence the rest of the organization (IT, for example). A business-level sponsor who doesn't have any influence over the IT organization will be a harder sell, because even if he or she is convinced to move forward, the person will still need to convince someone in IT to actually implement (and support) the solution. With any executives, make sure your initial discussion is specific to what you can do for them. Show them how the application can help their employees do their jobs faster, better, cheaper (or all three).

**HR/Training Organization.** These organizations are struggling with how to build community within an increasingly dispersed employee base and how to improve effectiveness of training. As a result, they tend to be willing to try new approaches to help them with this challenge. They were one of the first internal groups to experiment with virtual worlds in our company, and were also one of the first groups to want to pilot our virtual collaboration space. They used the collaboration space to run a global managers' meeting to discuss challenges of managing globally diverse employees. They were able to leverage the brainstorming wall to gather the challenges from participants, share and discuss their experiences with each other, and then document ideas from the discussion on addressing the challenges.

**Person Responsible for Unified Communications or Telephony.** This is not one of the most obvious places to look for advocates, but people in these roles have broad technical skills and are typically looking at new technologies to support communication across the organization. Use of virtual worlds, particularly when combined with VoIP, is a cost-effective way to provide enhanced communications/collaboration across an organization.

## Making the Case

**Support the Evangelists and Early Adopters.** In every organization, you will find these types of people—those who are willing to spend time and energy experimenting with new technologies (even on their own time) to be part of something new and innovative. Encouraging these kinds of grass roots efforts and allowing the good ideas to bubble to the top can help to create early proof points within the organization, with little investment. Certainly that was how our VW business was built—with a small group of dedicated "evangelists" who wouldn't take no for an answer!

Although it is true that this worked well for us in the early days, we really did end up with a two-pronged approach—thanks to those early evangelists. We started with a bottom-up initiative, which resulted in a top-down commitment to invest in what was a very early market, to help develop proof-of concept projects. The "emerging business opportunity" group that was created was put in place with an objective to develop prototypes and first-of-a-kind capabilities, and then figure out how to integrate those initial projects into the broader company. In fact, a measure of success for our unit was that, within two or three years, we would no longer need to be in place, as—if successful—VW would be adopted by other organizations within the company and become business as usual. As we enter year three, one initiative we began has become part of the corporate CIO office, and another is transitioning into the product groups, to be announced as an offering based on the early prototype efforts.

**Seeing Is Believing.** This is probably the most important way to demonstrate and help people understand the value. A virtual world is not something that one watches—it is something one experiences. The immersive nature of these tools makes hands-on demonstrations—where the people you are trying to convince actually experience it themselves—critical. Show demos not charts. Show videos if you can't do demos, but try your best to get them in-world. Over and over again I have seen skeptics turn into advocates before my very eyes. In the beginning, narrowly focused demonstrations are more effective, and customizing your demo to your audience is key. An attractive-looking general-purpose space is going to be less convincing than demonstrating how that space supports a specific business process that is relevant to your audience. Of course, it must be apparent to them when they see it that the activity is something that they can't do very well with web meetings, teleconferences, or other types of traditional channels. We have done a wide range of demo/research projects—from meetings/events including tours and team-building activities to mentoring sessions and training; from 3D data centers tied to real data to virtual green data centers to a wide range of collaborative meetings using our virtual collaboration space. Just get them in-world. My motto is "Creating virtual world evangelists, one avatar at a time."

## Going Mainstream

We are still in the early stages of going mainstream, although we already have a number of lessons learned. I am confident that there are many more lessons to learn along the way. Here are some of our early learnings:

**Personal Attention Is Key.** Once you get past the early adopters, you will quickly move into a community with a wide range of interests (or objections), incentives (or not), and technical skills (or lack thereof) that will make the widespread adoption a bigger challenge. It will take time, patience, and people to help your company move from early adoption to widespread, everyday use. As with your initial efforts, focus first on going mainstream with groups that can benefit most from the use of these technologies. Use your evangelists and early adopters to help support the mainstream users and expect to spend a lot of one-on-one time with people. Run weekly training sessions (at different times for different geographies) where people can stop by and ask questions of experts. I run a weekly "Open House" in our New User Test Space, where people are encouraged to stop by and have a tour or ask questions. The new user test space (an instance of our collaboration meeting space) is actually quite an interesting place, as you never know who you will meet there. One day, right after an announcement to a large internal community had gone out, I came in early one morning to find people from the United States, Germany, France, India, and Australia all exploring the space at the same time.

**Automation of Key Processes.** It is very different to run a pilot where you can, for example, manually create avatar names and passwords and send them to the small group of new users. But what about when there are one hundred people a week, or five hundred people for a single meeting, who all need to be set up for the first time? Make sure that the solutions you plan to use have mechanisms for integrating with existing services within your organization, or you will find yourself spending a lot of time on administration of your virtual environments. For example, one of the key components we created was a mechanism for linking to our internal employee directory (called Blue Pages), so we could use the same user authentication process for creating new avatars as we use for signing into our intranet. Each time users sign into our virtual collaboration space, they are prompted for their intranet ID and password, which is used to determine their identity (including their avatar name when they first sign in) in the virtual world. No user ID setup is required as a result. As you experiment with different tools and platforms, make sure you are considering what would happen if ten times or one hundred times the number of people in your pilots were suddenly looking to be involved, and consider whether the tools you pick can handle the ramp-up in participation.

**Good Documentation/Help Materials.** Although most tools will come with user guides, we ended up creating a lot of support materials in different forms to help people through the ramp-up. We had a "Getting a (second) Life" presentation, a wiki with sections on troubleshooting for common issues (which we updated as we found new common issues), a one-page reference sheet, and a lot of in-world help signage. Also, don't forget to think like new users when creating these materials. For example, if a user wants to "chat," don't forget to tell the person how to open the chat bar.

**Consider Platform Scalability and Usage, and Set Proper Expectations.** Many of the newer tools in the market are not yet proven for scaling to one hundred, much less thousands of end-users. Make sure you are setting clear and reasonable expectations with your end-user community and your sponsors—it is better to undersell the capabilities and delight the community than to oversell and disappoint them.

## Demonstrating Value

In our experience, value to stakeholders comes in different forms—some measurable and tangible, and other less tangible. We have collected many anecdotal stories from our employees' participation in meetings and events and with our discussions with clients, and we share those within the internal community.

We also try to collect more measurable feedback in the form of surveys of participants. For major meetings, for example, there is typically a participant survey. For our Academy of Technology conference, for example, we were able to report that, compared to a face-to-face conference, the content (54 percent/43 percent), presentation style (41 percent/21 percent) and amount learned (16 percent/18 percent) were reported as "the same"/ "better." Surprisingly, even for peer-to-peer networking, 41 percent felt the experience was the same as face-to-face, and 21 percent felt it was better. We have also calculated savings based on estimating our initial investment ($80k) and estimating savings from a combination of elimination of travel expenses and increased productivity as a result of time not spent in travel to and from an in-person event ($320k). These types of numbers can help get the attention of even the most hardened skeptics.

## Double-Loop Reflection

**Find the "Heat Seekers" in the Organization.** Find them and let them try out new technologies. Many of our evangelists (myself included) had supportive management who allowed us to experiment "in our spare time" (as long as we got all the real work done). We worked nights and weekends because we believed in the potential of the new technologies and wanted to prove it to our organization.

**Start Small and Work Hard to Realize Early Success.** Every snowball starts with just a few flakes.

**Measure and Report on Your Experiences.** Although some decision-makers make decisions based on intuition alone, real numbers make an impact on more people than something that just "feels right." Find ways to measure your virtual world activities.

# Essay 3

### Brian Bauer, Étape Partners
### Overcoming Objections

**Objection 1: Virtual World Technologies Are Not "Serious" Technologies.** Quite often technology that ends up becoming a valuable business tool did not start out that way. Public "chat rooms" and web forums also did not begin as business tools (for example, AOL in 1992 was not focused on chat rooms for "co-worker collaboration"). Virtual worlds can be as serious as you want them to be, but you must define your business objectives first, and rationally dissect virtual world technologies to clearly and explicitly identify the components that will help meet these objectives. For example, "implement a virtual employee lounge" is not a valid business objective.

Essential technology is defined as such only because it has displaced something else or filled a functional void within an organization. "Serious" technology is defined as such because it is used to accomplish a serious task or business objective. Much of the skepticism around VW technologies comes from people who have only been exposed to the not-so-serious side of the technology (whimsical avatars flying around fantasy gardens).

The same technology that is used to share presentations online (WebEx, Live Meeting) can just as easily be used to share photo albums and/or children's stories. Microsoft does not market Live Meeting by showing friends huddled around their screens looking at photos of a birthday party. They show their technology in context, they TELL you what the advantage is, and they show it performing a serious business task. We must do the same thing with virtual worlds.

**Objection 2: We Don't Have the Money to Invest in Non-Essential Technology.** Very few companies do. If your company is not able to make a commitment to investing in virtual world technologies and cannot spend the time/energy needed to understand how it can be leveraged as an essential technology, then your organization is not ready.

That being said, the economic environment today is ideal for introducing innovative technologies. Travel budgets have been slashed, flex time and work from home are becoming even more prevalent. And yet the necessity for co-worker collaboration and leverage of existing human capital are being pushed to new limits. Why would you believe that with legacy tools alone you can forever continue to squeeze more performance out of the same or reduced numbers of people? Is there a sound historical basis for this? Rather, let's focus on empowering the human capital that remains, and make every IT dollar count more than it ever has.

Define your highest priority business objectives. Define your most urgent organizational financial pressures, and work to construct a credible, successful argument for how virtual world technologies can address them more effectively and efficiently than the existing suite of collaboration tools within the enterprise. If you cannot define your business objectives down to an actionable level of detail, and if you cannot define your financial constraints (and opportunities), then you are not ready for virtual worlds.

## Objection 3: There Are Many High-Profile Cases of "Limited Success" in VW Technology Deployments. Why Should We Try It?

Virtual worlds are such an immature technology, especially in the corporate environment, that even the best business managers may forget everything they know to be true when it comes to this kind of technology. In other words, irrational exuberance could lead to certain failure. Many of the historical emerging technology failures have resulted from implementations that were not properly crafted for the target audience.

The application of virtual world technology as a corporate business tool is in its infancy. To do it well is not fast, easy, or cheap. It can be done well, but this requires a deep level of commitment. Today, there are a couple of major problems in the way that corporations are introduced to this emerging technology:

First, virtual world technology vendors sell what they have. This assumes that the customer wants/needs what the vendor has built. Microsoft can sell Word and Excel this way because, for most of the business world, the product is mature enough and feature-rich enough to meet the needs of the purchaser. With virtual world technologies, we are still in the proverbial garage tinkering. Selling the enterprise application of virtual worlds must begin with asking the question of customers: "What are your business needs?" not "What do you need a virtual world for?" and certainly not "Let me tell you how great my product is."

Second, virtual world marketing tends to "go big" rather than small. Big is quite often harder to achieve than small. It is much easier to accomplish a task than it is to accomplish a concept. For example, "collaborate more with your colleagues" is a concept, while "pick up the phone and call your colleague" is a task. We must define, and then explain to our target audience, not just the concepts that virtual worlds enable, but the activities and tasks that they improve or transform.

Goals are achieved through a process. A process is defined by a series of tasks. Tasks are accomplished using tools. A virtual world is a tool—like a hammer. A hammer does not build a house, but you can't build the house without one. This is the way that we must talk to our target audience about virtual world technologies.

## Establishing a Beachhead

The best reference and precedent for understanding what will ultimately be successful with virtual world technologies is to remember the "flight to the Internet" from 1998 to roughly 2000. Everybody became part of the movement. There seemed to be limitless potential for every idea to become a success.

But ten years later, we can see with some clarity that "good" ideas will always be good, and bad ideas will always be bad. So what can we take away from this? Let's understand what made the good ideas good and postulate that what has been a good, sound, business decision in the past may continue to be in the future.

The Internet delivered success onto:

- Services that could not be performed in physical reality due to physical constraints. eBay is a good example of that. It is not viable to attempt a physical auction where "everything" is up for bid. WebMD is another good example: it is not physically viable to try and bring together a large enough collective of doctors to provide such a clearinghouse of medical information.

- Services that could be delivered faster, better, cheaper on the Internet. Etrade is a great example of this.

Our intent by pausing to reflect on Internet success/failure is to reference the introduction of the last great "disruptive technology" and learn the lessons that are so important. When we look for low-hanging fruit with virtual world technologies, we can do one of two things:

- Take every unvetted idea that comes to mind, put it into virtual world technology space, and wait to see what sticks.

- Take a good hard look at those things that are simply not possible using any other technology and focus on them.

If time and money are not factors, and it's not important that your initiatives attain a high rate of success, the scatter-gun approach might be interesting. However, if your business, like most businesses, is highly scrutinized using ROI and program success statistics, our advice is to focus on a small number of real business tasks that, like the successful Internet programs, target services that really are not possible without the advent of new technology.

## Securing Sponsorship

When it comes to navigating the IT waters of a large enterprise, virtual world technologies are not really that unique. The same variables are in play:

- Who will pay for it?

- Who will support it?

- What is the business value?

- Do we already own this sort of technology? Have we tried it before?

In a utopian corporate environment, the dog will always wag his tail. But in many large institutions, the tail (IT) very often wags the dog (the business). We could spend an entire book (and this has surely been done already) trying to understand this phenomenon, or we can accept the rules of the game and play it with the following rules in mind:

First, we are going to spend money. This money needs to come from someone's budget. Therefore, we need a business sponsor. The business sponsor will almost always need to answer to a higher "business authority" before he or she can spend their money. The higher authority will want to see business value clearly defined. So have your business objectives mapped out to the real dollars of this project.

Second, you need to satiate IT. The best way to do this is to ask for IT's help as early in the adoption process as is feasible, even if you don't need it or want it. IT will need to host and support your product. This is more work for them. But the savvy IT manager will also recognize that:

- They can get their hands on cool, geeky new stuff.

- They can get credit for a successful project.

## Making the Case

In today's corporate environment defined by flexible work schedules, disparate physical locations, and functional alignment, providing an impactful tool that breaks through these process challenges is essential. The virtual corporate environment (VCE) is such a tool.

VCEs will help unify an organization's diverse population of associates who are both physically separated and functionally discrete. Efficiency and effectiveness can be raised to levels not currently achievable in the physical space, leading to favorably impacted business results. The VCE will be an environment that exists for bringing together associates who are separated not only by physical space, but by function as well.

The VCE will enable both structured and casual encounters with co-workers much in the same way people would interact with each other when they work in close physical proximity. The belief is that the facilitation of more frequent and impactful encounters with co-workers will enhance working relationships and ultimately yield improved business results driven by increased productivity and efficiency.

A VCE will create a collaborative and social environment that encourages both formal and informal co-worker encounters. It is anticipated that increased encounters between functional silos and physically separated associates will encourage communication and cross-functional awareness among individuals and groups that are all part of a cross-functional process.

Process awareness that transcends functional responsibilities is believed to be a key enabler of success when the goal is to improve a singular result. VCEs create a platform for ensuring that all associates are well equipped with an understanding of business priority, cultural principles, and process-oriented objectives. It is believed that if all process contributors are fully immersed in process and not just function, the unique ability of each contributor will help to improve the quality of the end result.

## Crossing the Chasm

High-quality virtual world technologies can be a very effective medium for gaining an employee's full attention. It is also a powerful tool that can be used for teaching and collaboration. But do we need a "world" to accomplish our business objectives? Or are we better served with a set of business tools that are deployed as needed in specific situations? After all, we are not trying to create the "matrix"; we are trying to achieve business results.

Employees use business tools to accomplish tasks that are part of a process followed to achieve a result. As such, we can think of virtual world technologies as a business tool, if deployed the right way. Think of it this way: when Microsoft first created MS Word, were they attempting to change the way in which people fundamentally did their jobs? Or were they looking to create a vastly improved typewriter? More than twenty years later, we might argue that Microsoft Office has fundamentally changed the way people work, but in the beginning, the goals were more modest.

Revolutionary change happens incrementally. Paradigm shifting tools are delivered discretely and become ubiquitous. When the timing is right, these tools can be conjoined, and we will find that the "office of the future" exists. The death trap of virtual world technology adoption in corporations is to attempt to create a parallel reality that is as large as your physical reality. Do you need a room, or a world? Be honest with yourself and your organization.

## Going Mainstream

We cannot force the issue of "mainstreaming" virtual world technologies. They are still bleeding edge and niche. This may change very quickly, but let's not take on the burden. Instead, let's focus on ensuring that our new technology has everything it needs to cross over, and does not have any of the constraints that would prevent it from crossing over.

The following is your recipe for success. Deviate from these priorities at your own peril:

- Ease of use;

- Stability;

- Business functions; and

- Performance.

## Demonstrating Value

How do you demonstrate value to your stakeholders? You start by asking your stakeholders what their business objectives are in terms of objectives, processes, and tasks. You survey the landscape of existing tools used to perform essential tasks. What are the strengths, weaknesses, gaps, and so forth. You explore what can be done (as opposed to what has already been done) using virtual world technologies and determine whether this approach provides a better tool for performing the objective, process, and/or task.

If you can establish that virtual world technologies do indeed provide value-added to the business issue, your last bit of work is building and implementing. But this is the easy part. Manage your project well, and the new tools will go into the toolbox and quickly be recognized as faster, better, easier than legacy methods of work.

## Double-Loop Reflection

**Do Not Get Involved in Virtual Worlds as "Me Too" Play.** Second Life is riddled with hundreds of millions of dollars' worth of "me too." The Internet is a similar graveyard. Take the time to understand what virtual world technologies can do for your business. And don't just ask the virtual world vendor. Do some soul searching and proper business analysis within your organization; document and think about your challenges and needs. Only then do you call the tool salesman.

**Define Your Business Objectives at an Actionable Level.** "Improve performance" is not actionable; "reduce costs" is not actionable. "Improve customer intimacy" is not actionable. These are all great business objectives, but as we know, objectives are met by following a process, comprised of tasks, performed using tools. Actionable change happens at the tasks and tool level (unless, of course, you are also changing your business objectives). Be clear about how the business objectives tie to task through process, and be sure that virtual world technologies being applied provide significant differentiated value over existing collaboration tools.

**Approach Virtual Worlds as Business-Critical Technology, Nothing Less.** It's not just about the money. Your employees are busy. They have methods of work that they employ because they are well understood, require less thought (than change), and are quite often efficient.

Introducing a disruptive technology as "hey, try this" is quite likely going to yield a different result than "this new technology is easy to use and will reduce your workload by 25 percent so you can spend more time with your family." While this may be an extreme example, the point is that you must manage people's perceptions of your virtual world initiative. If you do not tell them what to think, they will form their own conclusions, and that is not good risk mitigation.

# Essay 4

## John Hengeveld, Intel

"Enterprises of Great Pith and Moment with this regard their currents turn awry, and lose the name of action . . . "

*—Hamlet, Act III Sc. 1*

2D or not 2D? That is the question. Our physical world has been perceived in 3D since the invention/evolution of binocular vision. But our learning world, our intellectual world is the world of books, papers, blackboards, and computer screens—two-dimensional projections of insight, communication, and invention.

The revolutionary thought is not "Let's use 3D technology more," but "What is it that 'gives us pause and makes us rather bear those ills we have than fly to others we know not of.'" As we try to lead change in this area, understanding the mental perspectives that cause companies and people to stick to the comfortable is the first key step.

## Overcoming Objections

So what are the key perceptions people have about 3D? Most decisions don't map 3D with enterprise applications beyond product design and mechanical CAD. 3D makes nice pictures and is fun to play at. Overwhelmingly, the top three negative perceptions are

- 3D is recreational in purpose.

- 3D environments are not under our control and are therefore not secure.

- 3D environments are difficult to operate, manage, and sustain.

**Objection 1: 3D Is Recreational in Purpose.** As executives consider 3D environments, the G-word (game) gets inappropriately applied to learning and collaboration activities. Even the moniker "serious games" distracts from the key notion that learning and collaboration is not a game, any more than competition for profitability is.

However, most people who have experienced 3D environments have seen it in games: Some battle games (Battlefield 1942 and World of Warcraft), some social games (Second Life). As decision-makers consider putting their company collaboration and learning sacred jewels into this space, they are struck by images of furries frolicking in butterfly-filled fields (the Second Life problem) or of giants with clubs beating their enemies (the World of Warcraft problem). These images come from the fantasy nature of 3D environments, and the fantastical is the enemy of productive in the eyes of many executives.

So how do we deal with this issue? First, talk about serious scientific and technical applications of 3D technology. It is much easier for executives to think about applying technology for scientists' collaboration in physics to their work than to think about furries frolicking. Instead of talking about 3D spaces as a marketing space, leaders need to talk about 3D technology collaboration in protean folding. Leaders in collaboration and learning need to re-brand 3D away from socialization and play.

**Objection 2: 3D Environments Are Not Under Our Control.** "We can't have our corporate data and our corporate discussions running outside our domain." This objection is actually right. The industry has been providing toys to enterprise adoption so far. These toys allow folks to see the potential, but not to seriously use the tools. Enterprise 3D adoption will be predicated on operations that are securely within existing IT environments, demonstrate data security and manageability, and are rock solid in performance and cost.

If one of the value propositions for 3D learning and collaboration is lower cost per participant, the total cost (including manageability, support, etc.) has to be clearly understood. Having pilot projects to gain skills and understand the dynamics of these applications is essential to making the case. Intel has been exploring how to optimize performance of "immersive connected environments" through a collaborative activity called scienceism.

Part of doing this is to gain experience with the operating requirements for scaling out these environments to an enterprise scale. Armed with data, we can talk to the IT czars. Without it, we can't.

**Objection 3: 3D Applications Are Too Hard to Manage and Too Difficult to Scale.** Historically, much of this is true. The industry has been coming out with more focused tools that have "click and go" behavior necessary. I believe the industry must adopt a "thirty-second rule." From the time a user decides to enter a collaborative space *for the first time* to the time he is productively working with others should be no more than the amount of time it takes to load an e-mail in-box. Some flexibility (like making your avatar furry) is bad for enterprise learning and collaboration. The industry must strip down functionality to essentials to help drive mass adoption.

## Establishing a Beachhead

Sales training "the thing wherein we'll catch the conscience of the king."

So where are the best applications to get started with 3D? So far, it is clearly sales training and sales events. Sales events require center stage material delivery, person-to-person collaboration, and training simulation. These three areas are the highest value strengths of 3D collaboration technologies. When combined with low cost to get someone to participate, the relative tolerance for a physical abstraction, a much lower burden on the salesperson's schedule (a sales professional should be selling, not flying to training), this application is the best place to start when proposing investments in 3D learning and collaboration. The ROI is easy to demonstrate, and event planners can easily be convinced to add a virtual event track to a live event as a trial. What happens next is that a fair number of attendees want to attend virtually and 3D has taken its first step.

The problem with this is that many marketing executives were burned by poor investments in 3D marketing activities and so might have a bad taste in their mouths. So the right place to go is not the marketing exec, but instead the sales operations leadership. Reducing costs in sales training and improving sales competency are both critical to operational performance and business profitability.

## Crossing the Chasm and Going Mainstream

In his book *Avatars*, Bruce Damer describes the history of virtual worlds since the Seventies. He shows several epochs of experimentation, proliferation, hitting technology limits, and extinction of virtual world initiatives. Technology adoption has increased in each wave as each new generation of compute-and-display technology knocks down the barriers that killed the last wave.

So the question to ask is how to make this species of 3D technology persist and evolve into mainstream usage. I believe there are three conditions to ubiquitous adoption in the mainstream:

**The Technology Must Integrate Seamlessly with a Broad Range of Client Devices.** Mainstream adoption must not have high performance computer requirements at the client end. Today's platforms frequently require high-end gaming capability in the users' hands, and that doesn't correspond to how the mainstream customers will be experiencing their digital worlds in the future.

**Economics and Profitability Drive Innovation and Mainstream Deployment.** Somebody has to be able to make a buck from a robust and sustainable business model in order for solutions to reach the market. So achieving profitability requires having efficient development of new applications, a cost-effective means to support a high volume of users, and a very rational monetization model for the services or products involved. In order to enable efficient development, technology standards must proliferate so that web and cloud innovations enable better 3D experiences with a minimum of duplicated investment.

In order to enable efficient service delivery, the technology to scale applications to many users must be broadly deployed. In order to rationally monetize collaboration and training applications of 3D (distinct from gaming), mainstream software companies are ultimately going to have to deliver shrink-wrapped products to adopting end-users. The services model and advertising model cannot be the primary business models for these areas.

**Mainstream Users Don't Have the Time or Inclination to Manage Detail.** One of the keys to Moore's "Crossing the Chasm" model for mainstream buyers is they want complete solutions to their problems with the most focused delivery to their needs. These users want to extract value from their usage (be it entertainment, collaboration, visualization, or information) in as efficient a manner as possible. They want the "automatic transmission" of 3D that abstracts what goes on under the hood.

So application developers must simplify usage and cut out features that distract from the task at hand. The result will be targeted applications for mainstream usage built on highly efficient general-purpose platforms. This approach is distinct from the "one application fits all" approach. As we look at mobile augmented reality, its needs are distinct from group collaborative events, which are distinct yet again from scientific collaboration. Each user needs a subset of the feature set of the whole, and only those features should be expressed to them.

## Double-Loop Reflection

I believe very passionately in the application of 3D technology in our future. Yet I must temper that zeal so that those who follow see a coherent unbroken line from their present where each step makes sense to them.

Implied above are a couple of inviolate rules that I recommend to you:

- Shun the G-word and reposition 3D in the minds of your community.
- Adopt technology consistent with your company's IT philosophy.
- Have data.

Beyond this, my three pieces of advice follow.

**Understand Stakeholder Motivation.** Take the time to understand the fundamental motivations of executive leadership that you are trying to influence. What do they care about today? How do the gains in learning and collaboration efficiency manifest as part of THEIR vision and needs? Each executive I deal with is different. One is worried about legacy. One worries about profitability. One worries about his ambition. If what you say to each doesn't speak to his or her interests, the executive will not come behind the investments you propose. Take the time to connect.

**Sell, But Don't Oversell.** Don't oversell the benefits or the timeline. But make sure to sell. Like anything of value in this world, there is a line of argument and an emotional appeal that promote reaching a mutual exchange. The adoption of any technology is a long trek. I recall working on HDTV in the early Nineties. The technology was oversold, the pace of adoption overestimated, the timeline to transition the ecosystem was grossly misunderstood. The result of the overselling was a delay in this transition by probably five years. People turned off to the message and only turned on again when it was obvious and right before their eyes. 3D technology has substantial benefits, but sell the first step first.

**Make an Impression.** Each project leaves an impression within your company. Plan the impression as you plan the project. Take specific measured steps, each safe and secure in delivering value. Then after each step measure where the impressions stand and adapt the path you were on accordingly.

The 3D Internet and its applications in training, learning, and collaboration will not be built overnight. It will be a long path, and each small victory in every company helps build a compelling future for all of us. Thanks for your efforts on the journey. Good luck.

# Rules from Revolutionaries

The following rules are distilled from the essays above. While they in no way substitute for reading each essay in full, they are designed to provide the reader with the essence of the insights synthesized from our revolutionaries.

## Rule 1: Change the Name Game

The whole idea of a game as a productive use of time runs contrary to our mental models. Business is not about playing games. Games were for recess; real learning happens in the classroom. To overcome this issue, we must reposition the application of 3D technology to the enterprise away from "games" or even "serious games" and frame it based on the benefits it brings to enterprise training and collaboration. The person responsible for the business decision must be provided with solid evidence that real work can be done in virtual worlds.

## Rule 2: Build a Grass Roots Community

No revolution has ever emerged victorious without an army of passionate believers—those key individuals who are willing to volunteer their energy and effort to achieve a vision for a shared future. Purposefully seek out the evangelists within your organization and find ways for them to connect and commune. Within any organization, the 3D revolution will be built one avatar at a time.

## Rule 3: Begin with the Business Issues

You should approach 3D as a business-critical technology, nothing less. Define your highest priority business objectives. Define your organization's most urgent financial pressures and construct a credible, successful argument for why 3D technologies can address them. Identify the critical business gap that would be addressed through the use of a 3D solution, and gather the sponsorship and resources necessary to design and run a pilot. If you can't do this, it may not yet be the right time to bring 3D to your enterprise.

## Rule 4: Connect to Core Motivation

Motivation is everything. Take the time to understand the fundamental motivations of the executive leadership that you are trying to influence. What is their motivation to invest in a 3D solution? Value to stakeholders comes in many different forms. If the value proposition you present does not align with that motivation, the likelihood of them supporting you is slim. Be sure you understand the value they see in 3D and build your argument for investment around that motivation.

## Rule 5: Select the Right Pilots

Start small while thinking big. Beyond sponsorship, there are a number of criteria to consider when selecting a pilot. Where you start is largely a function of how well a 3D solution will address the needs of the client, how easily that value can be demonstrated, and how committed the client is to partnering with you. In general, it makes sense to start small, work hard to realize early success, show impact, and iterate.

## Rule 6: Pilot Early and Often

Seeing is believing. Each pilot leaves an impression within your company. Plan the impression as you plan the pilot. Don't oversell the benefits or short-change the timeline. Take specific measured steps that assure value. After each step, reassess impressions and re-vector subsequent pilots accordingly.

## Rule 7: Focus on the First Hour

Discomfort dissolves enthusiasm. The success or failure of any pilot usually comes down to the initial experience of the participants. Every effort must be made to ensure that the first hour of exposure to the 3D environment instills confidence and curiosity within participants. This requires significant planning and effort, but the benefit is well worth the cost.

## Rule 8: Begin with the Familiar

"You are here." That is the sign we all look for in the mall. While it is clear that there is much opportunity for learning and collaboration in virtual worlds, the road to mass adoption begins with engaging participants with what is familiar to them. Classrooms, presentation screens, flip charts, and sticky notes are all artifacts we have become very familiar with in the real world. Use them as affordances to familiarize participants with the virtual world, and then take them to the next level. Pushing too hard too soon results in disengagement.

## Rule 9: Build an Evidence Base

Proof is powerful. Each planned pilot allows your organization to gain more experience in understanding the operating requirements for building out these environments for enterprise scale. Each pilot should also be contributing to an evidence base that legitimizes the value proposition of the technology relative to a business need. Without proof of successful pilot experiences and evidence of business impact, the ability to scale is highly compromised.

## Rule 10. Prime the Scale Pump

Knowing that the IT tail often wags the business dog, it is wise to include them in the piloting process as soon as is practical. For the IT professionals, it is less about business impact or pedagogy and more about ease of use, business function performance, standards, security, and scalability. If you have worked to include the right stakeholders, identified the right learning need and target populations, developed the right 3D environment, and executed successful pilots, you will have several constituencies reporting positive experiences. This all helps when the enterprise-scale discussion arrives on the scene.

# Part Four

**Just Beyond the Horizon**

# Back to the Future

## Introduction

The Double Happiness Jeans factory specializes in customized jeans. The production process enables customers to customize orders to their exact specifications. The company offers several stylish cuts to fulfill different fashion needs—flare, skinny leg, boot cut, and relaxed. Customized details include a choice of rinse, pocket style, rivet design, hemline, and fly. The jeans are high fashion and have been featured at the Sundance Film Festival and other high-profile venues.

The company actively encourages customers to visit the factory to see how the jeans are made. Many customers make the journey. Upon arriving at the plant, customers find that visiting the Double Happiness Jeans factory is a lot like a visit to other typical textile manufacturers. There are familiar work stations like the loom, a bolt roll cutter, and a drill press. There are employee amenities like soda and coffee machines and even a nice clean break room. While touring the factory, customers find several work-related conference rooms used for brainstorming new products, a whiteboard for drawing up plans, and a large employee of the month poster.

What customers don't find on the tour is real equipment, real coffee, or even real fabric. While the Double Happiness Jeans factory is similar in many ways to a typical textile factory, it is anything but typical and it might just be the future of virtual immersive environments. The Double Happiness Jeans factory isn't a physical factory at all. In fact, the entire plant exists only on a computer server in Second Life and it has no physical assets or inventory. (See Figure 10.1.)

When a customer orders Happiness Jeans, they are "manufactured" by virtual workers sitting at different work cells. Each worker presses buttons and operates machinery that sends information to a file that configures the design of the virtual jeans. The jeans travel through ten or so work stations

**Figure 10.1.** Standing by the Laser Cutter at the Double Happiness Jean's Factory

until they meet the customer's design request. The data collected at each work station is fed into a server running the graphics application, Adobe Photoshop, via an application program interface (API) developed specifically for the Double Happiness Jeans company. At the end of a twenty-minute production process, the jeans enter the real world through a printing process—a large-format printer loaded with a canvas-like material that breathes and stretches when it is worn (similar to denim)—prints the jeans. The customer picks up the "print out" of the jeans, cuts out the separate parts, and stitches them together. He or she can then wear them around town.

This process, or one similar to it, is the future of VIEs and 3D worlds. The technology, in the form of such items as 3D resin printers, exists today to make in-world production of products possible and even desirable. Many information systems within factories transmit critical production information to customer service personnel, salespeople, and to the point of need on the factory floor. At a basic level, computer-aided drafting (CAD), computer-aided manufacturing (CAM), and even enterprise resource planning (ERP) programs are all forerunners to the concept of using a VIE to design and manufacture an item used in the physical world. In other environments where spreadsheets, documents, and other digital media are the end results of work efforts, the possibilities are even more immediate. People working, collaborating, and learning in virtual spaces to accomplish actual work is beginning to happen now and will accelerate into the future.

In a healthcare scenario, John Royer, director of sales training strategy at AstraZenca, sees a future wherein a patient can actually walk through a virtual rendering of his or her own heart rather than a generic heart. According to Royer, "A person's heart could be scanned via an MRI and an exact replica could be created. The doctor could then give the patient a tour of her own heart. He could show her the plaque beginning to clog her arteries. Since it is a virtual world, the doctor could even run a series of 'what if' scenarios to show the patient what would happen if her diet wasn't changed or what would happen if she decided to begin an exercise regiment."

The examples of Double Happiness Jeans and walking through your own heart are just two of the many future possibilities. In the near future, work, learning, and virtual worlds will merge. Real work performed in a virtual environment is the future of VIEs, and learning must follow or, ideally, lead the charge.

# Moving from 2D to 3D

Over fifty years ago, cell phones were nothing but science fiction. Then in April 1973 Martin Cooper made the first call on a cell phone to his rival at Bell Labs.[1] The rest is history. Over forty-five years ago, the Internet was science fiction until the Department of Defense commissioned ARAPANET for research into networking and in 2006, "You" became *Time* magazine's person of the year because of the ability for an individual to create and post content on the Internet—something not possible on a large scale a mere ten years ago. Once a technology is around for a few years, people tend to forget what it was like before. As Koreen Olbrish of Tandem Learning reminds us, "Today we say to ourselves, 'How did we look up information on the Internet before Google?' Soon there will be a time when will say 'How did we meet over distance without virtual worlds?'"

What seemed like science fiction a few decades ago is now reality. While creating products, working on deliverables, and collaborating across organizations on a large scale in VIEs seems like science fiction, the truth is that 3D environments for working, learning, and collaborating are the not-too-distant future. Today, for many, it is hard to imagine the Immernet when so much content and information are still presented in two dimensions. And while some of the first forays into 3D spaces have involved reproducing classrooms complete with slides shows and rows of front-facing desks, other pioneers have shown that much more is possible. VIEs allow data visualization not previously possible and applications for learning and collaboration not yet considered. To not be left behind, organizations need to evolve and begin working and learning completely within these spaces.

Unfortunately, some organizations are stuck in the process of merely mimicking 2D learning environments in 3D spaces. To help organizations evolve past that state, a framework in the form of a maturity model is needed. A maturity model provides a roadmap to move from the beginning level of using VIEs all the way to a scenario similar to the Double Happiness Jeans factory.

# 3D Learning Maturity Model

The concept behind the 3D learning maturity model is to provide a way that an organization can gage where it is in terms of implementing VIEs. Just as a software maturity model helps measure where a company is within its software development acumen, this model allows an organization to measure its use of 3D learning contexts. The 3D learning maturity model moves from mimicking the classroom in a 3D space to the creation of actual work products within a 3D environment.

It is worth noting that the 3D learning maturity model is meant to be applied to the majority of activities within an organization and not to individual activities. At each level of the model are elements that are required throughout every level of the model, including the highest level of maturity. For example, there is always a need for gathering spaces within a VIE. The difference between a Level 1 gathering space and a Level 4 gathering space is that in Level 1 the gathering space is used as the primary method of delivering instruction, and in Level 4 it is used as a quick meeting place while the participants are engaged in another activity—it is not the primary method of transferring knowledge.

## Maturity Level 1: Mimicking Existing Classroom Structures

This is where most organizations begin with their VIE implementation. At this level, instruction is based on replicating what is done in traditional educational settings such as a classroom. Actual physical spaces are reconstructed and learners are asked to sit in rows of seats, facing forward. Instruction is provided by an avatar/instructor standing in the front of the 3D space showing slides. Learners raise their hands to ask questions and rarely move within the environment. The model for the interactions and the hierarchy of control are based on the physical classroom. Transporting this type of environment to a VIE causes boredom and leads to a rather unruly classroom. Figure 10.2 is an example.

Other times, indoor auditoriums are produced and an effort is made to portray a campus or building as accurately as possible. While the realism provides a sense of location and identification with spaces in the physical

**Figure 10.2.** Holding Virtual Classes Is the First Level of the 3D Learning Maturity Model

world, it doesn't allow the full potential of VIEs to be leveraged. Realistically developed buildings and spaces in a VIE are too bound by constraints that exist in the physical world.

At Level 1 maturity, 3DLE often produce learning that is informative and helpful at the basic level for learners, but much of the knowledge transferred could be delivered as effectively with 2D synchronous learning software. This level focuses on the learning of facts, jargon, labels, and other types of declarative knowledge—information that must be memorized. This is the routinization level of using 3D environments for learning. In Level 1 instruction, the success of the learning event depends highly on having a dynamic instructor with interesting slides. The result is that potential adopters see little value in using a 3D version of a 2D virtual classroom. It appears that the 3D is superfluous.

To move beyond this level, the thinking must be more in line with field trips and site visits than classroom lectures. Think of places where learners should visit to learn more about a topic or what types of environments reinforce the content being presented. The goal is to think beyond the four walls of a classroom and transport the learners to environments in which they would be applying their knowledge and skills.

One way to escape this trap is to purposely develop activities in which the avatars need to move around the space. The focus on creating active learning within the 3D space will help push the design of instruction beyond the classroom. With a VIE, it is possible to take a field trip within every learning event or to transport learners from place to place with no travel worries and minimal time constraints. To force a movement away from routinization, create buildings floating in the air, re-create historic locations and other environments not possible within the parameters of a physical classroom.

## Maturity Level 2: Expansion of Existing Learning Structures

This is the level where learners are immersed and active within the VIE. This involves sending learners on scavenger hunts or guided tours. It involves having the avatars move around and interact within the 3DLE. The learning moves beyond a 3D classroom or even a realistic setting into a context specifically designed for the learners to interact with each other and the space. This level often involves group work and tours during which the learners are interacting with environmental elements such as fire hoses, a solar panel on a building, or a virtual kiosk. Figure 10.3 is an example.

The design of the instruction for Level 2 involves careful consideration of the spaces that are created. The spaces themselves are designed to serve as a catalyst for learning. The spaces contain elements such as items to be found in a scavenger hunt or note cards or other non-player characters (or bots), who provide information to learners exploring the spaces. This level provides declarative knowledge, but also teaches conceptual ideas through examples and non-examples of the concepts being learned. For example, the concept of discrimination was highlighted in the case study in Chapter 6 where students at Ball State University dressed as giant Kool-Aid men and experienced discrimination at a popular virtual dance club.

Maturity Level 2 3DLEs provide specific learning goals and objectives that the learners achieve during the course of their interaction within the 3D

**Figure 10.3.** Abbott Bundy/Karl Kapp Giving a Virtual Tour of the Onside of a Dell Computer to Bliss Yue aka Cammie

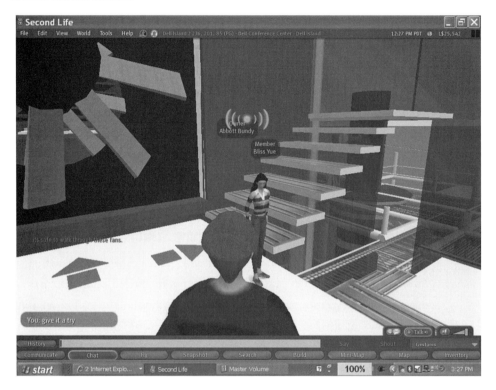

environment that would be difficult to convey via a lecture. In Level 2 the success of the learning event depends on how well the 3DLE is constructed and how well the tour guide or facilitator debriefs the learners on what they found or saw during the interaction.

To move to the next level of maturity, the goal needs to be the creation of realistic activities. While scavenger hunts are effective for basic learning, the real value of VIEs is that they can re-create actual situations. This doesn't mean that buildings and the environment have to be 100 percent authentic. It means the essence of the situation must reflect the conditions under which the work is actually performed. An example of this is when the students in the Loyalist College Border Patrol class are transported to a Canadian border station, mentioned in Chapter 6. They are inspecting cars and observing behavior in the VIE as they would in the physical world. This provides an actual context for which they can apply the skills they learned from reading and discussing situations within the physical classroom setting.

Think of the application of skills, the concept of "learning by doing." Often in work situations people must coordinate activities and work together to accomplish goals. Take these types of situations within the workplace and transform them into a VIE to provide authentic practice for the learners. When the majority of 3DLEs are focused on reproducing authentic behavior, the organization will have moved to the next level on the maturity model.

## Maturity Level 3: Practicing the Authentic Task

At this level, the learner is immersed in the task he or she would actually perform in the work environment. This could be assembling components for a manufacturing job, waiting on customers in a retail store, or negotiating a sale. The 3DLE created is as authentic and realistic as possible to encourage the transfer of knowledge, complete with actual people on the other side of the avatar making decisions in the same manner with the same criteria as actual co-workers or customers. Figure 10.4 is an example.

The learning that tends to occur at this level involves rules and procedures, psychomotor skills practice, and soft skill application—applying negotiation or leadership skills. This level of majority focuses on the application of skills.

An example of this level of maturity is the Ernst & Young inventory observation discussed in Chapter 6. In that environment, participants had to deal with inconsistencies in how incoming materials were counted, determine the difference between count sheets and tags, and what items needed to be test counted. The idea behind the 3DLE is to immerse the learners as deeply as possible into a realistic inventory audit so they can understand the unique challenges they will encounter during the actual process.

In Level 3 the success of the learning event depends on how closely it resembles the authentic work situation and how effectively the learner is debriefed after the process to improve what he or she is doing as well as how adept the other avatars are at fulfilling their roles.

**Figure 10.4.** Preparing to Conduct a Sales Call on a Physician in a Realistic Office Is an Example of the Third Level of the Maturity Model

To move to the final level of the maturity model, the organization must consider not just learning events in the VIE but also how work and work products can be created within a VIE. The process of creating work products of value adds to the learning process and provides opportunities for innovation. When work, collaboration, and learning occur simultaneously, innovation is the result.

## Maturity Level 4: Working

The highest level of maturity in a 3D synchronous learning event is the actual creation of value within the environment. This involves two or more people working together within the 3D space to create a deliverable that is desired by an internal or external client and the people working on the deliverable learn as they create the final product. One example would be a team of car designers creating a virtual prototype of a new car and allowing potential consumers to drive it. Another would be a group of architects observing how avatars travel around a space they have designed.

This level of the majority model involves helping people to problem solve and to network socially to gain new contacts. This level of the model focuses on addressing and solving actual problems through the collaborative nature of the environment. Figure 10.5 is an example.

An example of using a VIE for work is when IBM sent a select group of 330 thought leaders and technology innovators who are responsible for providing technical leadership to IBM into a VIE and then asked them for input and ideas about the direction of the technology. The purpose of the

**Figure 10.5.** A Customer Peers in from the Physical World as His Jeans Are Being Customized in the Virtual World

Image courtesy of Jeff Crouse and Stephanie Rothenberg. All Rights Reserved.

session was to create reports and trend analyses for IBM consultants to use to inform their work.

Success at this level depends on the group's ability to create something of value. One such example is when virtual real-estate moguls create houses in which other avatars pay money to live because of the architecture and beauty of the creation. Of course, the example from the beginning of this chapter of Double Happiness Jeans is a natural extension of creating something of value in a VIE and extending it to the physical world.

## 3D Majority Model Chart

Use the maturity levels as a guide for measuring the use of VIEs within a company to achieve organizational goals. As an organization moves from one maturity level to the next, the learning experiences will include the lower levels in the maturity level as well as the higher level.

The combination of the maturity levels, types of learning, and the learning archetypes will help you to craft effective 3DLEs. Figure 10.6 shows how

**Figure 10.6.** The Interaction of the Four Levels of the 3D Learning Maturity Model, Different Types of Learning, and the Learning Archetypes

**Putting It All Together**

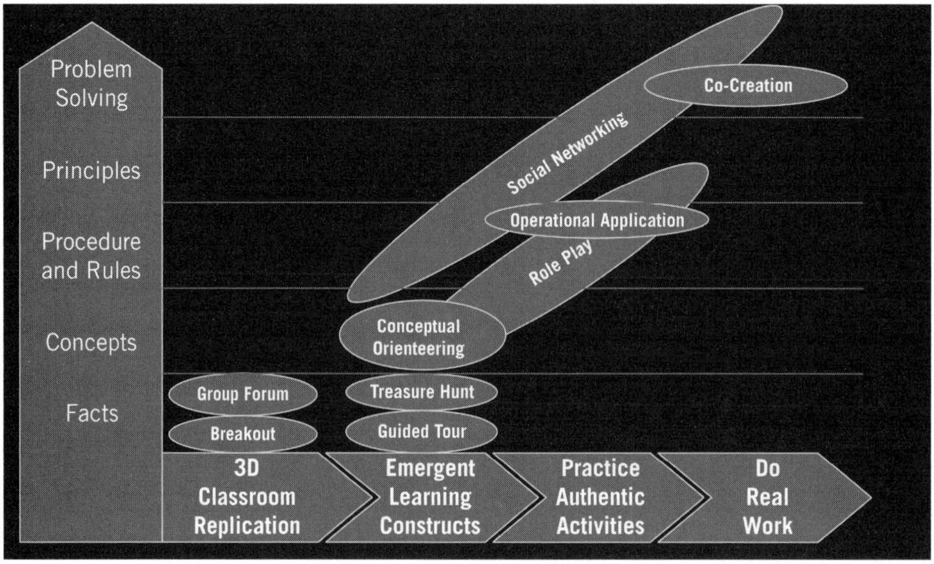

different types of learning are linked to different archetypes and maturity levels.

Organizations at Level 4 will routinely include all levels of interaction, including the act of conducting actual work within the 3D environment, as shown in Table 10.1.

## Table 10.1. Types of Learning at Various Maturity Levels

| Type of 3D Environment | Type of Learning | Archetype | Maturity Level |
|---|---|---|---|
| Virtual classroom | Facts, Jargon, Labels | Avatar Persona; Breakout Sessions; Group Forums | Level 1: Mimicking Existing Classroom Structures |
| Buildings, landscapes, miniaturized or enlarged spaces (walking around inside a computer) | Facts, Jargon, Labels | Guided Tour; Scavenger Hunt; Large Group Forum | Maturity Level 2: Expansion of Existing Learning Structures |
| Buildings, landscapes, miniaturized or enlarged spaces (walking around inside a computer) | Concepts | Conceptual Orienteering; Role Play; Small Group Discussion; Social Networking | |
| Authentic Work Environment (actual machinery, stores, factory, etc.) | Rules/Procedures | Role Play; Operational Application; Social Networking | Maturity Level 3: Practicing the Authentic Task |
| Authentic Work Environment (actual machinery, stores, factory, etc.) | Psychomotor Practice | Operational Application; Co-Creation | |
| Authentic Work Environment (actual machinery, stores, factory, etc.) | Principles | Role Play; Social Networking | |
| Any workspace open for co-development (virtual wind tunnel, virtual testing ground) | Problem Solving | Co-Creation; Social Networking | Maturity Level 4: Working |

# Conclusion

We are at the ground floor of the Immernet. The future of VIEs is expansive, impressive, and a little intimidating, but the upside is virtually unlimited. The examples, models, lessons learned, and paths forward have been forged by virtual world pioneers who have boldly taken steps to move the use of VIEs forward. Their hard work, virtual success, and virtual failures are the foundation upon which organizations can build the future of VIEs. The time is right for the application of this technology. The convergence of practice, applications, and opportunity has arrived. It seems fitting to conclude *Learning in 3D* with two essays outlining possible visions into the future of VIEs. Then the next step in the VIE evolutionary process is up to you.

If you would like to continue this growing, dynamic conversation and further explore of the potential of VIEs, please join us at www.learningin 3d.info.

---

## Campfire 3.0—The Next Generation Collaboration and Work Space

### Chuck Hamilton, Virtual Learning Strategy, IBM Center for Advanced Learning

Virtual social world spaces are so broad in type and application, and evolving so quickly, that it's impossible to predict their future. So I hesitated when the authors of this book asked me to suggest the future of virtual worlds. However, I believe early adopters often imagine or hope for the best applications and opportunities for emerging technology. I also believe there is value in reviewing future technologies in the context of historical precedents. Confucius said, "Study the past if you would define the future."[1]

I've divided my predictions into two parts. The first uses a campfire metaphor (perhaps the original social network) to understand why virtual worlds will contribute to the future of global collaboration. The second part lists upcoming opportunities as virtual worlds enter the workplace, where the modern incarnation of the campfire will take new and ever-changing forms.

## Part One

The campfire as depicted in Figure 10.7 (bringing people together in a circle to discuss life, the universe, and the significance of s'mores[2]) is an active part of today's global collaboration space. Contemporary campfires include boardroom meetings, classrooms, live events, conferences, evangelical gatherings, the assembly of governments, e-meetings, phone bridges, and in-person commingling of all kinds. These newer permutations are grounded in our fundamental need to bring people together to meet, work, and connect as human beings. By turning to virtual gathering places and collaboration tools, many of us are challenging the notion that a physical space and human proximity are the best way to form teams. We are upgrading to the next release—*Campfire 2.0.*

**Figure 10.7.** Sitting Around the Virtual Campfire

In 2007, one of IBM's first virtual world spaces brought people together from many nations to lounge and chat around a crackling fire. At the end of a long day, people still gather in this comfortable virtual space to catch up, learn from each other and discuss next steps.

In our increasingly global society, the classroom, our schools and universities, our workplace learning environments and meeting places, are just not big enough to support our needs. Front-line virtual spaces, like the web itself, work in infinitely scalable collections of people and technologies—a knowledge creation collective. Second-generation web spaces reach beyond physical boundaries and are growing exponentially.

At the same time, we are living in a "flatter world," as predicted in 2005 by Thomas L. Friedman in his book *The World Is Flat*.[3] The recent economic slowdown has rendered explicit the fundamental connection of our global financial systems, a powerful reminder and consequence of living in a flatter, more connected global landscape. Our workplace is also flatter, supporting virtual world spaces whether as functioning replicas of physical spaces or as newly conceived places for meeting, teaching, learning, mentoring, and the exchange of goods and services. A colleague from India once told me, "For us, geography is history." He felt that, as he navigated IBM virtual spaces, he was simultaneously in India and in other parts of the world, all from the comfort of his home. Combine this flat world with new, powerful, and often free global mass collaboration tools and it is no wonder that the use of virtual worlds is exploding for both work and play.[4] Accessible mass collaboration operations have helped to create a new era of web participation, allowing my mother at seventy-five and my youngest nephew at sixteen to be both producers and consumers in this flatter world.

Our search for the next campfire model, our flattening world, and increasingly available tools for collaboration provide us with new ways of coming together. Avatars do not replace humans, but they do augment our virtual selves. People gather, teach, and learn from each other, share code, walk through worlds, grow things, demonstrate and build new skills, searching for and finding value of global connectedness. Seeing and collaborating in real time with someone halfway around the world offers new benefits, including one big affordance we have identified: an emerging visual language that people understand regardless of where they come from. "Seeing is believing." Collaboration helps build trust and authenticity across virtual spaces, while allowing for anonymous connection when needed.

All these changes lead us toward a parallel and long-term, organically formed virtual space in which "the power of everyone" can be brought to bear. People reach across oceans to help others, demonstrating and teaching otherwise difficult concepts, in a virtual environment that is always on and always available. This offers a level playing field, even for those who are visually impaired or have only dial-up access.

In this context, I see our inherent playfulness as the oil for the innovation engine, connecting, reorganizing, and deploying hundreds of thousands of learners around joint endeavors, self-organized based on their capabilities, interests, and reputation. The combination of access, collaboration tools, and scalable innovation engine stacks up to an even bigger opportunity, hinted in the title—we are heading toward Campfire 3.0, and this is happening quickly.

## Part Two

Now that self-organizing virtual world spaces are flourishing, the question is: Beyond commingling and collaborating at a distance, what else will we all do there? Based on present adoption we will:

- *Create deep visualization of complex models in virtual spaces.* New concepts and tools will leverage the affordances of space in scale. We will interact with the enormous, the complex, or the microscopic using overlapping perspectives, point-in-context capability, and user-generated content.
- *Find places to express creative thinking—spaces for "right-brain thinkers."* Daniel Pink has described the emerging hordes of right-brain thinkers and why they will rule the future.[5] Guess what? These are high-concept, visual thinkers who will demand more from learning delivery teams. Pink asserts that design, which he describes as "utility enhanced by significance," has become an essential aptitude for personal fulfillment and professional success. In this context we can view an avatar-oriented virtual space as the "mash-up" for right- and left-brain collaboration.

- *Look for safer places to take risks.* Do you want to "dry run" a presentation, fly a hang glider, test live human reaction to natural disasters, operate on a heart, or simulate the operation of a nuclear power plant without the impact of real-life failure? If failure is a good teacher, then, by failing, we benefit from failing quickly and often in a comfortable, risk-free environment. One can take risks in virtual world spaces that would otherwise not be possible. This is an expanding learning opportunity.

- *Entrust tools for portable medical records.* Today avatars can carry our medical records.[6] Can they do more? Could your health profile be tagged like a living resume capable of seeking others with similar records and suggesting healthy approaches for your consideration? Could you observe a medical procedure virtually before undertaking it yourself? If you had a visual disability, could you navigate a space using another sense (such as touch) or organ (such as your tongue), and share your experience with others? Soon haptic technology will overlap with virtual spaces to permit touch and feel effects through an avatar. As technical capabilities converge, virtual spaces will offer richer opportunities for learning and collaboration.

- *Transfer knowledge to an avatar for safekeeping.* I routinely transfer knowledge to my personal information management (PIM) tool for safekeeping. Long gone are the little black books of numbers and addresses, birthday reminders, names of favorite pets and e-mail addresses. If an avatar can host my medical records, what else might I turn over for safekeeping? Credit information, site access passwords, and embedded chip information? In the overabundant, always on, information-rich world we share, filters become a way of life. Today three filters matter most. They are trust, authenticity, and presence. A well-appointed avatar could manage all of these filters and respond with information when we request it. "Avatar, call my doctor and book an appointment for Friday afternoon." Scary perhaps, but possible with emerging virtual technologies.

- *Leverage the power of many eyes for a common solution.* In Malcolm Gladwell's book, *Outliers*, we learn that success requires the understanding of outliers—those often hidden and markedly different factors we miss in understanding our own success and that of others.[7] When many eyes combine the right expertise with the right context, in the right place, and at the right time, can we spot outliers? Can we use our collective know-how to learn more about people, issues, and challenges that face us every day? Virtual social spaces may be our first examples of co-present collective intelligence environments, We need to learn where these spaces are headed. We need to create the opportunities for virtual learning interactions and observe what emerges in the virtual social worlds we are building.

• *Leverage multiple representations of self and* presence. Consider the possibility that there are only three places we occupy for any length of time. We are @Work, @Home, and @Play (somewhere in-between these is mobile), and increasingly our worlds are blended. We can develop representations of ourselves for these levels of interaction, each with varying levels of anonymity. My avatar already attends conferences with me (and for me), but this presence can deepen if we better equip our avatars. One opportunity is to do more virtually; another is to do more with mentors and advisors. We should explore and enable the ability to have more active participation and presence across the world and expand the notion of a workplace, a home space, and how we play. This concept is not lost on the makers of the Nintendo Wii, where haptic enhanced avatars have already entered many homes and are connecting similarly minded people for even deeper interaction.

• *Participate in places and activities to which we've not previously had access.* We cannot just hop on a rocket, fly to the moon, and walk around for a day. But we can go there virtually with friends, ride a dune buggy over lunar terrain, and explore this distant landscape in simulated gravity. We can learn about a carbon molecule while sitting in it or swim along the bottom of the ocean to study environmental issues. Given unlimited access, where else might we go? Would we mobilize as groups, voting with our virtual feet to shape global issues? Or would we explore what happens when many people come together in a simulated virtual city, designing what we need before the city is ever built.

We are working collectively on Campfire 3.0. Virtual worlds are a part of a converging tool set, blending community, culture, presence, marketplaces, learning, play, and collaboration into ever-simpler and more cost-effective interfaces.[8]

We hope that this emerging medium will not only support things we already do well, but also provide new opportunities and practices we could not previously have imagined.

3D virtual spaces are no panacea. We must weigh them against other spaces and practices that already work well. And although these spaces should be easy to use, they can be difficult to design. Even so, hundreds of schools, universities, and businesses have jumped into this space over the last sixteen months, looking for innovation and value for the ever-widening learning and collaboration community. Stay tuned as these early adopters and innovators shape these spaces over the next two years. Pull your blanket a little closer to the fire. The best is yet to come.

## Learning to Be 3D in 2020

### Randy J. Hinrichs

The next generation of learners is beginning to flood the market. If you're a digital country on the grid, the NetGen is bringing their multimedia, game rich, mobile, learning needs right to you! They are always immersed in streamed content with a high attention quotient. They have learned to research, synthesize, and produce results at fluid speeds. The 2020 learning environment is prepared for them. It is an immersive world, data rich and 3D, a place where learners solve problems using virtual worlds and geodata fed from the physical world. Learners display content on any flat surface, communicating seamlessly and mobile. The new tools enable story, digital actors, multimedia, collaborative teams, global data, and a global presentation platform.

Thank you for joining us into a future view of 3D learning. These forecasts for the year 2020 revolve around the notion that learners need to learn "to be" in 3D. No longer are they focused on learning about stuff and then going to apply it somewhere else; learners adapt to learning environments in which they are participating all of the time. Work environments are virtual, learning environments are virtual, connected entertainment environments are virtual. Learning is continuous and is integrated in all of our digital lives.

Here are some thoughts about learning in the year 2020 that reflect these changes. These are macro forecasts that shape the way we will think about learning, design it, and leverage it as part of the knowledge economy. I will then provide a comparative table of earlier predictions made by me and my colleagues in a report produced for the U.S. Department of Commerce, called *2020 Visions: Transforming Education and Training Through Advanced Technologies*. Those predictions were made seven years ago in 2002. What's changed?

## Forecast 1: We Live Inside the Data In 2020, Learning Through Adaptation

Data already surrounds us everywhere, in our homes, in our work, on the way to work, in our communication systems, in our entertainment and media systems. In 2020, learners will be immersed in virtual learning worlds. They will simultaneously move between the virtual and physical through mobile computing devices. They will operate in task-rich role-playing holodecks that read data directly from physical sensors. Connected to each other as avatars in virtual worlds, learners will jump into a virtual scenario to practice skills with others in-world.

Assessment will be continuous and will be tied to personalized recommender systems that feed relevant support material and job aids across multiple learning experiences, connecting common threads. Students will access their own personalized learning management systems everywhere. (See Figure 10.8.)

Laboratories will be virtual and provide software interfaces for remote control. On-demand supercomputing and on-demand storage will allow learners to access or create immersive 3D databases and peoplebases. Learners will be able to get data to support hypotheses that form their learning strategies, and they'll have a host of people to access as relevant teachers or advisers. When they move from learning problem to work problem, their personal library automatically creates the right interface for interaction.

Virtual-world tools will launch a social networking special interest group. Or they will call up a model of 3D visualization for the learner to inspect and manipulate to help understand how it works. Or the learner will plunge into a huge database and examine the stars, the ocean floor, or streaming video feeds of a telemedicine procedure for a medical student. For history, social studies, sales

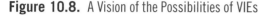

**Figure 10.8.** A Vision of the Possibilities of VIEs

training, or leadership coaching, an MMORPG game would appear to test your skills and allow you to defend your reputation.

In 2020, we will wear devices that enable us to compute on any surface in any location. We will set up multimedia meetings on the fly. Our bodies will generate biofeedback into the virtual environment, changing our avatars so others can possibly visualize our cognitive states and adjust their feedback. Our avatars will be driven by activities in-world in which they will exchange their best knowledge objects for rewards and reputation. We will try to add value to every learning environment we enter, stimulating a learning economy. Immersion in the data astronomically increases relevancy and imposes a set of digital biological adaptation rules to the virtual world. To defend ourselves and survive, we will have to use learning as a defense mechanism.

## Forecast 2: We Evolve into Problem-Based, Reflective Learners

In 2020, students will think of learning as what they need to know to solve a problem, not memorization. They are active in learning what resources are needed, what tools they'll need, who their collaborators and competitors are. They frame the problem in a virtual world, bringing together their customers and partners into their 3D learning environments to help them review the problem and form a strategy for pursuing a solution.

Since it's easier to meet and go into another's virtual world, learners will be able to use the virtual world to find places where their solutions may reside. They can teleport over to simulations, as if they were actually walking around in a virtual warehouse and watching people solve their kinds of problem. (See Figure 10.9 for an example.)

**Figure 10.9.** Customers and Companies Collaborating to Solve a Problem in a Virtual World

The learner becomes the group manager of a problem-solving activity. Virtual worlds serve as the nexus to bring the students' teaching community together to generate dialogue and make the most of the combined expertise and experience. Instead of taking a course and learning about something, the virtual-world learner identifies a problem and brings together resources to solve the problem. The learner owns the question and the problem-solving strategies. He curates a virtual learning object so others can see what he is describing. He tags the object and its components and links it to various trusted networks. When a student learns in 2020, he is basically creating a persistent problem-solving portfolio that is used to interact and transact through his lifelong learning years.

Group problem solving like this accelerates information and visualization literacy in the virtual world. There is nothing like asking someone how to do something and he or she shows you how, right then and there. Then you can practice using the same skills and receive immediate feedback from the person. The student then can reflect on how the two of you differ in approach or execution. Engaging in group learning creates a participatory learning and teaching cycle, leveling the burden of the teacher.

Another artifact of global group learning is that learning happens among diverse populations so individuals experience different approaches to problem solving. Some solutions are dependent on the surrounding environment, whereas some are global in nature. Viewing these differences and cultural identities in virtual worlds adds the ability to localize and globalize knowledge assets simultaneously.

Students record their engagement in videos and machinima and use them for reflection with mentors and peers. Students package their learning reflections as add-ons for others to watch or use during their learning experiences in-world. This exchange of "leveled experience" promotes an economy of peered learning objects, adding information to the learning experience that is more similar to the peer's way of looking at things and enhancing formal training material.

## Forecast 3: We Frame Our Learning into Visualizations

So much digital content in the 20th century manifested itself in word processing, spreadsheets, databases, photographs, video and sound files. Only the most literate computer users were able to produce the multimedia components. In 2020, learners have tools for combining all their expressions into rich 3D interactive visualization. 3D interactivity becomes a literacy, and students are immersed in 3D and producing 3D content rapidly. Software tools will enable learners to easily design, develop, measure, and demonstrate their learning through objects. Imagine a user learning how to configure his or her entertainment home system (See Figure 10.10). He or she shrinks down to the size of the device in order to look at it up close and learn what all the inputs and outputs are. The student re-creates the objects in 3D that aren't present in the environment. The student accesses voice instructions, referencing a Q&A system for clarification through knowledge bases and machinima of other users interacting with the content who might have had the same question.

**Figure 10.10.** Learning to Hook Up Electronics by First Checking Out the Proper Placement of Cord in a VIE

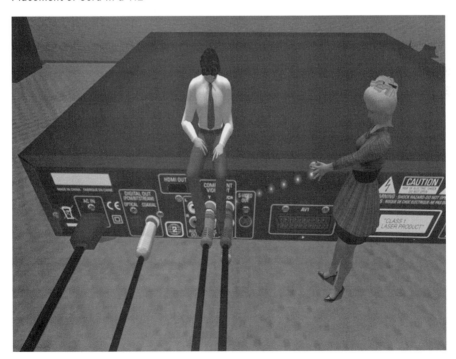

The learners create worlds that explain what things look like, what programmed behaviors should be, and how to interact within the world. This process demonstrates competency and provides additive 3D virtual learning assets into the market of universal educational objects. Learners support their visualizations by harvesting 2D content attached to wikis, blogs, web pages, social notebooks, games, and community information systems.

Linking-in context is helpful for understanding. Additional tagging, storing, and sharing among peers increase the usefulness of the learning. Because the learning objects are 3D, they extract information from the surrounding area and create holodecks for collective immersion. People visit each other's 3D objects or places and interact and respond to the other objects and people in the environment.

The learner and the data intertwine across connected cloud services, creating rich visualizations that store both expert and student learning data. The students store and integrate the interactive learning objects across their learning portfolios and can bring out full virtual objects into the surrounding virtual worlds of other learners or partners. The students automatically populate any given area with 3D objects that tell a story.

They include metric data in them so they can change rapidly with the introduction of new information. This process creates a virtual continuous cycle that helps learners learn to survive in 2020 virtual environments. So as they create and experience, they get the most out of the resources available to them and produce the best results.

## Forecast 4: We Create Everything New the First Time

Unlike content on the web today, which is always on, always the same information pushed to us no matter who we are, in 2020 the places that a learner goes to retrieve information change automatically upon their arrival. The learning environment evaluates all prior knowledge and begins an interactive dialogue with the learner, asking questions and listening to the responses. The users move information components around, sensing and reflecting on their appropriate place in the environment. The people who appear in the learning environment are paired to the learners because of their novelty and their emotional IQ.

Experiential interaction is the key outcome. The learner creates the environment by pulling forward those components that satisfy the learning needs.

Imagine creating a daycare center. (See Figure 10.11.) What components would you put into the environment? Several learners come together quickly and add items from their 3D library inventories to define how the room would look. They examine how the kids would move around in the environment, how they could be watched from various angles in the room, and look at the safety features of the equipment they would play on. Other specialists come into the environment and add their ideas by placing objects, changing colors, communicating compliance issues, and contributing new information. The co-creation component of virtual worlds creates dynamic development. Every time someone comes into the virtual world, he or she leaves new information—objects, scripts,

**Figure 10.11.** Creating Custom Content for a Child's Learning Experience

textures, audio, video, etc. The more the virtual world evolves, the more the learners graduate into experts over time.

## Forecast 5: Learners Filter Their Results into Transactional Interfaces

Because all sorts of people are available in-world, learners can buy nanoconsulting time from others to help them figure out components of their problems. They can use money or knowledge objects as transaction currency. Adding this layer to learning creates motivation and quality development.

Each learner has the potential to distribute outcomes to the rest of the world in 2020. Instead of document management tools, shared 2D web spaces, virtual worlds, are generated on the fly, adding context to each new location. Given the bandwidth and computing speeds in 2020, learners will easily be able to upload 100-gigabits of content per second. The more original content that a learner creates, the more valuable the learner becomes in his contributions.

It is recognized that brain fitness and the unique configurations of each individual can contribute significantly to the right project at the right time. Every learner manages a transactional system for distributing his or her expertise. Whether a learner is a consumer, a poller, a player, a collaborator, or a consultant, the tiny bits of unique information each learner has will be transferable and marketable. This means that the enterprise as we know it today has to accommodate a population of individual contributors, who will be just as inclined to work in non-corporate structures as they will to work inside the corporation. As long as the individual is given the freedom to construct, design, and package information and distribute it freely (or economically), the learning culture will prevail.

The idea of a learner becoming a knowledge entrepreneur is radical. It differs significantly from the passive, digital, lecture-based environments of 2010. Although we wish to transform our learning experiences, we often fall back into the formal lecture and PowerPoint presentation. We must believe we can change that. We must believe in learning by doing, putting the learner at the center of the learning, and in authentic assessment. We also must embrace the NetGener who requires more interaction, more game-like interfaces, more challenges in problem solving, and more innovation and ownership than before. Learning to be in 3D makes that possible.

## Looking Backward

In "A Vision for Life-Long Learning–Year 2020," in *2020 Visions: Transforming Education and Training Through Advanced Technologies,* I had the opportunity to share my predictions of learning in a document prepared for the Department of Commerce in 2002 and shared with ten other authors. These predictions are summarized in Table 10.2, compared with the forecasts I've presented here with my comments about what has changed in the past seven years.

## Looking at Now

So what does this mean to you? Why should you really care about 3D learning in your organization? As employee policy changes and national initiatives emerge to support virtual immersive environments and new technologies, success means creating and sustaining a competitive, digital global economy. (See Figure 10.12.)

This is an elementary call to arms—*you need to prepare for a different kind of workforce.* The era of small teams has arrived, and they offer outstanding and competitive service. Their businesses operate twenty-four hours a day. They've broken up their workdays to accommodate segmented hours with international members at significantly reduced overhead rates. They use every technology to connect partners, suppliers, and consumers. They are addicted to 3D game-like interfaces. So you should care because 3D businesses are creating a perpetual supply chain.

Secondly, in a historic tight economy, you can *eliminate the need for buildings and commuting.* You reduce costs by supporting telecommuting. Your workforce can work from anywhere in the world. You provide virtual office space, visualize business processes, conduct almost all training in-world, and can coach your co-workers daily. Lowering costs allows you to focus on team building, project management, and leadership skills. You create more jobs and pay better wages instead of paying for buildings occupied only eight hours a day. This move is based on speed.

**Table 10.2. Predictions for the Future**

| Prediction in 2002 | Prediction in 2009 | Comment |
|---|---|---|
| **Strategies:** Learning relies on technology to connect diverse groups together to work on relevant tasks and create digital arcVIEs of work. | **Strategies:** Learning relies on virtual worlds to connect communities of experts, mentors, and peers to co-create inside virtual environments. | Shift from just accessing technology to living in the data inside rich visual environments. |
| **Hardware:** Learners rely on broadband videoconferencing, interactive visualizations across interconnected networks, multiple devices, and an "Internet in the ear" device. | **Hardware:** Learners will wear devices that allow computing on any surface, access to supercomputers, and body sensors for determining cognitive state. | Move away from "the computer" to digital interaction with every device. More integration into the body for feedback. |
| **Software:** Software supports collaborative learning through video, audio, and voice recognition. Software personalizes all your information. | **Software:** Software supports production in multimedia virtual worlds, with personalized dynamic 3D digital libraries. Software focuses on relevance of your information. | Shift into production in 3D virtual worlds and interaction with data, rather than "searching" for data. |
| **Pedagogy:** Learning will be experiential and personalized in game-like environments. Q&A dominates interaction. | **Pedagogy:** Learning will be problem-based and driven by requirements, milestones, and acceptance criteria. | Learning is more directly connected to solving problems through visualizations rather than consumption. So users will create to learn. |
| **Content:** No one owns content as an end product. It is molecular at its origin and shared by everyone. | **Content:** IP ownership on content is discrete with embedded meta data to copy, transfer, and modify rights. | Learning environments provide experience and social networking, adding value to content and making it and the learner more a part of the knowledge economy. |
| **Toys:** Embedded technology captures learners' habits and preferences. | **Toys:** Embedded technology captures learners' habits and adapts. | Toys contain chips and can communicate to 3D printers for reconstruction. |
| **Mentors:** Virtual mentors will assist all learners. | **Mentors:** Virtual teams will assist all learners. | Guilds of professionals move as one in virtual worlds. |
| **Assessment:** Captive technologies record learners' cognitive achievement and provide constant feedback. | **Assessment:** Learners assess the learning environment's cognitive achievement and sends it constant feedback as well. | Assessment is the heart of interconnected learning and requires bi-directional feedback. |
| **Economics:** Transactions and recommender systems are integrated into the learning environment. School is tied more to industry and civic activities for content. | **Economics:** Every learner creates his or her own digital learning objects and sells them or gives them away. | Learning by doing by putting the learner in the center of the experience. 3D learning creates jobs and scales education to a universal model. |

**Figure 10.12.** From Ape to Avatar

Finally, the potential to increase revenue exists in building learning into your products and services. As your workforce consists of both internal and external employees and IP is managed in the learning objects created by both, the ability to package and distribute content and context to your customers might very likely hit the bottom line. The value added of individual content creation in every saleable object or service is part of the success of the knowledge economy burgeoning on our always-on network. With pervasive 3D technology, those who take advantage of both cost reduction and revenue generation will be the competitors you weren't expecting.

### Why Is This Vision Important?

Because you focus on innovation in your product, in your service, and in your team. And for the spirited, you just have more fun.

### Bottom Line

You need to look at integrating learning into every aspect of the job. Virtual worlds bring it all together in a way: mobile connectivity, global business partnerships, responsibility for the environment, innovating with conceptual design, "cloud services," social networks, and game-based computing. The fluid learning culture leverages these millennial software environments on a cloud of networked digital infrastructure using mobile phones, amazing interface surfaces, and virtual worlds to communicate uninterrupted.

You should care because virtual worlds are transforming worldwide collaboration and challenging the "determinants of competitiveness." Adaptation is imminent.

# Appendix

# Defining Learning in a 3D Virtual Space

## Introduction

Virtual worlds have been around even before computers. Humans have created virtual worlds while playing games like Dungeons and Dragons, when imagining invisible friends, and when kids pretend to be parents in a game of "house." Many professionals have a general and vague understanding of virtual worlds, but put a few of them in a room together and one quickly learns that not all concepts of virtual worlds are the same. This chapter outlines how virtual worlds are simply the convergence of existing technologies, defines some of the terms associated with virtual worlds, and provides definitions that can be valuable in understanding how virtual worlds fit into the context of learning.

# Convergence of Existing Technologies

Current 3D learning technologies are simply the natural extension and convergence of several technologies currently used for online learning. The converging technologies are synchronous learning tools, Web 2.0, social networking, and video games. These technologies are being consumed by a new generation of learners who were raised on 3D graphics and video game interfaces.

## Synchronous Learning Tools

The first software element that makes up the 3D web is that of a synchronous learning tool such as WebEx or Adobe Connect or Saba's Centra. Synchronous learning tools allow for real-time interaction on a computer among learners separated by great distances. At a designated time, an instructor logs into the software, as do the learners. Then the learners and the instructor can share the names of all the learners on the screen as well as share electronic slides, whiteboards, and even applications. The instructor and learners have the ability to speak with one another through text or voice-based chat.

## Web 2.0

The second technology element of the 3D web is the ability to easily create content within the virtual world. This is similar to the Web 2.0 capabilities of wikis or blogs, by which changes, updates, and additions are easily made to websites without the contributor needing to know HTML or any programming language. In the 3D web, learners can build their own items such as houses, cars, or even giant routers. This is accomplished by using basic building blocks within the program, allowing instructional designers to create customized learning environments to meet the needs of their learners without having to know coding or 3D development tools. The environment can be realistic, like a classroom, or it can be surreal, like the creation of a giant computer, drill, or the inside of an artery.

## Social Networking

Another important element of the 3D web is the social networking capability. The social networking aspects of a 3D web allow employees to interact and share data and information with one another while in the virtual world. When a person, in the form of an avatar, creates an object such as a briefcase or laptop, he or she can share that item with other people. Information can be exchanged through note cards or other tools that encourage social interaction. You can see when fellow learners are online and can initiate a text or voice chat with them. These virtual worlds are social and allow for a free exchange of ideas and informal learning.

## Video Games

While these software elements are available in many different programs, what pulls them together in a virtual world is the fact that the social networking, real-time interactions, and creation of content are done in a 3D world similar to video game interfaces. In these worlds, characters and the environment are rendered in 3D and the learners often have the ability to alter their characters or avatars to reflect their personalities. This provides a realistic feel to the interactions and helps the learners feel that they are in an actual space working, learning, and collaborating together. The learners walk up to each other and interact as if they were in the same physical space. This provides a high degree of engagement within the virtual world.

The convergence of these four elements creates the foundations for virtual learning worlds and, while virtual worlds can seem intimidating to some, they are just an extension of the evolution of software tools for communication and learning. Virtual worlds are the natural next step in learning environments because they provide even more opportunities than previous tools for the design, development, and delivery of effective online learning.

The combination of these elements creates the 3D learning environment, an environment that allows learners to interact and learn in ways not possible outside of virtual worlds.

## New Generation of Learner

While technology is enabling the creation and usage of 3D virtual worlds, the appeal of these worlds is being driven by a new generation of learners. A generation of learners who have grown up immersed in technologies like text messaging, social networking, and video games.[1] This generation is entering educational and business institutions with a different focus, mentality, and learning style than any previous generation—a mentality and learning style forged by playing video games and interacting in 3D worlds with names such as Nicktropolis, Whyville, Club Penguin, RuneScape, Mokitown, Toon Town, and Pirates of the Caribbean. Each of these worlds is inhabited by kids, some as young as six, who are spending time interacting, making friends, and navigating 3D virtual worlds. And these virtual worlds are inhabited by millions of kids, tweens, and teenagers. Nicktropolis, a virtual work created by Nickelodeon, a division of Viacom, has over eight million citizens, which is bigger than the population of London.[2]

The incoming generation of learners and workers blurs the line between the virtual and the physical worlds. It is not that they can't see the difference between the two. It is just that the new generation of learners is equally comfortable in either world—real or virtual. They bring a technology comfort level unachievable by generations who have not grown up with video games, gadgets, or the Internet.

These learners and workers have grown up in an age of the Internet, where they are able to create their own content, become avatars, and create their own realities electronically. They interact in 3D worlds comfortably and expect business and learning applications to have 3D aspects as well.

# Defining Virtual Worlds

If you place four or five learning professionals in a room and ask them to define a virtual learning world, you may hear six or seven answers. There are many different online environments that qualify as virtual worlds in one way or another. To truly understand the use of virtual worlds in learning, it is important to distinguish among the different types of virtual worlds and describe which ones are most appropriate for learning.

Having an awareness of the differences among virtual worlds and the impact they have on learners will help you make intelligent choices about which of these online worlds you might want to deploy in your organization. The terms and terminology of online environments can be confusing—with terms like MUD, MOO, MMORPG, metaverse, VSWs, HIVES, 3DLE, and others. But not all online environments are 3D or even appropriate for learning. A quick look at different online and 3D environments will help to clarify some of the terms and minimize confusion.

## Simulations

The term "simulation" has many different meanings. The most well-known type is the flight simulator. It is in these simulators that pilots learn to fly aircraft in a highly realistic environment. The concept of a simulator includes the use of software to emulate actual equipment. It is now possible to create an electronic version of multimillion-dollar equipment such as a plastics extruder. These simulators are typically not presented in 3D. They are more likely to be a representation of a control panel or other parts of a working machine.

Another type of simulator is a "social simulator." These are simulations in which a person is simulating interactions with others. A social simulation takes place in an environment similar to the actual environment and encourages the learner to interact. These are sometimes called "branching simulations." They can be created using photographs, video or, more recently, 3D characters. In these simulations, the learner is presented with a question and then given several possible responses. The learner encounters a virtual character such as a doctor, and the doctor responds to the learner based on a pre-programmed script. The learner, based on his or her answer, is branched to the area of the simulation corresponding with the chosen response.

Branching simulations are effective for learners who are novice or new to a subject matter. The choices provide an appropriate representation of responses and help guide the learner to appropriate behavior. When a learner is more experienced or knowledgeable in the content matter, the branching simulations becomes less effective. This is because an experienced learner typically wants to provide a response that is not listed in the simulation as an option. This frustrates the experienced learner. The experienced person typically ends up selecting what he or she thinks is the right answer and doesn't learn any new information or behaviors.

Simulations are typically solo activities. Although a group may work together to help make decisions while observing a fellow learner navigating a simulation, the learner is only interacting online with the program behind the simulation. In contrast, in a virtual world, multiple learners are "inside the simulation" at the same time, interacting and responding to each other.

## MUD—Multi-User Dungeon

One of the first virtual environments in which people could interact online was called a MUD. MUD is the acronym for "multi-user dungeon." The term "dungeon" was used because these text-based games were an extension of the board games in the genre of Dungeons and Dragons. The characters, rooms where chats took place, topics, and environment were similar to the Dungeons and Dragon games. They were also referred to as multi-user dialogue or multi-user dimension.

MUDs were real-time virtual worlds that were described entirely in text. The environment, characters, and interactions were all text-based. If you wanted to move your character, you had to type "Move two paces to the left" or "Explore cave." When you entered a room, it was described to the player, "You have entered a dark room with a table and chair and a small light in the far corner." While MUDs were great for fantasy games, they never caught on as a learning environment.

## MOO—Multi-User Object-Oriented Environment

MOOs were the next evolution of real-time, multi-player environments. The term MOOs represents the concept of a multi-user object-oriented environment. MOOs are text-based but offer the added benefit of being able to create codes and phrases that can be reused over and over again and that perform functions at specific intervals. For example, you could program a virtual instructor to say "Welcome to my classroom" any time a player walked into a certain room within the MOO. A number of university-based projects utilized the MOO technology to create virtual educational environments but, again, MOOs never achieved widespread educational or training adoption and have been replaced by more graphically rich applications.

## MMORPG—Massively Multiplayer Online Role-Play Game

The next evolution in the area of virtual worlds was the creation of massively multiplayer online role-play games or MMORPGs. In these virtual 3D environments, the player assumes a role and identity not typically related to his or her real-world self and attempts to earn points to move to a higher level within the game. Players become magicians, knights, priests, or warriors with special powers and interact within a persistent online world. Once a role is assumed, the player embarks on adventures or quests with a team, guild, or clan. They seek treasure, battle monsters, or accomplish other specific goals and objectives that are an inherent part of the world.

These worlds also are distinguished by the fact that they have a large number of players—all interacting with each other in a persistent world. A persistent world is one that continues to exist and function, even when the player has logged out of the world. Player-generated changes to objects or items in the world remain in a manner similar to the physical world. If you move a chair in the physical world and come back three hours later, the chair will remain in the same place providing no one else moved it. Moving a chair in a persistent virtual world provides the same result, unlike some environments that would "reset" when the player logs out of the game.

These worlds are also inhabited by non-player characters (NPCs), which are also known as bots (presumably short for robot) or agents (like Agent Smith in The Matrix). These NPCs are not controlled by people; they are actually programs that are designed to look like characters in the virtual world but are designed to perform certain tasks or play a limited role, such as providing a clue to the treasure. NPCs operate based on pre-programmed logic.

For example, in many online role-play games there are NPCs who can be defeated to earn points or to gain wealth. Defeating these NPCs typically helps a player progress to higher levels in the game.

Most MMORPGs require players to work together to achieve certain goals. In World of Warcraft, a variety of players with different skills and roles join forces to achieve success in many of the quests, for example, to defeat

Ragnaros, a giant seething fire god (and one of the game's signature foes), you need a guild of various people to assume such roles as mages, hunters, healers, or priests. Each player involved in the attack of Ragnaros performs a different task. The tasks are related and are interdependent. For instance, a player acting as a warrior may be doing battle and receiving a high level of damage but be kept alive by a spell cast by a fellow player acting as a mage.

MMORPGs can be used to teach concepts related to the real world through examples. It is possible to completely corner a market in an MMORPG and then observe the repercussions, whereas that is not possible in real life. One can also observe interactions between and among players to understand teamwork, group goals, and other social interactions. The *Harvard Business Review* published an article about how leadership skills learned in MMORPGs can translate to some skills within actual virtual teams. However, the fantasy aspects of most MMORPGs make it difficult to apply the use of these games within a work setting.

The term MMORPG is also sometimes shortened to MMO or MMOG to represent massively multiplayer online or massively multiplayer online game because MMORPG said three times fast is a mouthful.

## MUVE—Multi-User Virtual Environment

MUVE is a term coined by Christopher Dede, a professor at Harvard. Dede created a virtual world called River City with funding from the National Science Foundation. In this virtual environment, students become avatars and work together within a virtual environment to solve a health problem in a 19th century town. The environment is based on authentic historical, sociological, and geographical conditions. The goal is to have the students work together in small research teams to help the town understand why residents are becoming ill. Students keep track of clues that hint at causes of the mysterious illnesses. The learners form and test hypotheses, develop controlled experiments to test their hypotheses, and make recommendations based on the data they collect, all in an online environment.

The environment provides learning activities and the chance for the students to collaborate, problem solve, and apply critical thinking skills. The MUVE is a focused environment; tasks, hints, and tools are included specifically to address the task of determining the cause of the illness that is plaguing the town. Solving the medical crisis is an inherent part of the world of River City.

## Metaverse

Many of these terms and concepts sound like they are right out of a science fiction novel—this term literally is from a sci-fi novel. The term *metaverse* is from a 1992 science fiction novel written by Neal Stephenson called *Snow Crash*. The term embodies Stephenson's vision of how a 3D virtual reality-based Internet might evolve in the future. The term has come to represent the idea of a free-form online 3D world inhabited by avatars controlled by their real-life counterparts.

An avatar is how a person represents him- or herself in the virtual world. The word *avatar* is said to be a Sanskrit word meaning the incarnation of a form of god on Earth. While this may have been the original meaning, the term also now represents the virtual figure a learner decides to create to interact within a 3D world.

In most online environments, the players have the ability to change or alter their avatars. These alterations typically include body shape, clothes, and hair style. Avatars are controlled through the computer keyboard or mouse. They are able to move independently through the virtual environment controlled by their real-life owners. In the simplest terms, the avatar is an online version of the person who inhabits the metaverse—a virtual sock puppet. Other terms for metaverses are *synthetic worlds* and *cyber worlds*.

A metaverse is similar to an MMORPG, but with some vital differences. First, in a metaverse, players are not playing defined roles such as hunters or mages; they are playing characters they have created. And, unlike a MUVE, a metaverse typically does not have specific goals or objectives created by the metaverse itself. Players can create their own goals or objectives, but specific goals and objects are not an inherent part of these worlds.

Finally, the environment of a metaverse typically allows the player to create his or her own digital items, such as houses and clothing, using a scripting language or by dragging and dropping items. Because of the ability to create your own things in a metaverse, these environments typically involve the exchange of some type of currency tied to real-world dollars. People in a metaverse can buy, sell, or trade digital assets that they themselves create and then exchange the virtual currency for real-world currency.

Perhaps the best-known example of a metaverse is Second Life. However, Second Life is not the only metaverse commercially available. Other worlds such as Active Worlds and There exist. In fact, an organization called the Open Source Metaverse Project actively promotes a free, open source version of a metaverse.

A metaverse environment can be used for training purposes. Spaces can be established within metaverses for conducting learning activities and events. It is also possible to create many different learning environments in which people can interact to learn about items in 3D. For example, you can provide instruction on how to repair a laptop through a virtual tour of the laptop within the metaverse.

## VSW—Virtual Social World

Another term used interchangeably with metaverse is *virtual social world*. This term represents the concept of creating a virtual world in which social-ization is the primary focus. These worlds can be expansive virtual spaces in which different types of interactions between avatars can occur in different areas or it can be confined to a small "scene" such as a conference room that people enter to discuss a topic and then leave shortly after.

## Immersive Learning Simulation

The eLearning Guild, a community of practice for e-learning professionals, defines an immersive learning simulation as "a learning system that com-bines simulation, pedagogy, and 'hard fun' to create a truly engaging and behavior-changing form of learning." The umbrella term encompasses many different forms of immersive learning beyond virtual worlds. Included in the term "immersive learning simulation" are games, mini-games, virtual labs, serious games, and simulation/scenarios.

## Console-Based Virtual Worlds

A virtual immersive environment that is bound by a console, such as the Sony PlayStation 3's environment called "Home," fits in this category. As does the world inhabited by Nintendo Miis. A person must be logged onto the console to interact with the 3D world. The avatar interacts within the virtual world and can purchase items within that world and meet and greet other inhabitants of the VIE.

## MMOLE—Massively Multilearner Online Learning Environment

The MMOLE is yet another term for the genre of a computer-generated learning environment in which large numbers of learners interact with each other in a virtual 3D world with the specific goal of learning. The learning can occur formally through a class-like environment or through a scripted scenario (such as a role play). In that way it is like a MMORPG, as it has specific goals. However, learning also can occur informally through chats and discussions among learners in a fashion similar to a metaverse. So the MMOLE is a combination of a metaverse and a MMORPG designed for learning.

MMOLEs typically have two modes, one for an instructor and one for the learners. The instructor mode allows someone to facilitate a learning event and manage the interactions within the environment. This prevents everyone from chatting at once, and it provides a formal environment in which to learn. In other words, it allows the learning to be managed.

But managed learning is not the only kind of learning that can or should occur in a MMOLE. The fact that avatars can roam around the virtual space and interact with each other through pre-programmed jesters, voice over Internet protocol, or text chat means that the environment can foster and encourage informal learning.

## Virtual Event

This is a one-time event held in a virtual space. It could include a virtual conference or a virtual meeting space. Virtual events might have a life span of a few months, but the virtual world in which the event is held does not remain indefinitely. The primary purpose is to gather together people for a specific, targeted reason—with the virtual world most often being a conference setting.

## Data Visualization

This is more a function of virtual worlds than a type of virtual world. However, the process of visualizing data is a chance for virtual worlds to move beyond merely mimicking training that is done in a physical world and therefore deserves a special mention here. Visualization of data in virtual space could offer many possibilities for the representation of numbers, trends, and statistics. In these cases, data collected from sensors or within databases that typically consist only of numbers could be made more tangible within a virtual world and the participants could then see the data and manipulate it as they are surrounded by visual representations of the data.

## VIE—Virtual Immersive Environment

The term VIE was adopted for this book. VIE represents the concept of a virtual immersive environment, and it combines several attributes of other 3D virtual environments such as the VSW and MMORPG. The concept is that a VIE represents the technology in which learning can occur. It encompasses the technologies discussed above and represents a virtual 3D learning environment in which avatars can interact and learn from the environment, each other, and a facilitator. The learning events are called 3D learning experiences (3DLE).

## 3DLE—Three-Dimensional Learning Experience

The learning experience one has within a VIE is, in this book, referred to as a three-dimensional learning experience. This term describes the event in which the learner participates. The experience is designed within the VIE and requires the VIE to house the experience, but a VIE alone cannot facilitate learning without proper design and focus. Table A.1 provides a list of some immersive environments and representative vendor offerings and a definition of the type of environment.

**Table A.1.** Types and Examples of Immersive Environments[3]

| Type of Immersive Environment | Examples | Definition |
|---|---|---|
| Simulation | Virtual Leader, Branching Simulations | A self-contained world in which the person may be able to interact with the environment, but typically only one person can navigate the avatar and interactions are only between the computer and the learner. |
| Multi-User Dungeon (MUD), Multi-User Object Oriented (MOO) | Zork, Adventure, MirrorWorld, Medieval | Text-based worlds in which learners interact with the space and each other via text input. These were precursors to visually based virtual worlds. |
| Metaverse, Virtual Social World (VSW) | Second Life, There, Active Worlds. For Kids: Disney's Toon Town, Club Penguin, Pirates of the Caribbean; Console-Based: Sony's Home. | An online world in which there are no specific goals or objectives. It is a virtual world in which you create an avatar and then explore the world as that avatar. You are able to chat with others in the world and interact with their avatars. Typically, an inhabitant can create buildings, clothing, habitats, or any other items they can imagine. A metaverse usually has some type of economy in which goods are either bartered or paid for with virtual monies. At times those virtual monies are tied to an exchange rate based on "real" currency (such as the U.S. dollar or the Euro). |
| Massively Multiplayer Online Role Play Game (MMORPG) | EverQuest, RuneScape, World of Warcraft, City of Heroes | An online world in which the person assumes a role and typically teams with others to accomplish some sort of a mission or goal. |
| Virtual Event | InXpo, Unisfair, Qwaq Forums | Virtual conference, meeting, or other one-time event. The virtual world is not persistent in that it "disappears" or is taken off-line after a specified period of time. |
| Virtual Immersive Environment (VIEO) Also known as Massively Multi-Learner Online Learning Environment (MMOLE), Virtual Learning Worlds (VLWs) Multi-User Virtual Environment (MUVE) | ProtoSphere, OLIVE (Forterra), Icarus Platform, Virtual Heroes. For Kids: Whyville, River City | Environment in which large numbers of learners interact with each other in a virtual three-dimensional (3D) world with the goal of learning. Learners assume a certain appearance through the creation of an avatar. These avatars are controlled through a computer keyboard and/or mouse. The avatars are able to move independently through the virtual environment. The learning can occur formally through a class-like environment or scripted interactions with non-player characters or can occur informally. |

# Conclusion

This appendix described the context in which VIEs have come to be commercially available via the convergence of familiar e-learning and social networking software. It also defined common terms that are associated with the concept of interacting in a three-dimensional virtual world. Understanding a little bit of the history and the terminology provides a solid foundation for conceptualizing the myriad possibilities for learning in virtual 3D spaces.

# Glossary

**3DLE—Three-Dimensional Learning Experience**—This is the process of being immersed into a 3D virtual environment in which a learner acts through an avatar to engage with other avatars for the explicit purpose of learning, while being guided through a series of experiences that facilitate comprehension and application of formal learning objectives as well as enabling informal peer-to-peer learning.

**Anthropomorphic**—Having human-like characteristics or form. Something that is not human but has taken on human-like characteristics and/or form. The personification of an object. In this case, the characteristics of a computer-animated character that interacts with the learner in a human-like interface.

**Avatar**—The virtual character that players assume as they move about in a VIE or other virtual world environment. This Sanskrit word is often translated into English as *incarnation*. It literally means *descent* and usually implies a deliberate descent from higher spiritual realms to lower realms of existence, such as the embodiment of a god in the physical world. In today's virtual world environment, your virtual character becomes an avatar that is embodied and immersed within the 3DLE context.

**Bot**—An avatar that is not controlled by another person. Instead it is programmed to perform certain functions such as offering information to people-backed avatars who may be touring a particular space. This is similar to a non-player character in a MMORPG. No person is behind a bot; they function via their programming.

**Data Visualization**—This is the process of taking data and importing it into a VIE so it can be represented in three dimensions. Visualization of data in virtual space offers many possibilities for the representation of numbers, trends, and statistics. In these cases, data collected from sensors or within databases that typically only consists of numbers is made more tangible within a virtual world and the participants can then see the data and manipulate it, as they are surrounded by visual representations of the data.

**Digital Native**—Term coined by Marc Prensky to mean a person who grew up surrounded by digital technologies such as the Internet and video games from birth.

**Digital Immigrant**—A term coined by Marc Prensky. The term refers to those in society who did not grow up with digital technologies such as the Internet or video games.

**Flow State**—A state of mind in which a person playing a game player forgets his or her normal cares and the passage of time. The gamer derives intense satisfaction from the sheer pleasure of performing the activity required by the game and becomes engrossed only within the game itself. The gamer is so enthralled that the game becomes a sort of reality and the gamer reacts just as he or she would in an actual situation.

**Holodeck**—An enclosed room or space in which virtual objects appear in the form of 3D holographic images. The objects within the space appear real to the person standing on the holodeck. The person can then act and interact with the 3D virtual images. Originally, the term was associated with a recreation room on a star ship in the television series *Star Trek: The Next Generation*; since that time, the term has expanded to mean any type of room in which 3D objects are projected to create an immersive, life-sized reality.

**Immernet**—Term referring to the combination of "immersive" and "Internet." The term represents how the Internet is becoming more and more immersive.

**Immersive Learning Simulation**—This term was created by the eLearning Guild and represents "a learning system that combines simulation, pedagogy and 'hard fun' to create a truly engaging and behavior-changing form of learning." The umbrella term encompasses many different forms of immersive learning beyond virtual worlds. Included in the terms immersive learning simulation are games, mini-games, virtual labs, serious games, and simulation/scenarios.

**Machinima**—The act of creating a cinematic piece using animated characters from a 3D game or virtual world. The term is a combination of the words "machine" and "cinema" to form the concept of an animated recording created using computer- or machine-generated characters, backgrounds, and objects.

**Meatspace**—Slang term referring to the physical world.

**Metaverse**—The term is from a 1992 science fiction novel written by Neal Stephenson called *Snow Crash*. The term embodies Stephenson's vision of how a 3D virtual reality–based Internet might evolve in the future. The term has come to represent the idea of a free-form online 3D world inhabited by avatars controlled by their real-life counterparts.

**MMOLE—Massively Multilearner Online Learning Environment**—The MMOLE is yet another term for the genre of a computer-generated learning environment in which large numbers of learners interact with each other in a virtual 3D world with the specific goal of learning. The learning can occur formally through a class-like environment or through a scripted scenario (such as a role play). In that way it is like a MMORPG in that it has specific goals. However, learning also can occur informally through chats and discussions among learners in a fashion similar to a metaverse. So the MMOLE is a combination of a metaverse and a MMORPG designed for learning.

**MMORPG—Massively Multiplayer Online Role Play Game**—In these virtual 3D environments, a player assumes a role and identity not typically related to his or her real-world self and attempts to earn points to move to a higher level within the game. Players become magicians, knights, priests, or warriors with special powers and interact within a persistent online world. Once a role is assumed, the player embarks on adventures or quests with a team, guild, or clan. He or she seeks treasure, battles monsters, or accomplishes other specific goals and objectives that are an inherent part of the world.

**MOO—Multi-User Object-Oriented Environment**—These text-based virtual environments offer the ability to create codes and phrases that can be reused over and over again and that perform functions at specific intervals. A number of university-based projects utilized the MOO technology to create virtual educational environments, but MOOs never achieved widespread educational or training adoption and have been replaced by more graphically rich applications.

**MUD—Multi-User Dungeon**—A real-time virtual world described entirely in text. MUDs were one of the first virtual environments in which people could interact online. The term "dungeon" was used because these text-based games were an extension of the board games in the genre of Dungeons and Dragons. The characters, rooms where chats took place, topics, and environment were similar to the Dungeons and Dragon games. They were also referred to as multi-user dialogue or multi-user dimension.

**MUVE—Multi-User Virtual Environment**—This term was coined by Christopher Dede, a professor at Harvard. Dede created a virtual world called River City with funding from the National Science Foundation. In this virtual environment, students become avatars and work together within a virtual environment to solve a health problem in a 19th century town. The environment is based on authentic historical, sociological, and geographical conditions. The goal is to have the students work together in small research teams to help the town understand why residents are becoming ill. Students keep track of clues that hint at causes of the mysterious illnesses, form and test hypotheses, develop controlled experiments to test their hypotheses, and make recommendations based on the data they collect, all in an online environment.

**Netizen**—A term used to describe someone who spends a great deal of time working, collaborating, and learning on the Internet.

**NPC-Non-Player Character**—A character in a virtual immersive environment that is not controlled by a person outside of the environment. An NPC is actually a program that is designed to look like characters in the virtual world but that perform certain tasks or play a limited role, such as providing a signal clue, a greeting, or other information.

**Persistent World**—This is a form of virtual world that continues to exist even after a participant or learner exits the world. Changes made by a participant in that world remain after the participant logs out. For example, if an avatar moves a piece of furniture, that furniture will not reset; it will stay where the avatar has moved it unless another avatar moves it.

**Simulation**—A self-contained immersive environment in which the learner interacts within the environment in an attempt to learn or practice skills or knowledge. Typically, only one person can navigate the on-screen avatar, and interactions are only between the computer and the learner. One of the most common types of simulations is a branching story, which asks the learner a series of questions and the learner chooses the branch that mimics what he or she would say or do in that situation.

***Snow Crash***—The name of a 1992 novel by science fiction writer Neal Stephenson in which he defines the concept of a metaverse.

**VIE—Virtual Immersive Environment**—VIEs combine several attributes of other 3D virtual environments such as the VSW and MMORPG. The concept is that a VIE represents the technology in which learning can occur. It encompasses the technologies discussed above and represents a virtual 3D learning environment in which avatars can interact and learn from the environment, each other, and a facilitator. The learning events are called 3D learning experiences (3DLE).

**VSW—Virtual Social World**—This term represents the concept of creating a virtual world in which socialization is the primary focus. These worlds can be expansive virtual spaces in which different types of interactions between avatars can occur in different areas. These are most commonly the commercial virtual worlds such as Second Life or There.

**Virtual World**—A generic term for discussing a wide variety of online spaces in which participants, as avatars, interact with one another.

**Voice Over Internet Protocol (VoIP)**—This represents the concept of being able to speak within a VIE through the VIE itself. VIEs that offer VoIP do not require a separate phone line to hear what the other person is saying; the audio is integrated within the VIE.

**Webvolution**—Describes the evolving state of the World Wide Web. The web has gone from Web 1.0, which was static, to Web 2.0, which provides opportunities for participants to create their own content, to Web 3.0 (see *Immernet*), where web participants are immersed in the environment of the web. They act within the web instead of through the web.

# Notes

## Chapter 1

1. The concept of how profound the changes to society have been as a result of the invention of the browser are the result of Kevin Kelly's talk at TED. It can be viewed at www.ted.com/index .php/talks/kevin_kelly_on_the_next_5_000_days_of_the_web.html. And for more background on the Mosaic Browser: Mosaic (web browser). (2009, May 25). In Wikipedia, the free encyclopedia. Retrieved May 29, 2009, from http://en.wikipedia.org/wiki/Mosaic_(web_browser).

2. EBSCO is a research database that provides libraries, colleges and universities, and other institutions with searchable content in a large variety of subject areas.

3. Brown, J.S., & Duguid, P. (2000). *The Social Life of Information*. Cambridge, MA: Harvard Business School Press.

4. This perspective was raised in a conversation between Charlie Rose and Esther Dyson.

5. Yahoo! (2009, May 24). In Wikipedia, the free encyclopedia. Retrieved May 29, 2009, from http:// en.wikipedia.org/wiki/Yahoo!

6. Google. (2009, May 26). In Wikipedia, the free encyclopedia. Retrieved May 29, 2009, from http:// en.wikipedia.org/wiki/Google.

7. Amazon. (2009, May 29). In Wikipedia, the free encyclopedia. Retrieved May 29, 2009, from http://en.wikipedia.org/wiki/Amazon.com.

8. Chris Anderson's original *Wired* article on the Long Tail can be viewed at www.wired.com/wired/ archive/12.10/tail.html.

9. Napster. (2009, May 25). In Wikipedia, the free encyclopedia. Retrieved May 29, 2009, from http:// en.wikipedia.org/wiki/Napster.

10. Kelly, K. (2005, August). We are the web. Retrieved May 29, 2009, from www.wired.com/wired/ archive/13.08/tech.html.

11. Nielson Wire. (2008). Twitter Grows Fastest, MySpace Still the Social King. Retrieved May 29, 2009, from Nielson Wire: http://blog.nielsen.com/nielsenwire/online_mobile/leading-social-networking-sites-still-growing/

12. Rayport, J. (2009, May 18). OurSpace: The Shift to the Social Web. *BusinessWeek,* p. 67.

13. *Central Intelligence Agency: World Fact Book.* (2009). Country Populations. Retrieved May 29, 2009, from Central Intelligence Agency, www.cia.gov/library/publications/the-world-factbook/rankorder/2119rank.html.

14. YouTube. (2009, May 29). In Wikipedia, the free encyclopedia. Retrieved May 29, 2009, from http://en.wikipedia.org/wiki/YouTube.

15. This argument came from Library of Congress. (2008). Michael Wesch to Discuss "The Anthropology of YouTube" at Library of Congress on June 23. Retrieved May 29, 2009, from Library of Congress Press Release, www.loc.gov/today/pr/2008/08-104.html.

16. Hsiao, A. (n.d.). About eBay the Business: Holdings, Strategy and History. Retrieved May 29, 2009, from About.com http://ebay.about.com/od/ebaylifestyle/a/el_bus09.htm.

17. Loechner, J. ( 2005, July 26). eBay Supplements Income for One and a Half U.S. Entrepreneurs. Retrieved May 29, 2009, from MediaPostsblogs www.mediapost.com/publications/?fa=Articles .showArticle&art_aid=32378.

18. Jimmy Wales TED Keynote [Video]. (2005). Retrieved May 29, 2009, from www.ted.com/index. php/talks/jimmy_wales_on_the_birth_of_wikipedia.html

19. Howe, J. (2006). The Rise of Crowdsourcing. Retrieved May 29, 2009, from www.wired.com/wired/ archive/14.06/crowds.html.

20. Crowdsourcing. (2009, May 19). In Wikipedia, the free encyclopedia. Retrieved May 29, 2009, from http://en.wikipedia.org/wiki/Crowdsourcing.

21. Jimmy Wales TED Keynote [Video]. (2005). Retrieved May 29, 2009, from www.ted.com/index. php/talks/jimmy_wales_on_the_birth_of_wikipedia.html.

22. World of Warcraft. (2009, May 29). In Wikipedia, the free encyclopedia. Retrieved May 29, 2009, from http://en.wikipedia.org/wiki/World_of_Warcraft.

23. Cristina Jimenez, C. (2007). The High Cost of Playing Warcraft. Retrieved May 29, 2009, from *BBC News,* http://news.bbc.co.uk/2/hi/technology/7007026.stm.

24. Dibbell, J. (2007, June 17). The Life of the Chinese Gold Farmer. Retrieved May 29, 2009, from *New York Times* Online Edition, www.nytimes.com/2007/06/17/magazine/17lootfarmers-t.html.

25. IGE. (2009). Retrieved May 29 2009, from www.ige.com/

26. Hof, R. (2006, November, 6). Second Life's First Millionaire. Retrieved May 29, 2009, from The Tech Beat, www.businessweek.com/the_thread/techbeat/archives/2006/11/second_lifes_fi.html.

27. Wu, S. (2007, June 20). Virtual Goods: The Next Big Business Model. Retrieved May 29, 2009, from TechCrunch, www.techcrunch.com/2007/06/20/virtual-goods-the-next-big-business-model/

28. Craig, K. (2006, February 8). Making a Living in Second Life. Retrieved May 29, 2009, from www.wired.com/gaming/virtualworlds/news/2006/02/70153?currentPage=all.

29. Castronova, E. (2005). Synthetic Worlds. Chicago: University of Chicago Press, p. 225.

30. Yochai Benkler TED Presentation [Video]. (2005). Retrieved May 29, 2009, from www.ted.com/ index.php/talks/yochai_benkler_on_the_new_open_source_economics.html.

31. Massey, A.P. (2007). Industry Trends: Emerging 3D Internet (3Di) Multi-User Virtual Environments (MUVEs). Retrieved June 1, 2009, from TechQuarterly, www.cliftoncpa.com/Content/ ERRRMPHR8G.pdf?Name=TechQuarterly1207.pdf.

32. Global Innovation Outlook. (2005). Retrieved May 29, 2009, from IBM, http://domino.watson .ibm.com/comm/www_innovate.nsf/images/gio/$FILE/GIO_2005_for-printing.pdf.

33. This concept was originally introduced by Stan Davis in his book *Future Perfect*. Davis, S. (1997). *Future Perfect*. New York: Basic Books. The concept was further elaborated upon in the context of the Mollecular Economy in the book *It's Alive* that Stan co-authored with Chris Meyer. Meyer, C. (2003). *The Coming Convergence of Information, Biology, and Business*. New York: Crown Business.

# Chapter 2

1. Drucker, P.F. (1999, October). Beyond the Information Revolution. *Atlantic Monthly, 284*(4), 47–57.

2. Cutler, T. (2001, September). I never thought I would quote Bill Gates. Retrieved May 29, 2009, from Cutler and Company at www.cutlerco.com.au/activities/columns/20010920.html.

3. Gery, G. (2005, September 8). In Her Own Words: Gloria Gery on Performance. *Performance Improvement Journal, 44*(8).

4. Cross, J. (2007). *Informal Learning: Rediscovering the Natural Pathways That Inspire Innovation and Performance*. Hoboken, NJ: John Wiley & Sons.

5. Raybould, B. (2000). *Performance Support Engineering Part One: Key Concepts*. Ariel PSE Technology.

6. Hamilton, D.P. (2001, March 12). No Substitute: The Internet Does NOT Change Everything. *The Wall Street Journal*. Retrieved May 29, 2009, from http://people.kmi.open.ac.uk/marc/wsj/ index.html.

7. Stolovitch, H.D., & Keeps, E.J. (1999). Six Box Model from HPT. In *Handbook of Human Performance Technology: Improving Individual and Organizational Performance Worldwide*. San Francisco: Pfeiffer.

8. Dean, P.J., & Ripley, D.E. (1997). *Performance Improvement Pathfinders: Models for Organizational Learning Systems*. Washington, DC: International Society for Performance Improvement.

9. Ford, J.K., & Weissbein, D.A. (1997). Transfer of Training: An Updated Review and Analysis. *Performance Improvement Quarterly, 10*(2), 22–41.

10. Sugrue, B., O'Driscoll, T., & Vona, M.K. (2006, January). C-Level Perceptions of the Strategic Value of Learning Research Report [PowerPoint slides]. Retrieved from www.astd.org/NR/rdonlyres/ DB146C77-3205-4396-9211-5E29AEBE80DF/0/ASTD_IBM_StrategicValue_Report_2006.pdf.

11. *2004 State of the Industry Report*. Alexandria, VA: ASTD.

12. Cross, J. (2007). *Informal Learning: Rediscovering the Natural Pathways That Inspire Innovation and Performance*. Hoboken, NJ: John Wiley & Sons.

# Chapter 3

1. The term "metaverse" was coined by science fiction writer Neal Stephenson in his 1992 novel *Snow Crash*. Stephenson, N. (1992). *Snow Crash*. New York: Bantam Dell.

2. Hof, R.D. (2006, March). Virtual Worlds, Real Money. *BusinessWeek*, pp. 78–64.

3. Kapp, K.M., & O'Driscoll, T. (2007). Escaping Flatland: The Emergence of 3D Synchronous Learning. *Guild Research 360 Report on Synchronous Learning Systems,* pp. 111–153.

4. Gartner Says 80 Percent of Active Internet Users Will Have a "Second Life" in the Virtual World by the End of 2011. (2007, April 24). Retrieved May 30, 2009, from Gartner at www.gartner.com/it/ page.jsp?id=503861.

5. Halal, W.E. (2008). *Technology's Promise* (p. 56). New York: Palgrave Macmillan.

6. Avatar. (2009, May 26). In Wikipedia, the free encyclopedia. Retrieved May 30, 2009, from http://en.wikipedia.org/wiki/Avatar.

7. Bower, B. (2009, March 28). Playing for Real in a Virtual World. Retrieved May 30, 2009, from *Science News* at www.sciencenews.org/view/generic/id/41304/title/Playing_for_real_in_a_virtual__world. Vol.175 #7 (p. 15).

8. In Virtual World Real-World Behavior and Biases Show Up. (2008, September, 11). Retrieved May 30, 2009, from *Medical News Today* at www.medicalnewstoday.com/articles/121006.php.

9. Friedman, T. (2005). *The World Is Flat*. New York: Farrar, Straus and Giroux.

10. Kolb, D. (1983). *Experiential Learning: Experience as a Source of Learning and Development*. Englewood Cliffs, NJ: Prentice Hall.

# Chapter 4

1. These wonderful contributors are all listed in the About the Contributors section in the book. Again we'd like to thank them for their contributions to the model.

2. These macrostructures are based on the work done by Lesley Scopes and are further explained in Chapter 5.

# Chapter 5

1. Lesley Scopes, who has done some groundbreaking work with the archetype information developed by the authors (see reference 3 below), proposes an "assessment archetype." We've chosen not to include it here because we believe assessment cuts across all the archetypes, but further discussion may be necessary before a final definitive decision is rendered. However, for this treatment of archetypes, assessment is considered as an element that can be incorporated in all of the other archetypes.

2. The initial work describing the archetypes appeared in Kapp, K.M., & O'Driscoll, T. (2007). Escaping Flatland: The Emergence of 3D Synchronous Learning. *Guild Research 360 Report on Synchronous Learning Systems*, pp. 111–153.

3. Scopes, L. J.M. (2009). Learning Archetypes as Tool of Cybergogy for a 3D Educational Landscape: A Structure for eTeaching in Second Life. University of Southampton, School of Education, master's thesis, http://eprints.soton.ac.uk/66169/.

4. Some of this work describing archetypes appeared in Kapp, K.M. (2009). Real-World Instructional Design for Virtual World Learning. In *Michael Allen's 2009 e-Learning Annual* (pp. 137–148). San Francisco: Pfeiffer.

5. Carey, B. (2007, May 22). This Is Your Life (and How You Tell It). Retrieved May 30, 2009, from *New York Times* Online, www.nytimes.com/2007/05/22/health/psychology/22narr.html.

6. Carey, B. (2007, May 22). This Is Your Life (and How You Tell It). Retrieved May 30, 2009, from *New York Times* Online, www.nytimes.com/2007/05/22/health/psychology/22narr.html.

7. Scopes, L. J.M. (2009). Learning Archetypes as Tool of Cybergogy for a 3D Educational Landscape: A Structure for eTeaching in Second Life. University of Southampton, School of Education, master's thesis, http://eprints.soton.ac.uk/66169/. (p. 35).

8. The Next Best Thing to You. (2009, May 15). Retrieved May 30, 2009, from National Science Foundation www.nsf.gov/news/news_summ.jsp?cntn_id=114828&govDel=USNSF_51.

9. Scopes, L. J.M. (2009). Learning Archetypes as Tool of Cybergogy for a 3D Educational Landscape: A Structure for eTeaching in Second Life. University of Southampton, School of Education, master's thesis, http://eprints.soton.ac.uk/66169/. (p. 36).

10. Scopes, L. J.M. (2009). Learning Archetypes as Tool of Cybergogy for a 3D Educational Landscape: A Structure for eTeaching in Second Life. University of Southampton, School of Education, master's thesis, http://eprints.soton.ac.uk/66169/. (p. 36).

11. Scopes, L. J.M. (2009). Learning Archetypes as Tool of Cybergogy for a 3D Educational Landscape: A Structure for eTeaching in Second Life. University of Southampton, School of Education, master's thesis, http://eprints.soton.ac.uk/66169/. (p. 37).

12. Scopes, L. J.M. (2009). Learning Archetypes as Tool of Cybergogy for a 3D Educational Landscape: A Structure for eTeaching in Second Life. University of Southampton, School of Education, master's thesis, http://eprints.soton.ac.uk/66169/. (p. 38).

13. Scopes, L. J.M. (2009). Learning Archetypes as Tool of Cybergogy for a 3D Educational Landscape: A Structure for eTeaching in Second Life. University of Southampton, School of Education, master's thesis, http://eprints.soton.ac.uk/66169/. (p. 38).

14. Scopes, L. J.M. (2009). Learning Archetypes as Tool of Cybergogy for a 3D Educational Landscape: A Structure for eTeaching in Second Life. University of Southampton, School of Education, master's thesis, http://eprints.soton.ac.uk/66169/. (p. 39).

15. Phoenix. (2008, January, 18). America's Army medic training helps save a life. Retrieved May 30, 2009, from America's Army http://americasarmy.com/intel/article.php?t=271086.

16. Kafai, Y.B., Feldon, D., Fields, D., Giang, M., & Quintero, M. (2007). Life in the Times of Whypox: A Virtual Epidemic as a Community Event. In C. Steinfeld, B. Pentland, M. Ackermann, & N. Contractor (Eds.), *Proceedings of the Third International Conference on Communities and Technology.* New York: Springer. Retrieved May 31, 2009, from www.gseis.ucla.edu/faculty/kafai/paper/whyville_pdfs/Whypox_CandT_2007.

17. Raths, D. (2008, April, 2). Virtual Worlds Help Public Safety Officials Practice for Real-Life Threats. Retrieved May 31, 2009, from *Emergency Management News* at www.govtech.com/em/261426.

18. Scopes, L. J.M. (2009). Learning Archetypes as Tool of Cybergogy for a 3D Educational Landscape: A Structure for eTeaching in Second Life. University of Southampton, School of Education, master's thesis, http://eprints.soton.ac.uk/66169/. (p. 40).

19. Scopes, L. J.M. (2009). Learning Archetypes as Tool of Cybergogy for a 3D Educational Landscape: A Structure for eTeaching in Second Life. University of Southampton, School of Education, master's thesis, http://eprints.soton.ac.uk/66169/. (p. 40).

10. Scopes, L. J.M. (2009). Learning Archetypes as Tool of Cybergogy for a 3D Educational Landscape: A Structure for eTeaching in Second Life. University of Southampton, School of Education, master's thesis, http://eprints.soton.ac.uk/66169/. (p. 40).

21. Scopes, L. J.M. (2009). Learning Archetypes as Tool of Cybergogy for a 3D Educational Landscape: A Structure for eTeaching in Second Life. University of Southampton, School of Education, master's thesis, http://eprints.soton.ac.uk/66169/. (p. 40).

# Chapter 6

1. Visit http://www.ushmm.org/museum/about/ for more information about the museum.

2. See http://www.ushmm.org/museum/press/kits/details.php?content=99-general&page=01-facts#facts for additional facts and information.

3. Much of the content for this case study was based on an interview with Ken Hudson and material printed in the *Journal of Virtual Worlds'* research. Hudson, K., & Degast-Kennedy, K. (2009), Pedagogy, Education, and Innovation in 3-D Virtual Worlds. *Journal of Virtual Worlds, 2*(1), 4–11. Hudson, K. (2009, May, 17). managing director, Virtual World Design Centre at Loyalist College. Interview.

# Chapter 7

1. Kapp, K.M., & O'Driscoll, T. (2007). Escaping Flatland: The Emergence of 3D Synchronous Learning. *Guild Research 360 Report on Synchronous Learning Systems,* pp. 111–153.

# Chapter 8

1. Rogers, E.M. (2003). *Diffusion of Innovations* (5th ed.). New York: The Free Press.
2. Rogers, E.M. (2003). *Diffusion of Innovations* (5th ed.) (p. 35). New York: The Free Press.
3. The following definitions and examples are all based on the work of Everett Rogers. Rogers, E.M. (2003). *Diffusion of Innovations* (5th ed.). New York: The Free Press.
4. Rogers, E.M. (2003). *Diffusion of Innovations* (5th ed.) (p. 16). New York: The Free Press.
5. Gladwell, M. (2002). *The Tipping Point: How Little Things Can Make a Big Difference*. New York: Back Bay Books.
6. Walking the Virtual World Saves Money and Avoids Problems in Assembly Layout. (2006). *Modern Application News, 40*(10), 14–19.
7. Tambascio, S. (2004). The Virtual World Meets the Factory. *Tooling & Production,* pp. 38–40.
8. ARI Quick Start Program. (n.d.). Retrieved June 1, 2009, from American Research Institute at www.americanri.com/services/quick-start.php.
9. See the May 26, 2009, ThinkBalm report, *ThinkBalm Immersive Internet Business Value Study, Q2 2009.* http://thinkbalm.files.wordpress.com/2009/05/thinkbalm-immersive-internet-business-value-study-final-5-26-092.pdf.

# Chapter 10

1. Confucius, Chinese philosopher and reformer (551 BC-479 BC).
2. S'mores are associated with recreational camping. Part of the enjoyment of this simple dessert is the way in which it is made on such camping trips. http://en.wikipedia.org/wiki/S%27mores.
3. Friedman, T. (2005). *The World Is Flat* (p. 48). New York: Farrar, Straus and Giroux.
4. Tapscott, D., & Williams A.D. (2008). *Wikinomics: How Mass Collaboration Changes Everything*. New York: Portfolio. See Chapter 10, Collaborative Minds: The Power of Thinking Differently (p. 268), describing the potential impact of global mass collaboration, both the opportunities and the challenges we will face.
5. Pink, Daniel H. (2005). *A Whole New Mind: Why Right-Brainers Will Rule the Future* (p. 54). New York: Riverhead. MBAs and MFAs about critical hires in the age of high concept and high touch or the conceptual age.

6.  Avatars Innovate Medical Records, General Research. The American Society of Radiologic Technologists, May 21, 2009. http://www.asrt.org/Content/News/IndustryNewsBriefs/GenRes/avatarsinn090521.aspx.

7.  Gladwell, Malcolm (2008). *Outlier: The Story of Success.* Boston: Little, Brown and Company. See page 3, the definition of outliers.

8.  The website Dipity creates a very visual and compelling timeline for the convergence and the evolution of virtual social places at www.dipity.com/xantherus/Virtual_Worlds.

# Appendix

1.  Kapp, K.M. (2007). *Gadgets, Games, and Gizmos for Learning.* San Francisco: Pfeiffer.

2.  About Nicktropolis. (n.d.). Welcome Citizens of Nicktropolis. Retrieved June 1, 2009, from www.nick.com/nicktropolis/game/

3.  Special thanks to Koreen Olbrish, CEO of Tandem Learning, for her insights and assistance with this chart.

# Index

Page references followed by *fig* indicate an illustrated figure; followed by *t* indicate a table.

# About the Authors

K ARL M. KAPP is a professor of instructional technology in Bloomsburg University's Department of Instructional Technology in Bloomsburg, Pennsylvania. In Bloomsburg's graduate program, he teaches a course titled "Learning in 3D," which teaches graduate students how to design learning in virtual immersive environments. He also teaches a capstone course using problem-based learning in which students are formed into "companies," write business plans, receive e-learning requests for proposal (RFP), write forty-page proposals, develop working prototypes, and present their solutions to representatives from various learning and e-learning corporations throughout the United States.

Additionally, as the assistant director of Bloomsburg University's acclaimed Institute for Interactive Technologies (IIT), Karl helps government, corporate, and non-profit organizations leverage learning technologies to positively impact employee productivity and organizational profitability through the effective use of learning. He has provided advice on e-learning design, learning infrastructures, and e-learning technologies to such companies and organizations as AstraZeneca, Pennsylvania Department of Public Welfare, Toys R Us, Kaplan-Eduneering, Kellogg's, Sovereign Bank, and Federal Government Agencies.

Karl consults with several learning technology companies and government organizations. Additionally, he advises Fortune 500 companies on the use of technology for transferring knowledge to their employees. He has been interviewed by such magazines as *Training,* ASTD's *T&D, Software Strategies, Knowledge Management, Distance Learning,* and *PharmaVoice* and by general television and radio programs concerning his work with learning and technology.

Karl is a frequent keynote speaker, workshop leader, moderator, and panelist at national and international conferences as well as events for private corporations and universities. He is the author of three books on the convergence of learning and technology, *Integrated Learning for ERP Success, Winning e-Learning Proposals,* and *Gadgets, Games, and Gizmos for Learning.* Karl helps organizations devise strategies around virtual immersive environments, mobile learning solutions, learning through social networking, knowledge transfer, instructional design, and learning strategy development.

You can keep up with Karl's musings and occasional rants on his widely read "Kapp Notes" blog at www.karlkapp.blogspot.com.

TONY O'DRISCOLL is a professor of the practice at Duke University's Fuqua School of Business. Dr. O'Driscoll's current research focuses on how emerging technologies such as virtual worlds can rapidly disrupt existing business models and industry structure. His research has been published in leading academic journals such as *Management Information Sciences Quarterly,* the *Journal of Management Information Systems,* and the *Journal of Product Innovation Management.* He has also written for respected professional journals such as *Harvard Business Review, Strategy and Business, Supply Chain Management Review,* and *Chief Learning Officer* magazine.

During his eighteen-year industry career, Tony held several leadership positions with IBM and Nortel Networks in the areas of strategic business planning, new product and service development, services science research, management consulting, and human capital management. Throughout his industry career, Tony developed in-depth knowledge and extensive experience in leveraging technology to create sustained organizational growth and profitability in an increasingly networked and virtualized global economy.

Tony has been a keynote speaker, workshop leader, moderator, speaker, and panelist at over one hundred national and international conferences. He also frequently provides expert analysis and interviews to media outlets such as *The Wall Street Journal, BusinessWeek, Virtual Worlds News, Chief Learning Officer* magazine, *Wired* magazine, *Training* magazine, and for industry analysts such as Gartner and Forrester. Tony is also the corporate learning correspondent on Robert Bloomfield's popular Metanomics weekly show hosted in Second Life.

You can keep up with Tony's musings on his popular "Learning Matters" blog at http://wadatripp.wordpress.com.

# About the Contributors

While there are two primary authors listed on the cover of this book, this manuscript actually represents the insights and wisdom of a growing community of practitioners who are working tirelessly within their respective organizations to make the vision of immersive learning and collaboration a reality.

We could have not done it without them. If you find value in this book, know that you are standing on the shoulders of these brave pioneers who have been kind enough to share the wisdom of their respective journeys and experiences on the road less travelled.

## The Contributors

**Brian Bauer** is the founder and managing partner at Étape Partners LLC. He contributed an essay in Chapter 9, Rules from Revolutionaries. Brian's experience as a CTO for multiple firms shines through in this essay, and his words of wisdom should add significant value for those trying to convince their technology leaders of the value of the Immersive Internet.

**Ron Burns** is the founder and president of Proton Media. Ron saw the vision we present in this book long before most of us. He was kind enough to write the foreword of this book and to provide valuable feedback on early drafts of the manuscript that make the finished product a much more coherent work.

**Debbie Dalmand** oversees Ernst & Young's learning operations, providing world-class learning and personal growth opportunities for the 41,000 people of the Americas. Debbie led the efforts to build out Ernst & Young's Inventory Observation 3D Learning Experience in Second Life that is covered in Chapter 6. The lessons learned section of this case is right on target.

**Erica and Sam Driver** are co-founders and Principles at Thinkbalm, an analyst firm that is dedicated to the Immersive Internet. In Chapter 8, they were kind enough to provide us with a summary and synthesis of their Immersive Internet Business Value Study (completed in Q2, 2009). The work that Sam and Erica are doing at Thinkbalm is crucial to this emerging field, and their contribution to this book will be of value for those seeking evidence to bring to sponsors.

**Randy Hinrichs** is CEO of 2b3d. The fact that we reached out to Randy for two essay contributions in this book is testament to our respect for his insight and vision in this space. Randy contributed to the development of the 3DLE architecture presented in Chapter 4, where he also contributed an essay on rules for designing 3DLEs. Randy also wrote a wonderful essay for Chapter 10, where he takes us to the year 2020 and describes what he sees.

**Boris Kizelshteyn** is CEO of Popcha. Boris led the design of the FutureWork Island in Second Life covered in Chapter 6. This case demonstrates very clearly the creative expertise that Boris brings in applying new technologies in unique ways to achieve business results.

**Christopher Keesey** is the project manager with Ohio University Without Boundaries. Christopher contributed to the 3DLE architecture presented in Chapter 4. His years of experience in designing immersive and interactive environments was drawn upon heavily in this effort.

**Chuck Hamilton** is head of Virtual Learning Strategy at IBM's Center for Advanced Learning. Chuck's fingerprints are all over this book. From the early work on the seven sensibilities with Tony O'Driscoll, to providing advice on the 3DLE architecture, to writing an essay about upgrading the campfire in Chapter 10, to sharing his fantastic set of references with us. Chuck's untiring passion to learn and share is a model to which we should all aspire.

**Mike Hamilton** is chief learning and development officer for Ernst & Young Americas. It was Mike's original vision and willingness to experiment that culminated in the development of the Inventory Observation 3DLE outlined in Chapter 6.

**John Hengeveld** is a senior business strategist at Intel. John has spent a lot of time thinking about the Immersive Internet, and the essence of his insights is captured in an essay in Chapter 9, Rules from Revolutionaries. John's experience with bringing new technologies to market and his pragmatic sense on where things are going and how to help us get there will no doubt prove very valuable for the next round of revolutionaries.

**Ken Hudson** is the managing director of the Virtual Worlds Design Centre at Loyalist College. Ken is another person who has provided multiple contributions to the book. He contributed to the 3D Learning Architecture presented in Chapter 4 and a case study on Canadian Border Patrol Crossing Training in Chapter 6. This case brings a strong evidence base to suggest that learners who participated in the 3DLE experience fared better than those who did not.

**Karen Keeter** is a marketing executive with IBM's Digital Convergence EBO. Her e-mail tagline reads "Creating Virtual World Evangelists—One Avatar at a Time." Like so many others, Karen has contributed in multiple ways to this book. Along with Joanne Martin, she helped develop the case study on IBM's Academy of Technology Events in Chapter 6. Also, in Chapter 9, she shares her experience and wisdom in driving adoption for this new technology with an essay that is practical and to the point.

**David Klevan** is an education manager at the United States Holocaust Memorial Museum. His wonderful work in creating an installation in Second

Life to re-create the Kristallnacht experience is a wonderful example of kinesthetic learning in action. The Kristallnacht case is presented in Chapter 6 and is not to be missed for those who are seeking to understand how context figures into the 3DLE design process.

**Joe Little** is with BP's Chief Technology Office, where he leads the Virtual Worlds Game Changer Project. There are few people on the planet who understand as much about the technology and the creation of compelling 3DLE experiences as Joe. He has spearheaded multiple projects within BP. One of the most ambitious projects, the Global Graduate Challenge, is covered in a case study in Chapter 6. This case is a wonderful example of how participants from all over the world could work together collaboratively and create virtual networks.

**Steve Mahaley** is director of learning technology at Duke Corporate Education (Duke CE). Always on the cutting edge at the nexus of education and technology, Steve provided keen insight in the development of the 3DLE architecture outlined in Chapter 4 and shared his wisdom on getting "Across the Chasm" in Chapter 9.

**Joanne Martin** is president of IBM's Academy of Technology. The case study in Chapter 6 chronicles Joanne's journey and decision to host the first virtual meeting for the Academy. Reading this case provides a wonderful perspective of how leaders parse through decisions and will give the reader some insights as to the key benefits of Immersive Internet technology that Joanne experienced that led to her decision.

**Mary Ann Mengel** is a multimedia specialist in the Center for Learning & Teaching at Penn State University's Berks campus. Mary's case study contribution to Chapter 6 describes the creation of a virtual green home to teach environmental science. This case brings evidence that students not only learned within the environment, but they also liked it.

**Michael Pack** is director of the Center for Advanced Transportation Technology Lab at the University of Maryland. Michael's case study contribution to Chapter 6 describes the creation of a first-responder 3DLE developed to help reduce accidents by training emergency responders to more quickly clear crashes on interstates.

**Barton K. Pursel** is an instructor and researcher with the College of Information Sciences and Technology at Penn State University. Bart teaches several courses and works as a consultant with Education Technology Services at Penn State, helping to build a university-wide educational gaming initiative. Bart is responsible for the College of IST's Second Life and ProtoSphere initiatives, which involve working with faculty members on funded grants to explore the use of virtual worlds in academic areas such as network security and data fusion. He has great insight into how to create virtual learning spaces, which he shares by explaining how to design an environment within a VIE in Chapter 7.

**Koreen Olbrish,** CEO of Tandem Learning, a company that specializes in immersive learning environments and a frequent speaker on the topic of 3D immersive environments, contributed a number of insights concerning the implementation of VIEs and the future of the VIE space in Chapter 8 and Chapter 10. She helped to define terms in the Glossary and generally provided overall valuable information, ideas, and insights into the possibilities of virtual worlds.

**Margaret Regan** is president and CEO of the FutureWork Institute. Margaret saw the potential for someone to "walk in another's shoes" and experience diversity differently via the application of Immersive Internet technology. The case study presented in Chapter 6 outlines how Margaret's organization leveraged two different platforms to address the diversity and inclusion needs of clients. Margaret urges us all to be platform agnostic and to be led by the learning needs and technology maturity of clients.

**Sarah Robbins** is the director of emerging technologies for Kelley Executive Partners at the Kelley School of Business at Indiana University and is commonly known in the virtual world space as Intellagirl. Sarah is yet another multiple contributor to this book. She helped refine the 3DLE architecture in Chapter 4 and helped us all understand what it would be like to dress up as a Kool-Aid man and get kicked out of a virtual night club. The case study she shares in Chapter 6 on teaching rhetoric in a virtual environment demonstrates that is not just about being there, it is about doing there.

**John Royer** is the former director of sales training strategy at AstraZenca. He is a pioneer in implementing and thinking about using VIE for a competitive advantage. He has pushed through VIE technology and is pushing the barrier of what is possible while carefully considering the human factor issues involved with VIEs. John contributes his thoughts and insights about implementation in Chapter 8 and some ideas on the future in Chapter 10.

**Lesley Scopes** is a successful candidate at the University of Southampton, UK, for her master's degree in computer-based learning and training. She took some of our earlier work and really dug into its meaning and possibilities. Unfortunately, given the scope of this book, we could only touch on a bit of her work, but we strongly recommend serious scholars of VIEs to take a look at her master's dissertation "Learning Archetypes as Tools of Cybergogy for 3D Educational Landscape: A Structure for eTeaching in Second Life" for an in-depth study of the archetypes presented in Chapter 5 and a thoughtful discussion of the concept of cybergogy.

**Clare Timothy** led the Global Graduate Challenge project at BP. In the case study in Chapter 6, Clare provides practical advice on how to manage a large project with participants from all over the world. Her most important message is that it is not the technology itself, but how the technology meets business needs that matters most.

**Eilif Trondsen** is the research and program director of the Virtual Worlds @ Work (VWW), a research consortium for innovation and learning at SRI Consulting Business Intelligence (SRIC-BI) in Menlo Park, California. In this role, Eilif has seen more Immersive Internet implementations than most. In Chapter 7 he shares his insights on the questions you should ask any vendor before embarking on a project of your own. This is certainly a list you won't want to miss as you begin your own Immersive Internet journey.